PRAISE FOR *THE HOSTAGE'S DAUGHTER*

"Violent conflicts always entangle the innocent, and the scars they leave take decades to heal. Journalist Sulome Anderson set out to find her father's kidnapper; in the process, she found herself. Her brutally candid, fiercely intelligent, and beautifully crafted memoir is both a fascinating introduction to the shadow world of Middle East intrigue and an inspiring story of resilience and recovery."

—Stephen M. Walt, coauthor of
The Israel Lobby and U.S. Foreign Policy

"Sulome Anderson wasn't even born when her father, the American journalist Terry Anderson, was taken hostage by Shiite terrorists, and she was seven years old before he was released and she first saw him. In this heartfelt, moving memoir, Sulome retraces her father's path in life, returning to Lebanon as a journalist herself and courageously confronting some of the very men involved in his kidnapping and abuse. The result is both an exploration of the sometimes difficult love between father and daughter, and also an examination of a greatly changed Middle East and the groups that benefited from their hostage taking and other terrorist activities, but are far from atoning for them. Well worth reading for anyone who wants to understand that region and the human impact of war and terrorism."

—Rod Nordland, *New York Times* international
correspondent at large and author of *The Lovers*

"A gutsy coming-of-age memoir, beautifully written and always provocative. From wounded adolescent to fearless investigative reporter, Sulome Anderson confronts her father's kidnappers—and along the way, she shines a harsh light on the murky world of intelligence in a distraught Middle East. A poignant and astonishing mystery story."

—Kai Bird, Pulitzer Prize-winning historian and
author of *The Good Spy: The Life and Death of Robert Ames*

"Sulome Anderson's deeply personal and brutally frank memoir moved me to tears. This skillfully told tale of a life on the very edge and the quest for answers that brought Anderson face-to-face with her father's kidnappers in Beirut powerfully demonstrates that suffering need not destroy. Terry Anderson can truly be proud of his intelligent and spirited daughter."

—Terry Waite CBE, president of
Hostage UK and author of *Taken on Trust*

"If this is a book about personal reclamation, it is also about deliverance. Sulome Anderson has given us a remarkable personal story as well as penetrating insight into the adamantine world of the Middle East, where truth and politics are irreconcilable. She, like the terrorists, spooks, politicians, and bureaucrats she encountered, has had her own war to wage, and her personal victory in the face of great odds is deeply effective. This book is a testament to a talented and courageous young woman—every inch her father's daughter."

—Brian Keenan, former hostage
and author of *An Evil Cradling*

"With scorching honesty, Sulome Anderson takes us back to the grim world of the 1980s Beirut kidnappings and gives a rare glimpse of the lasting human damage done by events which for many of us simply came and went."

—Jim Muir, BBC World News
special Middle East correspondent

"There are times when you want to look away—this book is that personal. By telling the story of the author—and her famous family—it also traces the story of terrorism in the modern era, in gripping and intimate ways."

—Brian Williams, MSNBC

The
Hostage's Daughter

The Hostage's Daughter

A STORY OF FAMILY, MADNESS, AND THE MIDDLE EAST

SULOME ANDERSON

DEY ST.
AN IMPRINT OF
WILLIAM MORROW *PUBLISHERS*

DEY ST.

HarperCollins books may be purchased for educational, business, or sales promotional use. For information, please email the Special Markets Department at SPsales@harpercollins.com.

FIRST EDITION

Designed by Ashley Tucker
Frontispiece photo © AP Photo/Diether Endlicher

Library of Congress Cataloging-in-Publication Data has been applied for.

ISBN 978-0-06-238549-9

16 17 18 19 20   RRD   10 9 8 7 6 5 4 3 2 1

For everybody who believed in me
and
everybody who didn't.

And for my parents, who did the best they could.

CONTENTS

ACKNOWLEDGMENTS

When I was first shopping around the idea for this book, one editor gave me some well-intentioned advice. "You're only twenty-eight years old," she said. "You're too young to write a memoir." Needless to say, I didn't listen, and here we are.

I'd first like to thank Denise Oswald, my wonderful editor at Dey Street, who had my back like a true soldier throughout this process. But I wouldn't ever have found myself in the same room as Denise were it not for my lovely literary agent, Lindsay Edgecombe of Levine Greenberg, who believed in my work and took a chance on a first-time author.

Thanks must also go out to every digital security expert I harassed while writing this book, especially Dan Guido of Trail of Bits and Eva Galperin of the Electronic Frontier Foundation. I appreciate your patience and willingness to humor me.

To my friend Josh Wood: thank you for your valuable notes, and for all the late-night Domino's.

I'm indebted to every person who agreed to be interviewed for this book (regardless of whether they have come to regret that decision), but my special thanks go out to Terry Waite, Robert Fisk, Nick and Cass Ludington, Don Mell, Shazi Faramarzi, Gianni Picco, and Lou Boccardi, all of whom personally played various roles in the strange production that was my childhood.

To my half-sister Gabrielle: you forgave me for being the chosen one and became my friend, for which I will ever be grateful.

My gratitude also goes out to all the officials in the United States government and intelligence services who worked hard to help free my father and his fellow hostages. Regardless of the outcome, I know many of you had the best of intentions. Thank you for your service in support of my family.

Lastly, this book would not have a happy ending were it not for my fiancé, Jeremy, and his beautiful little boy, Ari, who are helping me build the family I've always wanted and never believed I deserved to have.

The
Hostage's Daughter

INTRODUCTION

In a mad world, only the mad are sane.
—AKIRA KUROSAWA

As far back as I can remember, maybe age three, I was aware of what was happening to my father. I didn't know exactly how dire the situation was, but I always knew, on some level, that he might be killed at any moment. Though my mother never came right out and said it, it's hard to protect a child from something like that.

Here are the barest facts: In March 1985, my father, Terry Anderson, the Associated Press bureau chief for the Middle East at the time, was kidnapped in Beirut by a Shiite Muslim militant group known as the Islamic Jihad Organization. It was one of the militias that came to be associated by most with the Hezbollah movement, which has since become the single most powerful force in Lebanon. My mother was six months pregnant with me when he was taken. Dad was one of ninety-six foreigners kidnapped in Lebanon during the 1980s, ten of whom died, in an episode known as the Lebanese hostage crisis. He was released after almost seven years, and I met him for the first time.

But facts are cold, impersonal things, and you can find those in any book about the kidnappings. You can find them in the hundreds of archived news stories about my father and mother and me; in the TV appearances that wrapped up our happy ending like a chocolate, soon to be discarded uneaten.

This is not that sort of book. This is what happened when the cameras went away and we were left unobserved, blinking in the dark. It's the legacy of trauma I was born with and how it led me to ask questions about the event that shaped my life.

I'm now a journalist working in Beirut, the city where it all started—just as Dad was. This is my story, but it's also the story of Lebanon, a place haunted by the phantoms of a bloody fifteen-year conflict, forever peering into the maw of another disaster. The tiny, politically exhausted country is currently sandwiched between war-ravaged Syria and Israel, its enemy and former occupier. As I write this in January 2016, Hezbollah, now the country's dominant militia and political party, stretches itself thin. In Syria, the Iranian-backed Shia group joins president Bashar al-Assad's brutal regime in battling rebel fighters and the terrorist caliphate calling itself the Islamic State. While spending itself in Assad's war, Hezbollah never stops warily eyeing Lebanon's southern border with Israel, preparing for an almost inevitable conflict with its longtime nemesis.

Meanwhile, sectarian Lebanese politicians are hopelessly deadlocked and unable to reach a consensus on electing a president—the country has been leaderless for more than a year and a half. The Lebanese parliament is so fractious it hasn't been able to agree on a company to dispose of Beirut's trash since last July. Stinking mounds of garbage decorate almost every main road in the city now. After watching it accumulate for months, the Lebanese have taken to burning the refuse. Across Beirut, plumes of reeking black smoke curl up to the sky. The once-lovely city is swaddled in a heavy smog you can almost taste, and when the roads flood with winter rain, they spread the filth with them. By some miracle, the country continues to sputter along, but it has become painfully obvious that the situation is unsustainable. As a friend recently put it, Lebanon now has the dubious honor of being the world's most successful failed state.

In November 2015, the Islamic State carried out coordinated suicide attacks in a neighborhood I often visit, killing forty-four people. It was the most recent in a series of bombings targeting Shia areas of Beirut, where Hezbollah reigns supreme. But a few short months later, life in the city continues and the incident seems to have been largely forgotten by all except the relatives of the dead. The Lebanese have lived with the daily threat of terrorism for so long that it has become almost unremarkable to them.

Americans are less accustomed to these perilous circumstances. The Islamic Jihad's spate of suicide bombings and kidnappings in Lebanon during the eighties was one of the first incarnations of modern-day terrorism against the United States. At the time my father was taken, these types of politically motivated attacks against Western civilians were unusual.

Nowadays, the threat of random political violence is part of our global reality. The day after the Beirut bombings in November, several Islamic State terrorists simultaneously attacked locations in Paris, including a café and a concert hall. One hundred and thirty people died, and the group claims to just be getting started. Its members have threatened to carry out more attacks in heavily populated areas such as New York City's Times Square and Washington, D.C. Shortly after the Paris killings, a married couple described as "radicalized" Muslims opened fire at a holiday party in San Bernardino, California, killing fourteen people. Muslims in the United States are being targeted with reactionary bigotry. Donald Trump, the unlikely front-runner in the race for the Republican presidential nomination, threatened to issue special IDs for American Muslims and ban all Muslims from immigrating to the country if he is elected. The world holds its breath, waiting for the next blow to fall.

This is a scenario I am not unfamiliar with. In many ways, my life has been defined by terrorism. I began the journey of writing this book in order to investigate the act of violence that shaped me, for better or worse. I had a goal in mind: I wanted to learn about the men who took my father and what they did. Their actions sent ripples of turmoil and chaos through my life; a series of little shock waves that molded my psyche. I thought perhaps if I could just understand something important about the situation that created these people, I'd be able to process the years of agony they had inflicted on my father, and in a very different way, on myself. I decided to report on Dad's captivity in order to discover what could drive his kidnappers to chain and torture another human being for political reasons. I wanted to know how a person becomes a terrorist.

I had no way of foreseeing that I would be confronted by more answers than I was ready for—answers that are especially relevant thirty years later, as we all struggle to make sense of our own boogeymen in the dark.

This book will follow two braided narratives. One story is my investigation of Dad's kidnapping; the other is the effect his captivity had on my life. With this approach, I hope to communicate that for each tale of grief and horror you read in the news, there are untold numbers of family members and loved ones who are never whole again.

The structure is also meant as a reminder to politicians and political actors: their choices are not without consequences. It's easy to make decisions that dictate people's lives while sitting in comfortable offices. Hurting others seems simple, when it's done for what they see as the greater good or to achieve maximum benefit for themselves. But they should know that people are not chess pieces. We are human beings, and their machinations do not exist in a vacuum. To everyone who has the power of life and death over others: Consider your actions in the long term. Try to calculate the ripple effect they might have, not just politically, but emotionally. Find your humanity before you play with our lives.

And lastly, my story is about reporting conflict in the Middle East. In many ways, this career was chosen for me while I was still in the womb. It has brought endless fulfillment and grief to my life in equal measure. This is about how journalism broke my family and my mind, and then helped put me back together.

1. THE SUPERMAN

All I know is just what I read in the papers,
and that's an alibi for my ignorance.
—WILL ROGERS

NOW

The Hezbollah press office is not easy to find. My taxi driver picks me up at my mother's house in the wealthy Christian neighborhood of Fanar, about fifteen minutes outside of Beirut proper. My boyfriend Jeremy, who constantly frets about me thousands of miles away in New York, made me promise to hire an armed driver who could "throw down if necessary." Jeremy's Orthodox Jewish background keeps him away from Lebanon. Despite my descriptions of the hipster neighborhood of Mar Mikhail or the lavish beach parties featuring gorgeous Lebanese women squeezed into tiny bits of cloth, as far as he's concerned, the country might as well be Somalia.

I am of the opinion that the last thing I need on a trip to Dahiyeh, the Shia neighborhood in south Beirut and Hezbollah's primary stronghold in the city, is a shady-looking driver/bodyguard packing a weapon. I assured him I would look for one, but I take taxis most everywhere; after all, Beirut is hardly an active war zone. Yet.

This particular driver, named Antoine, seems jittery as we pass a Hezbollah checkpoint. Given the Islamic State's series of bombings and attacks on Hezbollah over the past couple of years, his quavering under the steely gazes of the young men peering into each car is understandable. Besides, even in March 2014, twenty-three years after the civil war between Lebanon's opposing sects ended, many Christians still dislike venturing into Dahiyeh. During one of her customary interrogations this morning, my mother, who is Maronite, had a minor shit fit when she learned I was planning to come here, even in broad daylight. My overall policy with her has always been: do first; apologize later. I like to avoid her anxious diatribes whenever possible. Always the detective, though, she often manages to elicit information from me, and I had to fend her off before jumping into Antoine's car.

Most people—at least, most Americans—might be surprised to discover that Hezbollah has a press office. That's because most Americans don't fully grasp the concept that a group on the State Department's list of terrorist organizations is also the most influential political party in Lebanon. Its political power is exponentially strengthened by the fact that Hezbollah happens to be the country's most fearsome militia, dedicated (according to them) to resisting Israeli military designs on the tiny, war-weary nation. The group is armed to the teeth thanks to the patronage of Iran and Syria, and its military power outstrips that of the Lebanese army. In recent years, Gulf nations such as Saudi Arabia have tried to combat Hezbollah's military superiority by making extravagant donations to the army; another move in the proxy war between Sunni and Shia that joins the long list of proxy wars playing out in Lebanon since before the civil war.

In any case, the Hezbollah press office is a logical place to start my investigation into the circumstances of my father's kidnapping.

I've always been told that the Islamic Jihad Organization, the group that claimed responsibility for his captivity, was just another one of Hezbollah's many faces. According to the U.S. government narrative, the Islamic Jihad's acts of terror during the war, including bombings of the U.S. embassy and marine barracks as well as the kidnapping of Western hostages, should be laid squarely at Hezbollah's feet. If I want to understand the context of my father's kidnapping, who better to approach than the people charged with taking him?

I know the chances of Hezbollah officials agreeing to speak with me are slim, but I also know Hezbollah has tried hard to escape the accusations of terrorism that have dogged it since the war. Following his release, my father actually interviewed Hassan Nasrallah, Hezbollah's infamous secretary-general, for CNN. If Nasrallah himself spoke to my dad, perhaps someone from the group will give me a statement, even a vague one.

Now Antoine and I are driving around Dahiyeh in circles, stopping every five feet or so to ask passersby for directions to an "address" for the office I have found online. I use quotation marks because, like most addresses in Lebanon, it basically consists of instructions that read something like "the big white building by the *dekkane* [grocery] on the main street."

The passersby are less than obliging. Perhaps they don't know what to make of a nervous Christian taxi driver and his foreign-looking female passenger. In any case, most of them suspiciously deny knowing the whereabouts of the building, and some just shake their heads and keep walking. By some miracle, when asked where the *muqawama* (resistance) meets with *sahafiyeen* (journalists), one of them points us in the right direction, which of course bears no resemblance to the address I have written in my notebook.

They moved the office, the man says helpfully in Arabic, which I speak well, if not quite fluently.

We pull up to the unobtrusive building, where another serious young man motions for Antoine to wait in the tiny parking lot while I am to go upstairs. He's very polite to me as I make my way to the elevator.

"Ahla w sahla." He smiles. You are welcome here. His heavily accented English is jarring, like stones dropped into a river.

I encounter the same friendliness from the two hijab-clad women who seem to be in charge of dealing with journalists. They serve me coffee, then ask why I am honoring them with a visit. They speak perfect English.

"I'm a journalist," I begin. "I write for several magazines." I list them off: *New York* magazine, *The Atlantic, Foreign Policy,* and *Vice,* knowing most of the names probably won't mean much here.

"I'm also working on a book," I continue carefully. "It's about my father, Terry Anderson. He was held hostage during the war. They say the *muqawama* took him, but I'm trying to figure out the truth of that. I'd really like to speak with someone from the party, if that's possible."

The women look at each other, then at me, all smiles. "That will be very difficult," one says. "But please fill out this request form and we will call you back within a week."

I do so, thank them for their hospitality, and head downstairs. In the lobby, the man who greeted me upon my arrival stops me.

Thank you for coming, he says in Arabic. Please visit us anytime.

"Shukran." I thank him. *"Allah ma'ak."* God be with you.

I go outside and jump back into Antoine's taxi. He seems relieved to see me.

I wait a week, then two. They never call.

———

Throughout my father's captivity, I idealized him beyond all reason. Everyone told me he was a hero, and I always pictured an actual superhero. I kept a picture of him under my pillow and kissed it every night before going to sleep. On my birthdays my mother pretended some of my presents were from him—she even mailed them to our house, with letters she signed with his name, saying how much he missed me. I frequently asked her when he was coming home; every time, she said, "Soon."

Whatever shelter my mother tried to provide me from the dark reality of our situation wasn't enough to prevent me from absorbing it. She would close the door to her bedroom when she cried, but I could always hear her.

Besides, growing up as I did around war correspondents, death always seemed nearby. I knew people could be hurt; I knew they screamed when they were, and then sometimes, they were gone forever. I remember being four or five and walking into the living room to find my mother and some of my father's friends watching horrible, gruesome footage they had spliced together with that eerie, experimental Laurie Anderson song "O Superman." My mom had worked for ABC News before my father was taken, and they had hours of live coverage that was too gory to show on TV. Someone had decided to make a montage, complete with soundtrack, I don't know why. Nor do I know why they were watching it that evening; maybe my mom missed being in the field. She'd given up her career when she had me—a career for which she had worked hard, and she'd been very proud of it. Twenty-five years later, I still remember details from the video: bombs exploding, disembodied limbs decorating piles of rubble, blood painting the streets, rapid staccato gunfire.

I remember that we had a couple of false alarms, when they

thought maybe my father was dead. I think my mom sat me down one day and told me there was a chance he might not come home—the first and only time she wavered in her assurances that he'd be back soon. But then his kidnappers would release another video of him, or maybe some photographs. He would read from a script—angry anti-American propaganda I didn't understand—then look into the camera and tell my mother and me that he loved us. In retrospect, he looked half-dead already in those videos: paper white, with haunted eyes over a bushy beard. I grew up loving this frail image on a screen. At the time, I didn't think about how diminished he seemed compared to the hefty, smiling man in the photograph under my pillow. He was my daddy, thin now, but still perfect, and he loved me.

When I was five, Brian Keenan, one of the men who were held with my father, was released after almost five years in captivity. Mama and I visited him in Ireland. He was yellow-skinned and painfully gaunt. He tried to put sugar in his tea and was shaking so hard he spilled it all over the table. I promptly threw a massive tantrum, and my mother took me upstairs to try to calm me. I only stopped crying when she told me how we were going to nurse my father back to health when he got home. I often fantasized about that after seeing him in one of those videotapes—feeding him soup, taking him for walks.

And my father likewise got to see us on TV. This was thanks to my mother's decision to let film crews from various news channels visit our home in Cyprus to document special occasions like my father's birthdays, and my own. My mother didn't want to raise me in front of cameras, but she allowed it because she hoped my father's kidnappers might let him watch his daughter grow up on television. And so they did, permitting him to see us on the news from time to time. Later, my father said my tiny, freckled nose had looked like a button, there on the screen. That's what he called me sometimes after he came home—Button.

During the years my father was held captive, the U.S. State Department maintained regular contact with my mother and my father's employers, the Associated Press, ostensibly keeping them up-to-date on the government's efforts to free him. As a child, I was always confident my country was working as hard as it could to secure his release. And then it finally happened.

I was almost seven when my father was set free. There's a photograph in my bedroom of the night I met him. He's beaming, clutching an enormous bouquet of flowers in one arm. I'm attached to his other hand, wearing a little red coat and a confused smile. Cameras flash in the background. It's a famous, almost iconic image of the 1980s Lebanese hostage crisis—the man, the flowers, the little girl.

———

Nick Ludington, my godfather and former chief of AP services in the Middle East, was charged with avoiding bias while covering my father for the news organization my dad had been an integral part of before he was kidnapped—no easy feat, since the AP wanted desperately to help secure his release.

A couple of months before my jaunt to Dahiyeh, I interview Nick—who for some forgotten reason I've called Silly Turtle or just the Turtle for as long as I can remember—in the cozy, familiar little TV room behind my godparents' kitchen. Their house is one of the only places I consistently returned to during my nomadic childhood. It's at least a century old, a sprawling but unostentatious villa in Rockland County overlooking the Hudson River.

The Turtle is happy to reminisce about his days in Beirut, and my godmother, Cass, a grandmotherly woman from an old-money family, occasionally chimes in. She's like something out of another time—her beautifully antique American accent brings to mind mansions and yachts and ancient silverware polished to a bright shine.

Nick says he was heavily insulated from what the AP was doing behind the scenes—working with the government to try to bring an end to my father's captivity.

"These guys were doing things that were sacred and they were talking to intelligence services and this and that," he explains. "They were very clear that they were keeping me out of it because I had to cover it. They were absolutely right."

My mother and I had become close to my godparents while we were all living in Cyprus, before my father came home. I can't remember a time when I didn't know Cass and the Turtle.

"Mostly I try to think about the nice stuff from that time," Nick says with a smile. "We all lived in Cyprus, and you were so cute. You loved your mum, and Cassie and your mum were great friends, as you know. It was wonderful."

I ask them about the night my father came home.

"When your dad was getting out, we weren't told by anyone," Nick explains. "I think it was the American embassy in Syria that told us we maybe needed to get over there, so we took you and your mum.

"We were really worried, everybody was watching us," he continues. "They knew if Nick goes to Damascus—well, they were friends of ours, the journalists. Who was the guy I'm thinking of, the BBC guy—Cass, who was the BBC guy who was so interested in Terry's release, who was constantly sniffing around?" No one wanted the media to jump the gun on my dad's release. If it wasn't true, the brouhaha might have had severe consequences for him.

Cass responds with a name I will not disclose, then says, "Oh my God, absolutely, so we had to hide our departure. The morning we left, his wife calls and says, 'What are you doing today?' We were getting ready to leave with you and didn't know what to say and we certainly weren't going to—"

"He put her onto it, obviously," Nick remarks.

Cass jumps back in. "He had to have suspected something."

"Anyway, we flew into Damascus, but I had booked a room in a really skuzzy commercial hotel that wasn't the Meridian or anything where any of the journalists would be and they said we could stay there and we'd flown out quietly," Nick continues.

"Did I stay there?" I ask. A faint memory of a grimy hotel room stirs.

"Yes, you and Madeleine and Cass and I. It was a pretty awful hotel—it wasn't bedbuggy but just between bedbuggy and good."

"All I really remember is that my mom woke me up in the middle of the night," I say quietly. It's not an easy thing to think about. I know I cried because I had to leave my friends behind, and all the life I had ever known. Even then, I felt instinctively that everything was going to change, and I was afraid. "I remember Mom waking me up, and we rode on one of those army planes at some point and I remember throwing up. I think I threw up."

"Yes," Cass says. "You did. Anyway, we were there for a couple of days, and we were amusing you with games. But we couldn't go out, we couldn't show ourselves in public."

"So a couple of days later we find out it was true, that your father had really been released," Nick explains. "So there was a mad rush to get to the embassy, which was a zoo."

"Tell me about that night," I ask. "What was it like? If you can describe it for me."

"I remember seeing him, and we went crazy, everybody just went nuts," he recollects. "I remember Harry pushing forward and hugging your dad, he was the wonderful AP photographer, Armenian guy. He died recently."

"How did Dad look? I only remember him one way."

"I saw him from far away and he looked pretty good," Cass says. "Everybody expected this wraith to appear, but your dad wasn't that bad. They were asking questions and he was smiling and then he said, 'You'll have to pardon me but I have two ladies waiting.' He meant you and your mom."

"That's right, great line, that was a good one." Nick laughs.

"What was it like between me and my dad at first?" I ask. This is what I really want to know. Was it ever good for us? Was there some point when I was Button, the pretty little girl he had seen on television in the dungeon he lived in for seven years? Was he ever the father I needed him to be?

"Well, you know what, I didn't see much of it," Cass says. "I remember we were taken to somebody's house for a while. I saw you every so often, but your dad was busy. There was no sense of a relationship or anything at that time. All I knew was that he didn't want you out of his sight. But I remember a night or so before, when we were in that little hotel before your dad got free, you said, 'I know what my daddy is going to be like. He's going to be just like the Turtle.' Which was so cute. Nick was very flattered."

"I *was* flattered."

"Then we went to Germany, then we went to Antigua, right?" I ask.

"No, then we went from Germany to New York," Cass responds. "There was all this welcoming at Rockefeller Center. I have never forgotten the ride. We were part of the cavalcade from the airport to Rockefeller Center. It went without a stop the whole way. They cleared everything. The lights in the city . . . even the lights were turned off, and there were people standing along the streets yelling,

'Terry, Terry,' and some people were asking who it was, and they said, 'It's Terry—Terry.' It was really beautiful."

"I must have been petrified," I say. I remember being petrified.

At that exact moment, my phone starts to ring. It's Dad. I had been trying to get hold of him for days, but his number kept going straight to voice mail and I was starting to become worried.

"Hi, sweetheart," he says.

"Hi, Dad, I had a quick question for you, but I'm doing an interview with the Turtle, with Nick. Can I call you back in ten minutes? And why is your phone always off, by the way?"

"Oh, that," my father says absently. "I keep forgetting to charge it."

"Okay then, please don't do that because it's not safe. You need your phone on. Bye."

———

I actually remember the moment I met my father in startling detail. Exhausted, I had fallen asleep on a couch in a waiting room at the American embassy in Damascus. A thin, pale man in thick glasses woke me. He said he was my father, but he didn't look like any of the images I had of him in my head. He was smiling. Mama was sobbing. He hugged me and my mother hugged him. Dazed, I held on to his hand as we walked outside into a sea of people, all cheering and shouting their congratulations. The cameras flashed constantly, hurting my eyes. I noticed that despite his smile, my new father flinched at the noise and the lights. I wondered at his hand shaking in mine.

A couple of years ago, a man I dated for a bit slept over at my house. Forgetting he was there, I began counting out the handful of pills I take every night before bed. He saw what I was doing and asked what medication I was on. Thinking an abbreviated version of the truth would suffice at that stage in our relationship, I told him I was on antidepressants.

"Wow," he exclaimed, half joking. "Baggage."

I looked at the picture hanging on my wall. I saw that little girl and I wanted to put my hand to her cheek, wrap my arms around her, and never let go.

2. THE ABDUCTION

I feel utterly powerless, and that feeling is my prison.
—HARUKI MURAKAMI

NOW

The day my father was kidnapped began with the best of intentions.

"The night before, we were all at your dad's house," Don Mell tells me. "It was myself and Scheherazade [Faramarzi], a couple of others, and [Robert] Fisk. We were all drinking, and at some point we realized we weren't getting enough exercise. So tennis was kind of our thing, and you could play tennis for free at that little court by the lighthouse. We agreed to play and your dad picked me up at about seven the next morning."

Don Mell used to be an AP photographer in Beirut. He became almost a little brother to my dad as they covered the daily violence of Lebanon's civil war together. I've known him practically my whole life, but this is the first time I've seen him in years. He is just the same as I remember him: round, with a wry smile and a caustic sense of humor. My best memories of him were in our big old house in Bronxville, laughing with my dad, flirting with my mom. He always made me giggle, and I looked forward to his visits.

My dad and Don share a bond that's as unique as any I can

imagine. He was in the car with my father when Dad was taken, and although I know he's told the story countless times, he agrees to take me back to the morning he saw one of his best friends kidnapped in front of him. I'm interviewing him in his uncle's beautiful SoHo town house in Manhattan, which boasts a rare, lovely garden and what looks to be some priceless artwork. We sit on a slightly uncomfortable antique couch and he begins to talk.

"When we parked at the courts, I saw the car that would turn out to be the kidnap car drive by us, but I didn't really register it," Don recounts. "I mean, three creepy guys in a car in Beirut during the war, you know. We played tennis for about an hour . . . then we get in the car and I see them again, and I thought to myself, 'If I see them a third time I'm going to say something.' But I let my guard down."

After making a stop at my dad's building, they eventually pulled up in front of Don's apartment. I imagine it was probably starting to bustle in that part of Beirut at 8:15 A.M. The city would have just been waking up.

"I looked out of the front window and that car is sitting there in front of us," Don Mell tells me. "And I said, 'Holy shit,' and I got out of our car. I told Terry to get the hell out of here, because I thought they were after me. You've got to realize, all this happened in the space of twenty seconds.

"Your father is trying to get the car in gear, but he starts to panic, he can't do it," he continues tonelessly, a faraway look in his eyes. I suppose even after all these years, it can't be fun to relive this event. "One guy went across the street and he had a Kalashnikov. He was just there to make sure that nobody interfered. There was a little taxi stand and they all—everybody knew what was happening. And then another guy, a really big guy, came and literally reached in and grabbed your dad in a sort of bear hug."

"And Dad's not a small man either," I murmur. I'm trying to put myself in that car with them, imagining Ain el-Mreisseh in March, the quiet of the street shattered. The exhilaration of an early-morning tennis game devolving into panic. What must have been going through their heads? Utter helplessness, I'm sure—the impotence of knowing nothing you do or say will stop what's happening. The knowledge that someone else holds your life interlaced between their fingers, and they can snap it like a rubber band whenever they choose. The violation of having your body, your fate, belong to someone else. It's a feeling I'm not unfamiliar with, but I know my experiences can't compare to what that day meant for them.

"Right, he's not," Don answers with a brief grin that dies almost immediately. "So anyway, this big guy pulls him out of the car. The third guy came up to me directly, and he had a Beretta. He puts it to my forehead and I am thinking, you know, one of two things is going to happen here. I'm getting in that car or I am dead. But they threw your dad in the back of the car. And then the other guy with the Kalashnikov jumps back into the car. He was the driver. The guy who was with me, he starts to back up with the gun pointed at me. He backed up about three or four feet and then I took a step forward toward him, and another step, and he just looked at me and waved the gun." He mimes a dismissal at me.

"Like, get out of here."

"Right. None of them said a word, they didn't say anything to each other or me, he just went like, scoot. And then he got in the car and took off. I realized our car is still running, so I threw my stuff in the backseat and I got in."

"You actually drove after them?" I ask in disbelief. That must have taken some serious balls.

"I drove after them about three or four blocks and we kept

going toward the old Jewish court. We got past the Mirror Tower, and there was starting to be traffic. I mean it was Saturday, but the traffic was starting and I caught up to them. I saw the guy looking out of the window at me. And I thought, 'What the fuck am I doing?' I mean, all I had was a tennis racket in my hand. I was hoping to get to a checkpoint and then go around them, but they obviously had their escape route, and you know they had a safe house. So I just drove to the office and that was that."

"And then you told everyone?" I ask.

"Right. Of course, everybody in the office was hungover. I said, 'Terry has been kidnapped,' and they asked how I knew and I said, 'Because I was there.'"

I need more detail about the day my father was taken, and I know Scheherazade Faramarzi, another colleague of my father's, was present that morning, so I contact her and she agrees to an interview.

———

Iranian by birth, Shazi was invaluable to the AP, not just for her fluency in both Farsi and Arabic, but because, I'm told, she was fearless and fiercely dedicated to the job. She used to be my mother's best friend, although they've lost touch now, the consequence of some decades-old fight—my mother nurses her grudges with great care and attention—which is sad because she was a sort of aunt to me growing up. I've known her since I was a toddler in Cyprus, and her stories of what a cute but stubborn child I was are as much a part of my understanding of those years as the ones my family tells. In a Skype conversation from Iran, she shares how she remembers that day while I sit rapt at my computer in the living room of our house in Fanar, Lebanon.

It's highly uncomfortable because my mother, in one of her characteristic bouts of stubbornness, refused to get air-conditioning in the house when she had it built. I was forced to actually buy my own crappy little AC unit that I drag with me from room to room, where I sit sometimes with my sweaty face inches away from the grate. Months of my relentless complaining—and the rest of my family pointing out that even the Bangladeshi superintendent has AC in his little ground-floor apartment—have not convinced Mama to relent, so it's sticky hot, but I barely notice as Shazi begins her story.

"We didn't really become friends, Maddy and I, until the day Terry was kidnapped," she says in her slow, slightly raspy voice. It's always had a calming effect on me. "I was going to the office and stopped in a stationery shop. I saw a friend of mine and she said, 'Hey, did you hear they kidnapped an American in Ain el-Mreisseh?' I thought . . . it's either Terry or Don. I ran to the office and I saw Don Mell standing outside and I just said, 'It's Terry.'

"We went upstairs and the office was in like, just a hurricane," she continues. "Not physically but everybody was in shock, literally their faces were white, or that's how I remember them. Don was feeling guilty and so I was just walking around. Then Maddy comes in and she just came toward me and she was shivering and crying. I had no idea what to tell her. It's okay, it's not okay, he'll be fine. I didn't know. She just needed to hold on to something, and so I held her while she shivered."

Keep in mind; my mother was six months pregnant with me at the time. Her baby's father was gone. He was still married to another woman, from whom he was in the process of obtaining a divorce, who had a daughter of her own—my half sister, Gabrielle. Mama didn't even have the security of his last name. For all she knew, I would be denied U.S. citizenship because no one would be able to prove I had an American father.

My mother, all five feet of her against the world. She must have felt so frightened, so ripped away from everything that made sense—completely and utterly alone. I think Mama always felt as though she couldn't count on anyone but herself; a worldview that was likely the product of an almost completely absent father and a mother with a gambling addiction that became somewhat adorable in her old age—my *teta*'s affinity for chain-smoking at slot machines was a constant source of amusement to my cousins and me. I imagine it must have been significantly less cute to the five children she didn't attend to because she spent all her time and money at the casino. Mama basically raised herself, with the help of her older siblings, and this left her with a firm belief that no one can really be trusted, that leaning on others was unwise and bound to end badly. It was a message she constantly tried to instill in me when I was older: you can't rely on other people, because they always disappoint you. Like my father, who may not have been able to avoid it but nonetheless wasn't there when she needed him most. People always leave.

It was a belief I clutched inside myself for so long, and still haven't entirely let go of. People leave. But my mother used that conviction to fuel her stubborn independence, hold people at arm's length and push them away when they failed her, even in small ways. In contrast, the lonely child inside me always thought that if I clung to the people I loved hard enough, if I pressed as close to them as possible, maybe this time they'd stay. Needless to say, it rarely worked out that way, and my mother had little patience for my neediness as I grew older. I think subconsciously she wanted me to rely completely on her for my identity, because I was all she had for so long, the center of her galaxy. She swirled around me in a cloud of anxious concern, overwhelming love, and constant, haranguing criticism.

I need to be better, more like her. I'm weak, pathetic. I must be, because my iron-strong mother is so rarely happy with me as I am, and she's always right.

It was a thought that rooted itself in a dark, quiet corner of my mind after my dad came home, as Mama became ever sterner and sadder. It would grow longer, hungrier, wrapping its angry tendrils around my life—and when I would berate myself, almost tasting my own blood in my mouth as I raked deep mental furrows across the ugly, disfigured abomination I believed myself to be, I always did it in my mother's voice.

But the thought of her shivering, bereft of the man she let into her heart after turning so many others away out of fear—I can understand why she tried to bring her daughter up strong, fierce, and uncaring. She wanted to spare me the pain of losing someone. It wasn't a realistic goal, and it certainly didn't work, but I know she didn't mean to scar me the way she did. Parents rarely do. In the moment when she found out what had happened to my dad, she was a woman alone in a world where people were shoved into cars at gunpoint and ripped out of their lives.

"The men who kidnapped Terry weren't amateurs," Don told me seriously during our interview. "That big guy? He moved like a cat. They knew exactly what they were doing; they were frighteningly organized."

I know what happened next from Dad's book. After my father was thrown unceremoniously into the back of that car, one of the men who took him leaned down and said something.

"Don't worry," his kidnapper told him comfortingly. "It's political."

———

In my parents' world at the time—and to a certain extent, mine now—there has to be a kind of detachment from reality. You must put aside the very real possibility of your own death or you can't do your job. We drink and laugh that possibility away, bury it under cynical humor and work, the work, always this story and the next. We spend so much time around death and suffering as journalists; when you consider it, there's a deep strangeness to our habit of holding that one fatal story so far from our minds. We simply pretend to ourselves that they won't kill the messengers, the neutral observers, that all of us will end our lives peacefully in bed at a dignified age. It's a pretense that's becoming much harder to keep up these days as our colleagues fall in ever-increasing numbers each year.

"I think at the time, we felt we wouldn't die," Shazi tells me. "When we weren't working—there was no Internet or cell phones, we had to go and talk to people, see the devastation ourselves—we were always in the Commodore Hotel or reading the wires. Anyway, it was fun. We had parties in the middle of mayhem; we used to dance a lot. We clung to each other, I think."

Robert Fisk, who used to be my dad's best friend, is the man who embodies that generation of war correspondents for me, the reporter who brought Lebanon's heartbreak to life for so many people in his book *Pity the Nation*. He's still working as I write this, still making the news real for his readers. From what I understand, he remains the *Independent*'s crown jewel: the famous Robert Fisk, who has seen perhaps one too many wars.

Now well into his sixties, he's incredibly difficult to pin down, but he finally agrees to meet me for breakfast at Café Rawda on the Corniche, overlooking the crags and pools where poor Lebanese and Syrian boys dive and wade. The seawater is still blue, despite

Beirut's abundance of garbage, mounds of which carelessly litter the coast. Much like Lebanon itself, the shore is barely winning its struggle against the casual disrespect of the people who walk it.

Fisk, whom I used to call Fisky as a child, is an imposing figure, with his upper-class British accent, acid-tinged intelligence, and air of not quite caring. But he looks weary, much older than I remember him. Older than he should look, perhaps. But then again, this is a man who's witnessed more massacres than I even want to think about.

"During the civil war, you had enormous freedom to move around," Fisk tells me. "Another journalist once said to me, 'There are no good guys in this war, Robert. You'd better know that. And the only way to cover it is to go out, every day, and have an adventure.' And that's what I did, and you could do it then. The checkpoints respected you everywhere. They were cynical about what you wrote if they didn't like it, but you could go and be shot at by Syrian tanks from the Palestinian trenches or you could go to southern Lebanon and see the Israelis rearming what was then called the Free Lebanon Army . . . I had the house here, and I would meet with the others at the Commodore . . . There was great friendship in that; when somebody was in trouble, you'd immediately try to help them out."

Because I grew up around these Commodore stories, it's a time I'm as nostalgic for as any of my parents' friends, despite the fact that I was an embryo at the time. It was a different era of journalism, in some ways a more courageous, cleaner time, before Twitter, Facebook, and our hyperactive news cycle that churns out a tragedy each minute, only to discard it for another the next. These days, it seems as though massacres, refugee crises, episodes of human indignity and suffering are forgotten almost as soon as they're reported. Yes, it's harder for despotic regimes and militants to commit atrocities in secret, since practically everyone has a cell-phone camera and a social media account. Most of the time, we see the violence they inflict on the innocent. We see, but do we really notice? Or are we too busy clicking on the next horror show, the next bloodletting, the next listicle, gif, or meme, the next, the next, the next?

"The funny thing about Lebanon is that it's a tiny country," Fisk tells me from the lost place and time he's remembering. "If you spend all your time here, you understand the politics very well. But because it's got this huge mountain chain and Roman ruins in the Beqaa, it gives it a depth and height that is quite misleading. It was like this was the center of the world for us. You know, for the Crusaders, it was Jerusalem. When you came here during the war, it was Beirut."

Fisk shares one of the worst things he saw in that war of terrible things people did to each other: the massacres at the Sabra and Shatila refugee camps, an event that still haunts Lebanon's collective memory. The sickening gift my grandfather's friends, with the blessing and patronage of the Israelis, gave hundreds of Palestinian civilians living in those camps that September of 1982. The atrocity was executed by the Phalange, a Maronite Catholic political party/militia I'm told my *jido* (grandfather), Adib Bassil, helped found. An Israeli governmental investigation, the Kahan Commission, was formed after it was all over, in response to widespread international outrage.

The Kahan Commission found that Israel was "indirectly responsible" for the Sabra and Shatila massacres and Ariel Sharon, then the Israeli defense minister, bore "personal responsibility" for the violence. But a 2012 *New York Times* piece reveals declassified U.S. documents detailing the depth of Israel's complicity in the affair and how officials in the Israeli government manipulated and intimidated U.S. officials into inaction on behalf of Palestinian civilians in the camps.

"If you don't want the Lebanese to kill them, we will kill them," Sharon is quoted in the documents as telling Morris Draper, the American envoy to the Middle East. "When it comes to our security, we have never asked. We will never ask. When it comes to existence and security, it is our own responsibility and we will never give it to anybody to decide for us."

The declassified material exposes "how Israel's refusal to relinquish areas under its control, and its delays in coordinating with the Lebanese National Army, which the Americans wanted to step in, prolonged the slaughter." In short, the Israeli government appears to have been more than indirectly responsible for what happened at Sabra and Shatila, despite the fact that Phalange militiamen were the ones getting their hands bloody.

My grandfather's position in the Phalange is a legacy I don't much care for. Composed exclusively of wealthy Christians, the Phalange leadership seemed to be easily the foulest people in Lebanon, which was not known for the sweetness of its politicians and militiamen back then; still isn't. However, the Israelis seemed to decide the Phalange made promising allies in their strategy to rid themselves of the Palestinians once and for all.

The Gemayel family headed up that pack of murderers, rapists, and bigots, and from what I'm told, they made the Sopranos look like adorable babies playing with toy guns. A story I've heard multiple times while reporting this book involves Pierre Gemayel attending Hitler's Berlin Olympics and coming back to Beirut singing the Nazis' praises. You'd think that would mean the Phalangists hated Jews, but you'd be wrong. As an elite minority, they welcomed the citizens of the new country to the south as kindred spirits: educated, cultured sophisticates keeping the torch of Western values alight in a vast ocean of unwashed, ignorant Muslims. Don't be fooled, ladies and gentlemen, because according to these people, they were not Arabs, despite the resemblance they bore their fellow Lebanese. No, as the Phalange and many other Christians in Lebanon had each other convinced (some still are, sadly), they were Phoenicians, direct blood descendants of that great bygone merchant empire. And so an alliance was born.

"I can tell you, their names don't really belong in the dictionary under what you would consider Christian," an ex-Mossad agent recently told me with a chuckle, referring to the Gemayels. He was active at the time of my father's abduction. "They were quite ridiculous. Well, they were crazy. The whole place was crazy, and we just added fuel to it."

The Israeli government was on its quest to eliminate the PLO, which had moved into southern Lebanon following the Palestinians' abrupt need to relocate after the establishment of the Jewish state. The PLO quickly wore out its welcome by using its host country as a base from which to launch attacks against its powerful new neighbor and behaving badly in someone else's country, managing to piss off pretty much every faction in Lebanon. When Israel invaded southern Lebanon in June of 1982, causing Arafat and the rest of the PLO leadership to flee the country, the Phalange realized the Israeli occupation was going to be extremely helpful in their mission to keep the country safely in Christian hands. They hated the Palestinians too, so a little quid pro quo happened, backs were scratched, the Phalange killed a lot of Palestinian civilians, and Israel thought it would maintain a sense of plausible deniability by keeping its soldiers' hands clean of the actual massacre. They simply watched from afar, overseeing the bloodletting. But after Sabra and Shatila, the flames Israel fueled were too high to be ignored, because the people who died at those camps did not do so unnoticed. The Beirut press corps was there to hold the horrific things they saw up to the world in disbelief, and Fisk was one of the first to arrive on the scene.

"I went to the camp in the morning with [another journalist]," he tells me. "And while we stayed in the camp with all these corpses, there were still some men in armored trucks and vehicles there, so we hid in a backyard. Suddenly we looked around and we saw a woman dead on her back, with fresh blood—she'd just been killed . . . there were a lot of raped women. You could tell when you went into the houses—the smell was appalling, of course—but you'd see the tables overturned with food on the ground, and you'd go into the bedroom, and you could see that's where the killings and rapes had gone on.

"I came out and the Israeli soldiers were walking past Sabra and Shatila, and I'm just standing there watching them," Fisk continues. "They were running past me, stooped right down low . . . and this sergeant comes to me and says, 'You, go away.' And I said no. I think I actually said, 'Fuck you.' And he said, 'Why are you here?' And I said, 'For the same reason you are. Because all those people in there have been massacred.' 'No, they are terrorists.' 'Well they're all dead,' I replied. 'Yes, the terrorists are all dead.' 'No,' I said. 'Civilians. Women. Babies. All dead. Killed by your friends.' And then these other soldiers wanted to talk to me about what had happened. They were frightened of the terrorists. Terrorists, terrorists, terror, terror, terror, terror."

That's an incessant refrain now firmly established in our culture—the characterization of all Arabs, even defenseless ones, as terrorists. It's a conviction many Israelis still hold close. As recently as July of 2014, Ayelet Shaked, then a member of the Israeli Knesset [parliament] and now Israel's minister of justice, posted this on Facebook:

> *Behind every terrorist stand dozens of men and women, without whom he could not engage in terrorism. They are all enemy combatants, and their blood shall be on all their heads.*

> *Now this also includes the mothers of the martyrs, who send them to hell with flowers and kisses. They should follow their sons; nothing would be more just. They should go, as should the physical homes in which they raised the little snakes. Otherwise, more little snakes will be raised there.*

Little snakes. The depth of the dehumanization is utterly chilling, and very widespread. It's true that plenty of Arabs return the favor with gusto, but the media has become so saturated with their bigotry that we often miss the fact that the hatred happens on both sides.

Fisk knows all about it. "Sabra and Shatila changed my life as a journalist," he tells me. His eyes go bright for a moment. "The job of a journalist is to be neutral and unbiased, on the side of those who suffer. It is not our job to treat the Middle East like a fifty-fifty game of football. What they teach you at your first newspaper—equal time to both sides—well, even when you think you're being equal, the Middle East is a bloody tragedy. And what happened there—I interviewed an Israeli soldier who was quite psychotic. He was a young officer from France who said, 'I know you are tape-recording this, but the Palestinians are all cunts and I want them dead.' They knew what the Phalange was like."

I can't stop thinking about those people, the women and children cut down like animals, like little snakes. But if I shudder at the thought, how must it be for Robert Fisk, who keeps watching the dead pile up, unable to stop working, to retire and tear his eyes from the Middle East as it burns itself to dust?

"Can I ask you a personal question, Robert?" I say.

"Go ahead," Fisk replies, but a wary look crosses his face.

"Do you still see those people when you close your eyes at night? The ones from Sabra and Shatila."

"No, not at all," he says quickly, firmly. "The only thing that happened was one night after I'd written the big story, I thought the corpses were lying around me on the bed. The reason was that my clothes stank of dead people . . . And we were so tired during the Israeli invasion and siege, absolutely exhausted, that I had strange dreams. I had a dream at one point—I'd been in so many air raids—that through the window of my bedroom, a little tiny Israeli plane came. I could see the pilot, and he whizzed out of the other window."

He gives a short, bright burst of laughter. "That's what happens when you're very tired."

"But you must know about PTSD," I argue. "You're saying all of it never affected you?"

"No, not at all," he repeats. "However terrible the things I've seen . . . I can come home to Beirut, go to a French restaurant, and forget about it. You have to be tough to work in the Middle East, and if you're affected by it very badly, go home."

"But the toughest people I know in this job—they see ghosts at night, most of them," I persist.

"I don't see ghosts," Fisk insists. "I never see ghosts. Never seen a ghost in my life."

"Well, not ghosts. But my friend is a tough guy. He's seen some bad shit. And he freely admits, and I've heard him because I've slept on his couch, that he has terrible nightmares."

"Well, I've never done that," Fisk says uncomfortably. "No, I've been fine. I think you can turn the recorder off now."

"Wait, wait," I respond quickly. "I grew up with journalists, Robert, and I never deluded myself that anything I wrote would make a difference. For me, it was never about changing things—"

"I don't think we do change very much, sorry to say," Fisk interjects shortly. I can see I'm losing him.

"It must bother you, though, seeing all this and writing about it—"

"No. It doesn't."

"And never seeing anything change," I finish. "Did you ever feel as though you detached?"

"No," he says again, with finality. "I felt very sorry for dead people. But when you're around a lot of dead people, you're quite frightened, not because it reminds you that we're all going to die, but because you know the killers aren't far away and they're not going to care about your life. Especially with the indignity at Sabra and Shatila—with the heat of the summer, the bodies were corrupting very quickly. Within two days, they were leaking chemicals all over the road and the stench was indescribable. I remember I did a film interview with Irish television, and I kept having to swipe the flies off my face because they were going from the bodies to me. When I got back to Dublin, they told me they could see me swiping at my face but they couldn't see the flies on TV. The immigration officer said, 'Oh, we know you, Bob. You're the fella that keeps slapping yourself around the face.'"

Fisk barks another quick, loud laugh, like a gunshot.

"I think now I regard the dead as friends who would want me to tell what happened to them, and if the soul exists, if they're moving around, they'll see me and say, 'That's Bob Fisk. He'll tell the world what happened to us.' But that's not posttraumatic stress. That's just my view on it. Now please turn off the recorder."

I turn it off. But I can't turn off the way his face closed like a shutter being snapped when I asked him if he saw ghosts. It's the same look my father gets when anything comes close to the wounds at his core, the ones I watched him drown in food, wine, and money, ignoring them with every fiber of his being.

Because you can't be around the dead that much without seeing ghosts. I watched them flit across Robert Fisk's eyes myself.

Whether he admits it or not, he's haunted by them, just as my father is. I imagine their whispers can become quite loud in the dark
and quiet. I think they must weigh on a person, heavy as the rocks
and crags of the Lebanese coast.

THEN
June 1992

I knew right away things were not how they were supposed to be.

After the glorious, star-spangled homecoming, the AP asked
my dad to choose between a chalet in Switzerland and a private
island off the coast of Antigua in the Caribbean. We were to have
a vacation; some time for our squeaky-new family to bond, away
from the reporters. Luckily, my dad picked the island.

The trip should have been a dream realized. An active, playful
seven-year-old unleashed upon a stretch of white sand and crystal
waters, full of creatures to marvel at: I should have been over the
moon. Instead, it felt like some sort of half nightmare, the kind
where you float above your body and watch it move without your
consent. I cringed at my father's hugs, which felt unnatural and
forced. Who was this man? He wasn't kind and nurturing. He
didn't know me, and didn't seem like he genuinely wanted to. His
attentions were mercurial, fleeting—like the sun across the surface
of the island waters. Only a mirage. Some part of me sensed that his
attempts at connecting with me were stunted, and I shrank from
them.

Now I understand how he must have strained, trying to reach
past the wall he had built in his head—his only protection from the
nightmare he had lived for seven years. How he must have wanted
to hold the child he had only ever seen on TV; how frustrating it
must have been to feel my rigid little body reject him.

What a strange little almost-family we were; my mother, my father, and I. Like puppets on a stage, we jerked and flailed through the awkward script the world had written for us.

The fights started almost immediately. The first one was the Nintendo fight. Someone—I can't remember who now—gifted me with a Super Nintendo, one of many toys presented to me by well-wishers after my father was released. I had never played a video game before. Growing up in Cyprus, I barely ever even watched TV. My mother had been reading to me since I was still in her womb, and at age three, I started reading to her. By seven, I was reading at a teenage level, and much preferred books to cartoons. But the Nintendo was a novelty, and I would sit in our beautiful condo on the beach and play it for hours, moving the little figures around on the screen. Perhaps I liked having control over something in my environment. Or maybe I'm overanalyzing. In any case, it was certainly an escape from the weirdness of our situation.

One day, I had been in front of the TV for hours, and my father decided I should stop playing for some reason I can't remember—maybe to eat dinner at the table or go outside or something. I would learn that his decisions regarding what a child should and should not do were often arbitrary and harsh—likely a product of his childhood, which I later understood was probably much more traumatizing than mine.

I don't remember the fight verbatim. I was seven, after all. All I can recall now is how his face twisted with anger as he shouted, and my tears when he lost patience and yanked the Nintendo out of the TV. That was my first confirmation that the father I got was not the father I needed. I spent the remainder of the day tearful, sullen, and confused.

After Antigua, we moved around for the first few months, then landed in Westchester, New York, where we settled into an unhappy domesticity. My father would constantly berate me for minor infractions—sitting on my feet at the table, not finishing my food, being too hyper and loud. I had a moderate case of ADHD, so I was often possessed by surges of electric-quick energy that had to be released by running, dancing, making shrill, strange noises. We had mandatory family dinners, and I dreaded them, marked as they were by forced conversation and raised voices; they usually ended with me in tears.

I felt completely betrayed: I had waited for his return for as long as I could remember, fantasized about it, longed for it. And then all it brought us was a new kind of pain.

I was very much aware that my father was jealous of the bond my mother and I had formed in his absence. I understand now how difficult it must have been for him, trying to find a place in our somewhat unhealthy attachment to each other. At the time, though, I was heartbroken by his obvious irritation with my presence, and felt as though I had lost my mother as well. I thought of myself as unwanted, inconvenient. He would vacillate between offering me an awkward sort of love and bellowing at me, calling me a spoiled brat or a smartass. He told me on more than one occasion I was the reason he and my mother were always fighting. And it was true. My mother wanted my father and me to build our own rapport, so she hardly ever interfered in his treatment of me while I was in the room. But I heard them screaming at each other downstairs after I had gone to bed.

For her part, my mother became quiet, sullen, and even more preoccupied with me, though in a darker, more complicated way. She would criticize me constantly, and her expectations became almost impossible to fulfill. Mama was always vigilant when it came to my misdeeds and I started to feel as though I was under constant surveillance by a government agency, like I was out on parole and my PO was sure to catch me doing something awful. When I misbehaved, she would punish me, then refuse to speak to me for days, even weeks. I remember prostrating myself outside her bedroom door once, begging hysterically for her to forgive me. She would always say the same thing: "Sorry isn't good enough."

So I retreated into the only place that felt safe: my imagination. I would play in our backyard for hours every day, creating a fantasy world that seemed much more real than the painful isolation waiting inside our house. I began acting out, fighting at school. I cut off my hair, wore boys' clothes; I was always climbing trees. My behavior, as well as my thick glasses, buckteeth, and strange name, made me an easy target for bullying. I had few friends, so there was no solace for me at school, apart from my talent for academics. I was always an honors student, and I still read constantly—books about faraway places, elves, talking animals, demons, and witches. I must have gone through almost everything Tolkien wrote before I was eleven. Things made sense in those books. Characters were either good or bad, heroes or villains. People who were supposed to be heroes weren't inexplicably, bafflingly cruel. And the endings were genuinely happy.

We were constantly in the news—the world expected us to be content, assumed my parents' marriage was solid. It used to make me furious to have to lie to reporters and tell them how thrilled I was to have my daddy home, when in reality, I would cry at night and pray for those men to take him back.

Of course, I had no idea what that really meant. About three years after my dad came home, his book, *Den of Lions,* was published. My mother cowrote it, and it was a huge success. I don't remember how many weeks it was on the *New York Times* bestseller list, but it was a while. I read the book for the first time soon after it came out. I must have been about ten years old. That's when I began to understand exactly how terrible those seven years were for my father. He's a wonderful writer, and he recounted every facet of his fear and misery in excruciating, captivating detail. I've avoided rereading the book for years—there's a copy on my shelf, and I suppose I'll go back to it eventually, but the prospect doesn't thrill me. I'm old enough to truly grasp the horror of his experience now, and I'm afraid to awaken those terrible images in my head.

At the time, certain details and scenes stood out, and have never left me. They broke his glasses when he was taken, for one thing. My father and I have the exact same eye prescription; we're so nearsighted that without glasses or contacts, we might as well be blind. I thought about what it would be like, chained in a basement without being able to see, and I was just as terrified as if it had happened to me.

They eventually taped his glasses back together and gave them back, but the brutality continued. There were regular beatings and psychological torture, of course. They would put a gun to his head, tell him he was about to die, and pull the trigger, but it wouldn't be loaded; he would just hear a click. One year, they wouldn't let him send us a Christmas message and he became so hopeless, so consumed by anger and desperation, that he beat his head against the wall until he was covered in blood and they had to restrain him before he seriously injured himself.

Because, of course, my father was valuable to them. He was a commodity they needed to keep alive, the human equivalent to a fistful of cash. I was also struck by his descriptions of the times his kidnappers had to move him: they would wrap him in duct tape from head to toe, with only his nose sticking out, and throw him in a compartment under a truck. I remember that he and his fellow hostages used to make chess pieces out of tinfoil left over from their meals. They would hide them from their captors and play to escape the endless, silent passage of time, but every now and then, the men who held them would find the pieces and throw them away. There are other things I recall now, similar horrifying vignettes of his captivity, but I try not to think about them too much. It's why I won't watch *Homeland,* why I can't bear being confined or restrained in any way. His experience is burned into my brain, and for years, it was the stuff of my nightmares.

The book answered some of my need to understand what had made him so closed off, so numb and dismissive, but it didn't bring us closer together. My father remained remote and casually, unintentionally hurtful, and I never stopped desperately longing for the daddy I had invented as a small child—the gentle, nurturing man who would hold me close to him and make me feel safe and loved.

My father almost never discusses his captivity with me. Before I started investigating it myself, everything I knew about what happened to him I learned from the book or from watching him speak. But the book ended with his happy return, and it didn't address the very real misery I was experiencing at home.

Some years ago, when I was in my early twenties, my father came to visit me in New York. We went to dinner, and one of us made the mistake of bringing up those years. I still try to avoid broaching that topic with him as much as humanly possible, but it does come up from time to time. My father and I remember my childhood very differently. "I don't understand why you're so upset," he's said to me more than once as I fight back tears, not wanting to break down in front of a restaurant full of strangers. "Things weren't that bad."

But my father didn't live in my head, and as far as I'm concerned, things *were* that bad. At this particular awkward meal, my father mentioned a little vignette from my childhood. He seemed to think it was funny.

When I was nine, we were having one of our innumerable fights. I was a stubborn little girl, and as year bled into unhappy year, I became more and more angry at my situation. Maybe it was the books I was always reading—stories that pitted good and right against bad and wrong. Perhaps it was just a child's innate sense of fairness. Either way, on some level, I knew someone my age should not feel so desperately alone, and it pissed me off.

I don't remember what started the fight that day, but we were screaming at each other, my father red-faced and furious.

"You think you're smarter than me?" he shouted.

"I'm just as smart as you!" I countered shrilly.

"We'll see about that, you little smartass," he said. And the next day, I was whisked away to a child psychologist to have my IQ tested in order to prove I was not actually as smart as he was.

Turns out, we have the exact same IQ.

Decades later, as we sat across from each other at the restaurant in New York City, I gaped at my father, who was laughing about the incident.

"Dad, can't you see how fucked up that was?" I asked him plaintively. The tears started to well up.

"Come on, Sulome," he huffed. "It was a long time ago."

Some months after that dinner, I was recounting the story to a friend. "Jesus," he said when I was through. "It's actually a fucking miracle you turned out this normal. I mean, you're crazier than a bag of cats, but still. You should probably be dead of a heroin overdose."

"Uh-huh." I smiled as I railed up a line of cocaine. "Welcome to my life."

3. THE BOOGEYMEN

Monsters come in all shapes and sizes. Some of them are things
people are scared of. Some of them are things that look like things
people used to be scared of a long time ago. Sometimes monsters are
things people should be scared of, but they aren't.

—NEIL GAIMAN

NOW

The first whispers of the Islamic Jihad Organization were lost in
the noise of the civil war.

Twelve people were killed and twenty-seven wounded in the
1982 car bombing of the French embassy in Beirut. The culprits
were elusive. There were a few mysterious anonymous calls to newspapers by people taking credit for the bombing on behalf of various entities, most of which had never been heard of. One of these
previously unknown names was the Islamic Jihad.

The French had been pissing people off in Lebanon for decades.
Their long-term sponsorship of the Lebanese Christian minority
was an open sore to many Muslims, especially given the outrageous
wartime behavior of Christian factions such as the Phalange. The
country's long-marginalized Shia population, which had already
begun looking to Iran for support, often clashed with the Christians. As if that weren't enough, France's then-president François
Mitterrand was becoming very cozy with Israel, which would in-

vade Lebanon a month later. So the fact that French installations had become a target in Lebanon made sense at the time.

Despite that first phone call, the IJO would go largely unnoticed until April 1983, when a suicide bomber blew up the American embassy in Beirut, killing sixty-three people including eight CIA agents. Robert Ames, the agency's top Middle East analyst and Near East director, died in the blast. It was a devastating blow to the U.S. government, which had joined a multinational intervention force with other Western nations in an attempt to restore some semblance of order and governmental authority in a war that was rapidly spiraling out of control. Although this force was originally intended to be a neutral player in the conflict, it was quickly perceived by many as supportive of Israel, which wasn't making any friends in Lebanon following its invasion. Resentment against America had been mounting in the months preceding the attack, but no one expected such a brutal retaliation.

Ironically, my father covered the embassy attack. In an article for the AP, he quoted an anonymous call by his future captors to a Beirut daily newspaper. The bombing, the caller claimed on behalf of the IJO, was "part of the Iranian revolution's campaign against imperialist targets throughout the world."

Then, an eerie foreshadowing: "We shall keep striking at any imperialist presence in Lebanon, including the multinational force."

Until the embassy bombings, these types of attacks against Western targets were rare, and the emergence of such a tactic was extremely worrying to Western intelligence agencies. Ryan Crocker, a career diplomat with the U.S. State Department, was one of the lucky survivors of the attack. At the time, he was serving as the embassy's political chief, and he would eventually be appointed as U.S. ambassador to Lebanon in 1990, making him the chief State

Department official dealing with the hostage crisis. In a phone interview, he explains the initial U.S. perception of the Islamic Jihad.

"The first concrete indication that there was something new and bad out there came pretty early," Crocker tells me. "I think looking at it just from my perspective, we knew we had a militant Shia Islamic phenomenon supported by Iran and Syria. It was going to be something that we would have to reckon with that would be a real danger to us. It never had the clarity, if you can call it that, of the Palestinian guerrilla movement . . . They were deliberately careful to avoid labels or recognized offices."

It wasn't long before another spectacularly violent display convinced Washington it had a major problem on its hands. On October 23, 1983, two suicide truck bombs simultaneously struck buildings that respectively housed American and French armed units. Fifty-eight French paratroopers and 241 U.S. servicemen lost their lives, making the Beirut barracks bombing the single deadliest day the United States Marine Corps has experienced since its battle at Iwo Jima during World War II.

Again, a mysterious phone call. Again, that name: the Islamic Jihad. My father also covered that event for the AP. Dad had left his home in upstate New York to join the marines when he was seventeen years old and served two tours in Vietnam before becoming a professional journalist. He once told me that in the aftermath of the bombing, he saw someone he had fought with in that ill-fated war. Well, he saw parts of him, enough to recognize, anyway.

This was a catastrophe of epic proportions for the United States. The marines had come to Lebanon to keep the peace, until politics made enemies of the people they were supposed to be protecting. Scores of Americans were dying in a new kind of warfare—one almost impossible to anticipate or prevent, given its nature. It was the dawning of a fearful era.

These days, we live with the constant threat of random bomb-ings and hijackings. Terrorism is a demon we recognize, a familiar evil. At the time of its debut, though, this type of violence perplexed U.S. authorities and horrified the American public. Surely the gov-ernment must know something, people thought as they turned on their televisions to see plumes of smoke rising and shrouded corpses wheeled from ruined buildings. Surely our country can find and punish these monsters.

But U.S. intelligence agencies were stymied. Fred Burton is now vice president at Stratfor, a private intelligence firm known as the shadow CIA. He's written several books and has become a prominent expert on counterterrorism. He joined the U.S. Diplomatic Security Service in 1985, right around the time my father was taken, and worked extensively on the Islamic Jihad file. In a phone conversation with me, he describes American efforts to unearth the identity and motivations of the terrorist group. According to Burton, U.S. intelligence agencies didn't have enough local informers and experience to understand or anticipate the IJO's tactics, which were alien to them at the time.

"I've got to tell you, Sulome, in many ways we were some-what dysfunctional," Burton says. "We just consistently lacked the human intelligence to tell us basics. Who were the IJO? What did they really want? We just didn't know."

I don't know either, and that's troubling. Hezbollah was never shy about expressing what it wanted: an end to Israeli occupation and American "colonialist" influence in Lebanon, legal retribution for the Phalangists' war crimes, and the right of all Lebanese to choose the system of their own government, preferably an Islamic one.

In February 1985, Hezbollah "came out," so to speak, as a po-litical and military movement. It published a manifesto describing those very objectives. Interestingly enough, the manifesto included a reference to the IJO's terrorism:

The US has tried, through its local agents, to persuade the people that those who crushed their arrogance in Lebanon and frustrated their conspiracy against the oppressed were nothing but a bunch of fanatic terrorists . . . such suggestions cannot and will not mislead our umma *[community of Muslims], for the whole world knows that whoever wishes to oppose the US, that arrogant superpower, cannot indulge in marginal acts which may make it deviate from its major objective.*

So even back in 1985, at the time of its birth, Hezbollah was denying involvement in the kidnappings and bombings. Maybe its members were just trying to distance themselves from the terrorism, as the conventional narrative of the hostage crisis dictates. Perhaps I should unquestioningly bow to U.S. government wisdom on the matter, as have countless analysts and reporters who have written about this topic. But their fathers hadn't been kidnapped by these men, so perhaps I have more incentive than they did to pull at the dangling threads of this story.

If I pull long and hard enough, maybe I'll see a pattern there that no one has seen before. Maybe then I can end that sense of uneasy confusion that's been nibbling at me for years before I began this investigation; that little faraway murmur I've been hearing since I was old enough to understand the complexity of what happened to my father. *Something doesn't fit.*

———

Even before social media spurred the short attention span of today's news cycle, television and print media brought these atrocities to American homes. One-off attacks like the embassy and barracks bombings make for compelling airtime: the blood, the bodies, the wails and moans of survivors. But the thing is, TVs switch off, and news stories are plentiful. Our collective memory is brief. The bombings happened in a place as unfamiliar to most Americans as the surface of Mars, an alien region of strange-faced people who speak a strange language. Those disturbing images quickly faded for viewers snug and safe in our national bubble. Lives must be lived, after all, and shock can last only so long.

The terrorists needed a different approach, one that would linger in our minds. The suffering of the dead is quickly forgotten, but the long-term pain of innocent people held against their will—that has staying power. So the kidnappings began.

Robin Wright, a fellow at the United States Institute of Peace and the Woodrow Wilson International Center, both think tanks in Washington, has written several widely acclaimed books on militant Islamist movements. At the time of my father's kidnapping, Wright was also a familiar face at the Commodore Hotel, reporting on the civil war for a number of prominent publications.

"[The Islamic Jihad] discovered that the Americans were quite emotional about their hostages," Wright tells me in her colorful, chaotic office at the Institute of Peace. There are books and documents scattered everywhere; it's a work space I quite identify with. "They learned that was a far more effective technique, and the suicide bombs stopped."

David Dodge was one of the first to be taken, in July 1982. He was president of the American University of Beirut—perhaps the single most valuable gift the United States ever gave Lebanon. It remains practically the only Lebanese institution for higher education from which a degree holds some value outside of the country. The important thing about David Dodge's kidnapping is that he was initially held in Lebanon, but his captors eventually took him to Iran. From what's been documented, Palestinian militants controlling West Beirut, which was the site of Dodge's abduction, were originally implicated in his capture. But Yasser Arafat, then chief of the Palestinian Liberation Organization (PLO), was perceived to be searching desperately for the kidnappers, hoping to see Dodge freed. The Palestinians seemed to already be aware that their cause did not need more bad PR.

It wasn't long before there were indications of Iranian and Lebanese Shia involvement. "Unofficial sources" suggested to the Associated Press that Dodge had been taken with the intention of using him to secure the release of an Iranian diplomat and three of his aides who had been kidnapped in Lebanon, likely by Christian militiamen, earlier that month. This motive seemed to be confirmed when Dodge was released a year later and explained that he had indeed been taken to Tehran and interrogated about the missing Iranians.

Wright says Dodge's kidnapping was a clear cause-and-effect scenario. "The sequence of events was quite logical," she explains. "The Iranians were picked up, and when the outside world did nothing, Iran kept appealing: 'Do something about them. Find them; tell us what happened to them. Look for them. They had diplomatic plates. They had protection. This is the route they were taking, these are the checkpoints.' There was this plaintive appeal, but in the aftermath of the embassy takeover in Tehran, in the midst of the Iran-Iraq War, there was a sense of, 'Why should we help the Iranians?' Nobody really cared, and the Lebanese weren't very helpful."

The motives for the next abduction of a U.S. citizen seem less clear-cut. Reverend Benjamin Weir was captured in May of 1984 while he was taking a walk with his wife. Weir lived in Shia West Beirut and worked for Muslim charities, so it was sadly ironic that Shia Muslims would kidnap him. The Islamic Jihad claimed responsibility for this as well. In another telephone message, they expressed their ultimate goal: "We will not leave any American on Lebanese soil."

At this point, the State Department issued an urgent warning to all U.S. citizens in Lebanon: essentially, get the fuck out of the country, or stay at your own peril.

There's another very important hostage who was kidnapped almost exactly a year before my father was taken: William Francis Buckley, the CIA station chief in Beirut. His kidnapping was another catastrophic blow to the agency. As station chief, he had plenty of secrets inside his head that the U.S. government was deeply invested in keeping from terrorists. Also, his friends in the CIA must have had an idea of the vicious torment an agent would be subjected to at the hands of people like the Islamic Jihad. The first of three videos showing Buckley being tortured that were sent to the U.S. embassy removed any doubt. From what I hear, by the third tape, the man had been abused into insanity. At the end of it all, he was "a gibbering wretch," barely able to string words together into a sentence.

A little over a year later, Buckley would die in the same room my father was being held in. Apparently he was talking to himself as his life slipped away; Dad wrote about it in his book. I remember crying as I read that passage for the first time, at about age ten.

"Oh God," Buckley had muttered in the dark place they shared, no longer cognizant that he was speaking his thoughts aloud. "I've lasted for a year, and now my body is failing me."

————

Dad was well aware of the dangers he faced before he was taken. But until my father was kidnapped, journalists in conflict zones hadn't become the walking bull's-eyes they are today. There was an implicit understanding that parties on all sides should avoid targeting reporters, who were, ostensibly anyway, neutral witnesses.

I still have an AP T-shirt my father gave my mother before he was taken. I often sleep in it. It reminds me of a different time in journalism, one I fear will never return. On the back, it reads PRESS, DON'T SHOOT in five different languages. The idea of wearing such a T-shirt in most wars these days is ludicrous. Advertising oneself as a member of the press basically means issuing an invitation to every asshole with a longing for ransom money or a hankering to televise the gruesome death of a Westerner.

So maybe it was that Dad felt a false sense of safety as a reporter documenting the atrocities of the Lebanese civil war, many of which were being committed against Muslims, both Shia and Sunni. Or perhaps it was just the arrogance and delusion of invincibility that plague so many of us, not only journalists. Either way, while most Americans in Lebanon listened to their government and skedaddled, my father stayed put. I wonder if he would take that back now. If he were given a ride in a time-traveling car, *Back to the Future* style, would he return to 1985 and abandon the innocent people dying, starving, and suffering—the ones he felt such a calling to tell the world about? I'm not sure. Knowing my dad as I do, there's a good chance he still wouldn't have left Beirut, even if he had known what was in store for him. My father is a reporter to the core. He considered it his life's work to tell the truth about war—no matter the price.

Then, another whispered name. A culprit began to materialize: the ultimate boogeyman. I'm not sure when the U.S. government first heard of him, but two of my father's friends would see his name scrawled on a napkin in a Cyprus bar, and soon after, it became clear that this man was a key player in the Islamic Jihad's twisted game.

All of Dad's circle of friends were reporters. They had their own sources, and after he was abducted, they all worked their connections as hard as they could, trying to find information on his whereabouts and condition. During my first Skype conversation with Shazi, as I sit sweating at my dining room table in Fanar, she tells me about how she and Robert Fisk began their quest to find my father.

"I had a very good source in Tehran," she begins. "We used to call him Annie so that nobody would know who we were talking about, but it was a man. Anyway, this guy used to be part of the Iranian regime, but at the time when I got in touch with him, he had left his job and was doing business. I called him in Tehran and I said, 'Can you do something? What can you do?' He said, 'Let me find out.' After a few exchanges, he told me he had talked to the Iranian regime and they wanted to know what happened to the four Iranians who had disappeared."

Shazi and Fisk made some inquiries into the whereabouts of the missing Iranians. Most of their sources seemed to think the men were dead, and they relayed this to Annie. But their dialogue with him continued.

"I put Fisk in charge of contact with this guy, but of course we kept your mother informed, and she became very dependent on Annie," Shazi murmurs softly. "I think she was clinging to him, to his information. It made her keep going."

This hurts my heart a little. I remember how my mother's face would tighten and turn ash gray sometimes when I was very small. I can still hear her sobbing behind a closed door.

"This guy started coming into Cyprus to talk with us, because it was very dangerous to talk over the phone," Shazi tells me. "We [Shazi and Fisk] went one night to a pub, because it was dark and noisy. We didn't want anybody to hear us. It was like a James Bond movie. He wrote down—and I still have this piece of paper; it's become yellow now—he wrote down the name Imad Mughniyeh. We had never heard of him.

"He didn't even want to utter his name," says Shazi. I shiver.

———

It wasn't long before the United States became aware of Mughniyeh's connection to the IJO. The common understanding of his motive at the time—which has largely stayed the same—is that he was kidnapping Westerners to force the United States into putting pressure on the Kuwaiti government. Supposedly, Mughniyeh wanted to free seventeen Shia men imprisoned for bombing the U.S. and French embassies in Kuwait earlier in 1983. One of the prisoners was Mustafa Badr al-Din, Mughniyeh's friend and brother-in-law. The IJO communiqués always demanded that the "Kuwait 17" be freed in exchange for the Western hostages.

But I don't believe that could have been the sole factor driving Mughniyeh to commit such acts of violence. Besides, his seventeen cronies were all freed when Iraq invaded Kuwait in 1990—yet my father wasn't released until December 1991, a year and a half later. The United States clearly didn't have much influence over Kuwait, or the men would have been freed right away. I need to find out more about why Mughniyeh kidnapped my father and the other hostages, because this explanation seems inadequate.

A year or so before my father was released, Barbara Bodine would become the U.S. State Department's acting coordinator for counterterrorism. As such, she was extremely preoccupied with the hostage file. Her name caught my eye in some documents on my father's captivity Dad requested be declassified under the Freedom of Information Act shortly after he came home. Well into my investigation, I travel to D.C. to view them at George Washington University's National Security Archive. I'm shocked to discover that despite the fact that Dad was requesting information on his own kidnapping, what seemed like a good 80 percent of the documents he received from government agencies were completely redacted.

Apparently, when presented with a list of the names my father and his lawyer believed were members of the Islamic Jihad, the Drug Enforcement Administration, which had agents in Lebanon at the time and was monitoring narcotics activity among Shia Muslims, gave him a politely worded response I still laugh about. In a letter, they expressed their regret that they were unable to provide him with any information on these people, as doing so would violate their privacy. However, if Dad would kindly print out letters of authorization, find his kidnappers, and get their signatures, the DEA would fulfill his request.

Whatever happened to Dad, the U.S. government was in no hurry to tell anyone about it; not even him.

I do manage to get some sources out of the declassified papers, though, and Bodine is one of them. I interview her shortly afterward in her office at Georgetown University, where she now teaches. She's a kind, competent-looking woman in her sixties, and she's unusually frank with me during our conversation—well, unusual for a diplomat, anyway.

"There are some people who are fundamentally pathological," Bodine says firmly when asked about the IJO and Mughniyeh. "These groups will attract them and give them a purpose and a reason . . . These are murderers and kidnappers and hijackers. To them, the political cause is utterly and completely irrelevant."

Part of this makes sense. Anyone who would take a man against his will, keep him in chains for years, and treat him like an animal is clearly not morally sound. But as far as I know, there were dozens of men involved in the bombings and kidnappings. Could all of them have been psychopaths without consciences, men who reveled in hurting others? Or were there some who told themselves they were doing all this for the good of their country? Did they justify their actions as they lay awake at night, reciting like a poem the wrongs perpetrated against their people? Were they convinced that committing these atrocities was their only weapon against the powerful nations that opposed them and the world that stood by and watched as they suffered?

When asked about this, Bodine acknowledges the complexity of a situation that breeds terrorism.

"There is a very high correlation between being occupied and terrorism," she admits. "Probably that's the highest correlation. It's higher than a poverty correlation; certainly higher than a religious correlation. In the case of Lebanon, there was Israeli occupation. That tends to make people far more militant and desperate.

"All I can imagine is that you would have to be at a level of hopelessness and anger to sign up to die," she continues thoughtfully. "It is almost inconceivable to the rest of us. On one level, it's harder to understand than even the drive to kill somebody. You might kill somebody for self-preservation, but killing yourself is a very extreme step . . . the occupation aspect is very interesting and says a lot about Lebanon, which has been occupied by someone almost continuously. The Lebanese and the Palestinians are in a race for longevity of occupation by another country, and what you will sometimes do if you can't actually get at your immediate occupier is to go for their outside supporter."

In this case, that was America, of course. The United States' close relationship with Israel seems to have cost it dearly during the Lebanese civil war. But that's an alliance rarely questioned in

Washington. It's become as familiar as the national monuments we immediately recognize, as American as the Statue of Liberty or the Lincoln Memorial. Our special friendship with the Jewish state is automatic, knee-jerk, like a child yelling "Polo" in response to "Marco." But I think the years have proved it comes with a price.

———

Around the same time that Mughniyeh was leading the Islamic Jihad on its terror spree, a different name was being whispered in the south of Lebanon. A group of extremely religious Shia Muslims seemed to have nominated themselves as the chosen defenders of their tiny, beset nation. Sponsored and trained by Iran, they emerged from a religious movement into a militia and began to engage in effective guerrilla-style warfare against occupying Israeli troops as well as Israel's local Christian proxy, the South Lebanon Army. These people have also gone down in history as the first Islamic group to embrace suicide bombings, a tactic they employed with great success against Israeli convoys and checkpoints. The group would become known as Hezbollah, the Party of God, and it quickly became a serious headache for Israel.

"I remember very well," Randa Slim tells me in another D.C. think-tank office. She's director of an initiative at the Middle East Institute and a research fellow at the New America Foundation. Slim is a well-known expert on Lebanon and Hezbollah. She's also Lebanese Shia and grew up in Dahiyeh, where Hezbollah would eventually entrench itself as thoroughly as it did in the south.

"I remember my cousin coming to me and saying, 'There are these young men who will wear their shrouds before they go to the front lines, fighting the Christians,'" she continues. "I said, 'What? Wearing their shrouds?' You know, their *kafan*, for burial. Their burial shrouds. He said, 'Yeah, they're called Hezbollah. They go and fight the Christians.' This is in Dahiyeh, where we were sitting. I remember exactly the scene. The electricity was cut off, and we were sitting on the balcony. It was summer. It was definitely before the Israeli invasion . . . that was the first time I heard about Hezbollah."

All my life, I was convinced that Hezbollah and the Islamic Jihad were the same thing. The Western narrative that's coalesced over the years has always maintained that the Islamic Jihad Organization was just a cover for Hezbollah, a name they used to provide themselves with plausible deniability for the terrorist acts they perpetrated against the West. It's an explanation that makes sense, given both groups' use of suicide bombings as well as the angry rhetoric they employed against Israel and its American sponsors. Known members of the Islamic Jihad were associated with Hezbollah and would eventually rise high in the militia's ranks. Some of them still hold influential positions in the organization today.

Also, at the same time as the Islamic Jihad was waging its terror campaign, Hezbollah consolidated a significant amount of power in Lebanon, essentially replacing Amal, the more secular Shia militia, as the representatives of their people. It was assumed that nothing could happen in Dahiyeh or the Shia regions of the Beqaa Valley, both areas where my father was held, without the approval of Hezbollah. My father always believed that to be the case, and he told me that at one point, he was actually imprisoned in one of Hezbollah's headquarters.

Hezbollah's responsibility for the Islamic Jihad's actions is a narrative that goes largely unquestioned these days. Even as the militia expanded into the monolithic political party it is today, the group still can't escape the legacy of terrorism that has haunted it since the war. And until I started examining the circumstances of my father's captivity, I didn't question it either.

But as I would discover, Lebanon's history is as intricate as its landscape, which shifts from lush valleys to snowcapped mountains to rocky coasts. The truth about what happened to my father would prove complex and elusive, much like the nature of the country that stole so much of his life, and mine.

THEN
February 2003

Clink, clink, clink.

There was a moment when I wasn't sure what had fallen out of my coat pocket onto the floor of my dormitory common area. Just a few seconds, really. Then realization dawned. *Oh, fuck,* I thought helplessly. I rushed to grab it, but it had dropped not three feet from my dorm master's sensible shoes, and she got there first.

"What is this?" she asked, holding up the marijuana pipe. I'm pretty sure she knew what it was, so the question was rhetorical.

I said the first lie that came to my lips. "It's not mine."

"Uh-huh. Then whose would it be?" Her skepticism was palpable. I was positive she could smell my terror. Private boarding school teachers have a nose for fear.

"A friend gave it to me. To hold for him. So his parents wouldn't find it."

The dorm master raised an eyebrow. "Okay, well, you'll have to tell me who he is," she said, but I could see the doubt cross her face. A glimmer of hope. Was it possible I'd be able to bullshit my way out of this? I unleashed the tears.

"This can't be happening!" I wailed. "I'm graduating in three months! I was just trying to help a friend! Please don't tell the dean, please . . . I'm supposed to go . . . to NYU . . ." I dissolved in sobs.

The dorm master put a hand on my shoulder. "Sorry, Sulome," she told me, sounding honestly regretful. "I have to tell the dean, otherwise my job is on the line."

She shook her head. "It's a shame, though, it really is. You're such a smart girl. Why do you have to do this stuff?"

After a long, tearful conversation with the dean and what basically amounted to the Holy Inquisition by a "peer committee" of my schoolmates (three of whom I'd seen getting drunk and high at the last house party someone threw) that ended with a vote to expel me, I asked myself that same question in the passenger seat of my father's car as my school disappeared behind us. *Why do I do this stuff?*

I was set to graduate cum laude. I knew because a teacher on the committee all but told me I was next in line. I had just been accepted to New York University's Tisch School of the Arts, early decision, no less. I finally had a group of close friends. We weren't the most popular clique on campus but we weren't losers either. After I spent two long years nursing an incredibly cliché crush on the football team quarterback (who also starred in all the plays), he finally agreed to put a label on our hurried trysts. I had a boyfriend, albeit a reluctant one. Why did I have to fuck it all up so thoroughly?

My father was furious, of course, but it was this almost befuddled anger that clawed at my heart, as if he walked outside that day expecting snow and was hit by an avalanche. He just looked confused, like he didn't know who I was or where I had come from. He barely said a word the entire ride back to hell; otherwise known as Athens, Ohio. The only words that came out of his mouth were "I'm not going to tell your mother. You have to tell her." Mama was in Lebanon for a couple of months, and the thought of calling her to say I'd just been expelled from the school my parents had spent probably $100,000 on at that point made my mouth go bone dry.

———

My parents had decided to move to Ohio around the time I was turning fourteen. My father had experienced a sudden urge to become Old McDonald and buy a farm. He got a job teaching at Ohio University in Athens, and we moved right before I started eighth grade—probably the worst time in a teenager's life to find oneself in a place where everyone at school has known each other since kindergarten. Also, I had very little in common with my peers there. I had lived in about six countries by then and traveled to many others. Many of my classmates hadn't even left the state, and I'm pretty sure they thought I was really weird for talking about Lebanon or Cyprus or any of the other places I'd been.

I was also at the tail end of an incredibly awkward phase. I decided right before we moved to cut all my hair off again, and frizzy Arab-girl hair does not look good in a pixie cut. It mostly just grew out instead of down. I still wore glasses because my mother wouldn't let me get contact lenses, acne abruptly grew to be a concern, and as if that weren't bad enough, I had a mouthful of braces. A late bloomer, I still had the body of a child. Overall, like most teenagers, I was in a hurry to grow up and felt like a complete alien in my own skin.

Typical adolescence stuff, right? But there was the added weirdness of literally everyone knowing who my father was and our family's strange history. Since Dad was teaching journalism at the university and it was a small town, word spread quickly. Kids at school would ask me about it, but their curiosity seemed detached, as if they were examining some strange species of animal at a zoo. Let's just say it didn't make me any cooler, just more out of place.

Although I had no idea how to talk to boys, I also had no idea how to say no to them, so after a rather unpleasant make-out session at a party, I suddenly had a reputation for being slutty. Few kids in my grade showed any interest in being friends with me, and I was completely fucking miserable at school.

Then there was my home life. My parents were fighting more and more, and I started acting out in earnest. Screaming matches became a daily occurrence. My mother seemed to think forbidding me to do any of the things other girls my age did—wear makeup or dresses above the knee, watch R-rated movies—would trap me safely in my childhood forever. I understand now that she was just trying to keep me protected, in her dysfunctional way. But at the time, it felt like her strictness was nothing more than pure spite. My punishments seemed way out of proportion to my misdeeds—I was constantly being grounded for weeks at a time, and she would still give me the cold shoulder for what seemed like relatively minor infractions. As her criticisms and nagging became almost compulsive, I began to feel like everything about me displeased her, and started to believe somewhere inside me that I was disgusting right down to my core.

As for Dad, he remained remote and brusque for the most part, and our interactions became almost entirely limited to my shrieks and his bellows. I was a stubborn girl, and angry at what felt like his lack of concern for me. Subconsciously, I knew I'd get his attention by being sullen and talking back to him, which always got results, albeit negative ones. I think I just wanted to feel as though I mattered enough for him to become emotional about me, even if that emotion was fury. He once told me, "Sulome, you're the only person who can infuriate me to the point of rage." I remember being strangely comforted by this.

Finally, there was the lawsuit. Sometime after we moved to Athens, my family sued Iran for sponsoring the terrorists who kidnapped Dad. The legislation that allowed American victims of terrorism to sue governments proven to have sponsored the groups that victimized them was relatively recent. I remember testifying in court and crying when I recounted how I used to ask God for them to take my father back, because he was so damaged after he came home. It was the first time I had really thought or talked about how my father's captivity affected me. My parents and I actually filed three separate lawsuits, and when I was fifteen years old, I was awarded somewhere in the neighborhood of $6 million in frozen Iranian assets held in the United States, after taxes and lawyers' fees.

All my money went straight to a trust fund, of course, but my parents collectively received settlements of around $40 million, and our lives abruptly changed. We had never been poor, but not particularly rich either, and it was great in many ways—we could suddenly afford all the things we wanted. But Dad didn't handle the money well. He started to throw it around in public and became what I saw at the time as pompous and arrogant. Our fights increased in frequency. My mother adopted the opposite stance and grew disapproving and judgmental of his spending habits. She would also constantly harangue him about the fact that he was putting on a lot of weight. The distance between them grew ever wider, and they would often end up screaming at each other as much as they yelled at me.

Looking back, I realize why they reacted so differently to our newfound wealth. My father grew up dirt-poor in upstate New York, a region I've heard called the Kentucky of the East Coast. His dad was a chicken farmer and a truck driver, and their large family— Dad was one of six kids—lived on very little for much of his childhood. He left home at seventeen and built a successful career as a journalist through sheer force of will and his vast, lightning-quick intelligence. Because he was raised with nothing in a culture that prized wealth and rampant consumption, he wanted everything, and he suddenly had the means to buy it. So he did.

Mama grew up dirt-poor as well, but in Beirut during a horrific civil war. She was raised scrimping and saving as her family struggled to eke out a living under the most dire of circumstances. During the tremendous uncertainty of war, she never knew how long money would last, especially when my grandmother was constantly spending whatever they had to feed her gambling addiction. To this day, despite the millions she's managed to hold on to while my father's wealth is gone, the woman still refuses to spend more than forty dollars on an item of clothing and has shopped at T.J.Maxx for as long as I've known her. When I was a child, instead of name-brand cereals like Lucky Charms or Cookie Crisp or whatever the other kids ate, we had to get the giant bags of knockoff brands like Charms O'Luck and Crispy Cookies.

Some of the difference in the way they handled the money was cultural and personality-driven, of course. My mother has the traditional Lebanese trait of thriftiness and financial savvy, and she is by nature a careful, calculating person. Dad's very American consumerism, as well as his impulsivity and inability to think long term—traits I inherited—made it easy for him to spend thoughtlessly, almost compulsively. But I see now that much of their conflict was rooted in their respective upbringings, and it's a sad thought. It reminds me of a bitter little poem by Philip Larkin:

> *They fuck you up, your mum and dad.*
> *They may not mean to, but they do.*
> *They fill you with the faults they had*
> *And add some extra, just for you.*

In many ways, my parents' families and childhood environments dictated the rest of their lives. I live in constant terror of the same thing happening to me.

At the very least, you'd think the money would have earned me some popularity at school, but Athens is a poverty-stricken town, at least for people not associated with the university. Most of the kids seemed to think of me as a snotty little rich girl, and their envy led to much nastiness and shit-talking. I was snubbed even more frequently for my nice things and the impressive mansion my parents decided to build atop a hill right outside the town.

I suppose it's no surprise that I quickly discovered alcohol and pot. Right before I began high school, I realized my unhappy awkwardness was much less immediate when I was drunk or high. Unfortunately, my mother had an uncanny knack for catching me every single time I snuck a drink or a joint, which just cemented my idea of her as an implacable archenemy I had to constantly outwit. One particularly unpleasant incident took place in the middle of ninth grade, and over fifteen years later, I still cringe at it.

I had managed to get a role in a school play, which was very exciting to me, as I had recently decided I wanted to become an actress. I finally had a best friend, a pretty, popular girl named Jessica who was dating one of the cool, artsy older boys in the play—increasing my popularity quotient by association. A bunch of senior boys offered to give us a ride home one night, and they lit up a joint on our way to my house. I took a couple of puffs and felt fine, but Mama was all over me as soon as I walked in the door.

"Why are you late?" she asked suspiciously.

"I don't know, Mom; they took forever to leave."

She sniffed at my clothes. "You've been smoking pot."

"No! I swear, I wouldn't do that. I mean, how dumb would that be, smoking right before I came home?" I prayed my stupidity would save me.

My mother was unmoved by my protestations. "You're high, Sulome. Tell me who you were with. What were these boys' names?"

Hours of screaming and begging ensued, but she eventually

managed to pry their names out of me, and the next day, my father called up the parents of each senior boy and told them their son had been giving marijuana to a freshman girl. After that, I was a pariah. Kids practically spat at me in the hallway, and I heard "narc" and "tattletale" whispered as I scurried to class, trying desperately to avoid their glares. I became quietly, profoundly depressed, and even started cutting at my wrists from time to time, just because I couldn't stand the pain of my own existence and needed release from it somehow.

Another rather horrific incident cemented my conviction that I had to leave Athens. Sometime after the pot affair, I was finally released from my three-month home incarceration. Jessica's mother was going out of town, so she was throwing a party, and I managed to talk Mama into letting me sleep over at her house. The party was huge, and all the cool kids were in attendance. I started drinking early, enjoying the way the alcohol lubricated my conversation, made it easier to loosen up and tell jokes or show my personality in a way I was too self-conscious to do sober. At some point, a partygoer broke out a bottle of 151-proof liquor, and after a couple of shots of that, the rest of the night went mostly black.

I do remember puking violently, and someone saying, "We need to call her parents. She might have alcohol poisoning." I was unceremoniously deposited on the front step of Jessica's house at my parents' feet and they took me to the hospital, where I had my stomach pumped. After that, we were all in agreement that it would be best if I enrolled in a boarding school about three hours away, near Cleveland. I was dying to get away from both the town and my parents, so off I went.

At boarding school, the braces and glasses were quickly discarded. I grew into my body and became more attractive, confident, and socially adept. I discovered my sexuality got me attention and approval from boys, something I had started to desperately crave—though it came with its share of mean-spirited gossip. But I had real friends for the first time in what felt like years. I was challenged by and excelled at the school's rigorous curriculum. In other words, I found some self-confidence and a small piece of happiness that was just mine, and I held it close.

Until I was kicked out, of course. Then I had to go back to Athens and finish my last three months of high school in disgrace. That's when things really started to go south. Athens is a quiet, boring place to be a teenager, and there's a significant amount of drug abuse. My boyfriend at boarding school had broken up with me hours after I was expelled and I found myself in a place I hated, with barely any friends. The empty place in me grew canyon wide. I needed something to fill it and was soon dabbling in harder substances; cocaine became my favorite way to erase my misery. Luckily, NYU didn't withdraw my acceptance, so I was still off to New York in the fall, which was a light at the end of the tunnel. But I would often find myself doing lines off the toilet lid in the school restroom or running around town with some guy, rolling on Ecstasy. My parents seemed to just give up and let me do what I wanted, which was both painful and exhilarating.

One night that summer, I was spread-eagled on the grass in my friend's yard. The night jittered and danced, full of color and mystery, thanks to the mushrooms I had eaten earlier and the coke that followed. I remember lying on the damp earth, looking up at the sky, and thinking, *Maybe this has gone too far.*

4. THE RESISTANCE

If someone puts their hands on you, make sure they
never put their hands on anybody else again.
—MALCOLM X

NOW

The way Hezbollah tells it, they saw God leave their ruined country,
and they wanted to bring him back.

I'm at a house in Dahiyeh, the Shia suburb of Beirut, sitting on
a couch facing Hamza akl Hamieh. He looks to be in his early sixties, grizzled, with a calm demeanor and a patient smile. He used to
be an Amal militiaman and one of the most prolific airplane hijackers in the world. Hamza completed six hijackings between 1979 and
1982, including Kuwait Airways Flight 561 in 1982 and the longest
hijacking in history, that of the Libyan Arab Airlines 727, which
he took control of midair and proceeded to fly six thousand miles
in three days, making multiple stops throughout Europe and the
Middle East before landing in Beirut. He claims he never harmed a
single person he hijacked. Whether that's true or not, he certainly
saw the Shia uprising in Lebanon with his own eyes and fought in
their war to be heard by the world.

"Where did your journey begin, *hajj*?" I ask him through my
interpreter. *Hajj* is an honorific for men who have completed the

Islamic pilgrimage to the holy city of Mecca, in Saudi Arabia. I generally have someone translate interviews like this for me, so as not to miss anything. It's also quite useful to pretend not to speak any Arabic in these situations. That way, I can listen to what they're saying about me when they think I can't understand them.

"We had demands of our government," Hamza begins. "In the early seventies, there was a movement headed by Imam Musa al-Sadr to demand the improvement of the lives of less fortunate people in Lebanon. We wanted the development of Akkar, Baalbek, Hermel, the south, and the misery belt on the outskirts of Beirut. It was for all the oppressed people in Lebanon, but we, as Shia, were the ones suffering most. So it became a Shia movement."

"This was before the civil war?" I ask.

"Yes, but then the war started, for several very complicated reasons," Hamza responds. "At the time, Israeli incursions into the south of Lebanon were increasing. So Imam al-Sadr called for the establishment of a Lebanese resistance to defend the south, because the government refused to send troops there. We called this the Movement of the Deprived, and it was a political, social movement. Amal, or the Lebanese Resistance Detachments, was the armed wing of this movement. We started training and organizing local youth."

In August 1978, Imam Musa al-Sadr disappeared while traveling in Libya. Libyan leader Muammar Gaddafi was widely blamed for his disappearance, although Gaddafi's motives remain unclear to this day. Amal is still around, of course. Its cartoonish green-and-yellow flag flutters from many buildings in the Shia areas of Lebanon. But Amal, which means "hope" in Arabic, is now a shadow of its child, a breakaway faction that would eventually become the most powerful militia and political party in Lebanon: Hezbollah, the group many believe is a latter-day incarnation of the Islamic Jihad Organization.

Today, in Hezbollah territory, there is little unregulated crime, because criminals aren't remanded to the corrupt and inefficient Lebanese justice system. Hezbollah has its own justice, and it's usually better avoided. Dahiyeh, part of what was once known as the misery belt, isn't exactly luxurious, but it's not so miserable these days. Hezbollah isn't just a militia; it also provides many social services for the poor and runs the areas under its control with order and precision. It's as much a part of Lebanon now as the grotto at Jeita or the Roman ruins in Baalbek. But Hezbollah started as a murmur of discontent; a rebellion within the ranks of the Deprived.

———

In 1978, the United Nations Interim Force in Lebanon (UNIFIL) was formed by the UN in response to a request from the Lebanese delegation. They wanted Israel out of southern Lebanon. Israeli troops had just invaded and occupied the region in response to PLO incursions into Israel. Always the considerate houseguests, Palestinian militants had been using Lebanon, their reluctant, fragmenting host country, as a base to launch attacks against their hated enemy.

But according to some historians and observers of the Middle East, what the PLO actually, inelegantly did was kick down a door the Israelis had been trying to open for years. Veteran journalist David Hirst's *Beware of Small States,* an excellently sourced history that traces the origins of the Arab-Israeli conflict, makes the case that Israel had been eyeing its little northern neighbor for a long time. According to Hirst, who uses documented statements by the very first Zionist leaders to support this narrative, Israel's founding fathers had hoped to add some enviably lush Lebanese territory to the rapidly expanding Jewish state. In what was left of Lebanon, they planned to install a sympathetic Christian government that would be an ally against the hordes of angry Muslims that surrounded them.

I'm going to digress for a moment here and address the elephant some of you may have noticed stomping around in the middle of the room. It's no secret that I disagree strongly with Israeli government policy, both then and now. A glance at my Twitter feed will remove all doubt about that. I never quite saw the point of hiding my personal opinions about the Middle East in an attempt to be perceived as "objective." It always felt like lying. This is an approach I've been attacked for, but journalists are people too, and we see things most Americans don't. What we see shapes our beliefs about the regions in which we work—and because we are close observers, our opinions are important. I still believe in the value of objectivity in journalism, but I think one can have opinions and still write as fairly as possible.

In my reporting, I try my hardest to quiet my own views and imagine what it's like inside the heads of the people on both sides of whatever conflict I'm writing about. That requires more than just including a perfunctory, requisite quote from the side I don't agree with, a tactic many news outlets use as a nod to "objectivity." Accurately portraying the complexity of these issues demands a certain level of empathy, even for people whose actions I have the most trouble understanding. It's not a perfect process, and I don't always succeed, but I do believe in its importance.

I came to my current beliefs through half a lifetime spent in the Middle East, and the evidence I've accumulated through research and on-the-ground reporting. I've examined this conflict in all its ugliness and horror, and I've learned one thing: there are no good guys here. There are assholes and bigger assholes. Moral of the story: don't be an asshole, and if you are, I'm going to write about it.

It would be naive in the extreme to believe Hamas or the Palestinian Authority are morally pure or motivated simply by concern for the Palestinian people. Certainly Lebanon and other Arab nations have demonstrated that Israel is not the only country willing to persecute and marginalize Palestinians.

However, any real examination of the facts, uncolored by political agenda or propaganda, will reveal that we in America are not getting the full story of what goes on in the West Bank or the Gaza Strip. While every instance of Palestinian violence against Israelis is fairly well publicized, for instance, there is barely a whisper in international news coverage when an Israeli soldier shoots a Palestinian boy, sometimes in the back as he flees, or a Palestinian child is deliberately run down by an Israeli settler's car, as is reported to have happened several times in the past two years alone. In these instances, arrests are seldom made and the killings continue to occur with impunity. To be clear, any act of violence offends my nature, including those committed by Palestinians. I'm simply pointing out that by and large, the West is primarily hearing one side of this issue.

I once called Dad from Beirut, shortly after I had started working there, in a rage at what I felt was the injustice of the things I was seeing and hearing about. "Sweetheart," he said. "You're certainly not the first journalist—nor will you be the last—to take a look at the Middle East and notice things aren't the way you've been told they are."

I'm certainly not an anti-Semite with an ax to grind. The man who put the diamond ring I now wear on my left hand grew up Orthodox Jewish. Which God you pray to or where you come from means nothing to me. As far as I'm concerned, you can paint yourself purple and worship the moon. You're a person, I'm a person, and I will treat you with the respect you deserve by virtue of your humanity. It's not about whom you were born to, because that's essentially the only difference between us: an accident of birth.

I think the Jews and the Shia have more in common than either would like to admit. Both have been pushed around for generations; both carry a tremendous legacy of oppression around their necks. Both have emerged from their suffering with a drive to make sure no one ever pushes them around again. Both have been stockpiling money, power, and weapons for decades, determined to break from historical patterns. *This time, world, you try to hurt us, and we'll make you wish you hadn't.* It's an underlying mantra I hear in the rants of Iranian ayatollahs and the threats of Israeli generals. *No more. Not this time.*

Unfortunately, this approach to the world is much like an ouroboros, that familiar image of a snake eating its own tail. When you live in constant fear of persecution, you often act in ways that create situations certain to invite more persecution. Human nature being what it is, instead of learning from the suffering of our people and trying not to cause suffering in return, we often disregard those hurt in our quest to make sure we don't suffer again.

If I were an Israeli in 1978, living in my still-new homeland not long after the Holocaust, with millions of furious Arab faces glaring at me from across my fragile borders, I might be frightened and angry enough to justify the kind of aggression Israel demonstrated in its repeated invasions of Lebanon as well as its brutal treatment of the Palestinians. I might grip handfuls of the earth on which I built my house, the land I'd been promised for so long, now warm and real between my fingers. I might look at the enemies who wanted to take it from me and think, *No. Not this time.* But that doesn't make the Israeli government's actions any more right than kidnapping human beings and holding them against their will to achieve political goals.

Let me be clear: Israelis have not escaped unscathed from this conflict. While Israeli casualties are dwarfed by the total number of Palestinian deaths resulting from hostilities, that doesn't mean the Israeli lives lost were any less valuable or precious to the people who loved them. Also, living in a constant state of terror that your country will be attacked—regardless of why—must take its toll on the collective Israeli psyche. I imagine that kind of fear must generate a lot of preemptive aggression. I also think it's probably just an exhausting way to live.

But what seems even more apparent to me is a burgeoning cultural identity crisis: who are the Jews? What do they stand for? Increasingly, large numbers of secular Jews have turned away from the hardline policies of the Likud government. Many diaspora Jews, Americans in particular, seem to be losing faith that Israel's current government is on the path to a peaceful, prosperous existence for the Jewish people.

By and large, American Jews tend to be liberal in their politics. They care about the poor and disenfranchised. As social media exposes the ever-mounting inequality of the Israeli-Palestinian conflict, I believe it's becoming more and more difficult for them to reconcile Israel's treatment of the Palestinians with their own values. Simultaneously, the expanding population of ultra-religious Jews has embraced Likud policies wholeheartedly. The resulting fracture is increasingly noticeable to me.

And let's not forget the Israeli army. I'm sure that much of the IDF believes strongly in their government's message and mission. But the voices of soldiers who have lost faith in their country's policies are growing louder. One organization, Breaking the Silence, brings together former Israeli military personnel who disagree with their government's occupation of the West Bank and Gaza Strip. After reading an essay I wrote about Lebanon's disintegrating security situation, a former Israeli soldier reached out to me and personally apologized for how his country had treated my mother's nation. He served in Israel's 2006 war with Lebanon—a conflict I witnessed while in Beirut for a cousin's wedding. Being American, I was evacuated to Cyprus via U.S. Navy destroyer. Lebanese people living on the country's southern border with Israel were not so lucky. Almost twelve hundred Lebanese died in the 2006 war, the majority of whom were civilians.

"Jewish kids were not raised to blow up villages," an Israeli friend recently told me. "It causes a lot of trauma, for them as well as for the villagers." He happens to be staunchly pro-government. But he's respectful and well spoken, and my conversations with him have given me new insight into how the right-wing Israeli mindset has developed over time. I've started to comprehend how otherwise good people can justify some of the horrors I've seen and heard about in this part of the world.

All of this may not be easy for some to swallow. These ideas are not tidy; they don't fit neatly into traditional conceptions of the Arab-Israeli conflict. But it's called nuance, and we could use a lot more of it in this discussion.

In any case, following the first Israeli invasion, UNIFIL was given the Herculean task of policing the nebulous "Green Line" separating the Jewish state from its vulnerable, self-destructing neighbor. Originally from Turkey, Timur Goksel was appointed spokesman shortly after UNIFIL was created, and he became the voice of a long-suffering organization.

I interview Goksel at Café Rawda, overlooking the Mediterranean Sea, the same place I would have my conversation with Robert Fisk over a year later. Goksel has helped me with a few stories before, so we have a good rapport. He's an elderly man now, well into his seventies, still quick and energetic. He tells me about what he observed as he tried to mediate the conflict between Israel and Lebanon during the civil war.

"It was a Shiite awakening," Goksel says. "I don't think Hezbollah and the Islamic Jihad or all those other groups were specifically formed or shaped to oppose the Israelis. This was not their primary motive at first. They wanted to have a say in the Lebanese context and in the civil war. The Shiites were being pushed around. They didn't have their own representation except Amal, which wasn't very [religious]."

"Didn't Amal end up working with the Israelis?" I ask.

"Well, they were easier to work with, let's say, and Amal was a very local establishment. The local villagers, they didn't have a structure, but they had numbers. Meanwhile, all the Shiite youngsters with guns in their hands were working with other groups, mostly the secular groups, the Communists and the Palestinians."

"Then they ended up hating each other, right?" I ask. "I heard some Shia actually threw rice and rosewater at Israeli tanks when they rolled into the south in '82, because they disliked the Palestinians so much." From what I understand, Palestinian militants angered the Shia population by running roughshod over south Lebanon when they arrived in the country after being displaced.

"I was there," Goksel responds. "It was not very widespread, but it happened, yes."

"Then the Israelis behaved badly, or so I've been told."

"Stupidly, actually," says Goksel, rolling his eyes. "The seeds were already there, and Ashura became the ignition. That was when the clergy started to have a say in the Shia awakening."

Goksel is referring to an incident in the fall of 1983, when an Israeli convoy tried to drive through the southern city of Nabatieh during the sacred Shia festival of Ashura. It's a bloody, violent event meant to commemorate the death of Husayn Ibn Ali, the prophet Muhammad's grandson, and is marked by much wailing and self-flagellation. So many Lebanese Ashura celebrants wound themselves during festivals that the streets of Nabatieh are said to turn red. But Ashura is revered by Shia Muslims, and there were over fifty thousand of them taking part in the ceremony that day. Nonetheless, the Israeli convoy insisted they get out of the way to let the tanks pass, the mourning Shia refused, and at some point, the Israelis opened fire, killing two and wounding fifteen. It wasn't a large number of casualties and didn't seem that important in the context of the war's violence. But to the Shia, the Israelis had committed an unforgivable act, a desecration of their religion, and that's when opinion began to turn against Israel in earnest.

"I started hearing that it is a blessing to kill all the Jews," says Goksel seriously. "I took it to the Israelis. There were a couple of bright Israelis who were really careful about the Shiites and all that, but they were the minority. Nobody took notice because they were so spoiled, so arrogant."

Goksel recounts how the Israelis ignored his warning that the once-friendly Shia in south Lebanon were beginning to militarize against them.

"I just told them, 'Enjoy yourselves.'" Goksel laughs, with an edge of bitterness. "And that was how it started."

From what I understand, fresh from its Islamic revolution, Iran quickly recognized an opportunity in the Lebanese Shia discontent. I ask Robin Wright if the Iranians prompted the Amal-Hezbollah split.

"Well, Amal was a Lebanese movement, and Nabih Berri [Amal's leader] was always a secularist and a nationalist," she responds. "I don't think he was always happy with the Iranians or willing to be their surrogate on the ground. As the Iranian revolution mobilized clerics as allies, they looked to some of the clerics in Lebanon as alternative vehicles to work with. They were threatening to create allies in every country in the region, to have pockets that would propagate their ideology, that would do their bidding, and they were willing to pour resources into it."

So the Iranians sent a special contingent of their Revolutionary Guard to train and mobilize the increasingly radicalized Shia in Lebanon during the early eighties. Their attentions prompted the more religiously inclined Shia to break off from Amal and form their own militia. They would come to call it Hezbollah, the Party of God, and its members announced its presence in 1985, with a manifesto swearing to expel Israel and its Western allies from Lebanon. It began to coalesce while battling the Israelis in south Lebanon following the 1982 invasion, using coordinated suicide bombings and other guerrilla tactics against occupying Israeli forces. However, Hezbollah as we know it today appears to have emerged out of a loosely organized patchwork of various Shia militant groups with Iranian ties in the mid to late eighties, when it reorganized into a cohesive entity with the help of Iran.

"Right, but I mean, look, arming and sponsoring whatever you may call them, Shia resistance movements, is quite different from exporting terrorism against civilians," I point out to Wright. I'm still confused as to how Iran went from supporting an armed militia defending their country against invaders to becoming the Islamic Jihad's benefactors, and I'm curious about Hezbollah's repeated insistence that they were not responsible for the IJO's acts of terror. But of course, that's not the kind of legacy any group trying to establish political legitimacy would rush to claim responsibility for.

"I'm not talking about exporting terrorism; I'm talking about exporting an ideology, and that's how the Iranians looked at it," Wright says. "They would not call it exporting terrorism."

"When did you, as a journalist, first hear of Hezbollah?" I ask. "What was your understanding of who they were at the time?"

"One of the things we noticed first of all, in terms of tangible physical evidence, were all these Hezbollah symbols that started being spray-painted all over the southern suburbs," Wright responds. "It was kind of staking out their turf. 'This is where we are.' Then we started hearing names, Abbas al-Musawi, Sobhi al-Tufayli. They'd have these meetings in the Beqaa and you'd hear people spouting off about things. Journalists had a lot to cover, so a lot of us didn't pay much attention."

Musawi and Tufayli would both go on to become secretaries-general of Hezbollah, the same position now held by Hassan Nasrallah. But I still need to know at what point Hezbollah and the IJO became two hands of the same body—one for resistance, one for revenge. There's an element to this story that seems to be dancing right out of my line of sight.

"Then the terrorism started, right?" I ask. "Did people at the time assume it was Hezbollah?"

"Well, there were a lot of different names, and we were having a hard time figuring it out," says Wright. "At some point, though, it became clear that whether they were all directly linked or not, they probably had a common agenda, a common philosophy, and there may be different cells doing different things."

Maybe. Probably. But something still isn't sitting right with me so far. I've started to feel like there's a hole in the narrative of this event that I've been hearing all my life. I want to find it, stitch it back together with what I've been told. Perhaps that will help me wrap my mind around the moment in history that led to shackles snapping shut on Dad's leg, holding him fast as six of my birthdays came and went. Maybe if I just knew the truth, I could understand the men who trapped my father on the ground while I slipped from his hand and drifted away into the sky like a little red balloon.

———

In another house in Dahiyeh, I'm speaking to a different *hajj*. He prefers not to be named, so I'll just refer to him as the Hajj. He's about the same age as Hamza, but shorter, heavier, with a jolly air about him. The Hajj was one of the very first to join Hezbollah when it split from Amal. He's "retired" now, just a party supporter and educated observer. I tell him I'm working on a book about the civil war and ask him about his experience in the Party of God.

"The idea of a group like Hezbollah started back in 1978, around the same time as the victory of the Islamic revolution in Iran," he tells me. "But until the Israelis invaded in 1982, we were only involved in Islamic [cultural and social] activities or *daawah*, not under the designation of Hezbollah . . . and as people of the south, we started resisting the Israelis before there was a Hezbollah. The seeds of Hezbollah started in secret . . . there were small groups, and then they made themselves known and announced themselves as Hezbollah in 1985."

I ask him about the Islamic Jihad's terrorism, whether it was committed under the umbrella of Hezbollah.

"In America they say, Hezbollah did the killing, Hezbollah did the bombings and kidnappings, but that's not true," the Hajj complains. "Before it rose, Hezbollah was not well organized. There might have been some extremist groups outside Hezbollah, not necessarily within our ranks . . . but those groups are now gone."

Now is the moment. "My father is Terry Anderson," I tell him. "He was kidnapped for nearly seven years and treated very badly by the Islamic Jihad. Do you know anything about the people who did that to him?" I like to save this information for well into interviews like this. It generally throws the subject off his guard.

The Hajj is clearly taken by surprise, but he recovers quickly. "Ignorance makes a human being do something like that," he says, looking into my eyes. "We actually can't call someone like that a human being. He doesn't serve his cause, and he has nothing to do with Islam or humanity. Many people who are enthusiastic to help Islam only harm our religion . . . This is a barbaric act that goes against all religions. I can assure you that Hezbollah did not do something like this. It was meant to harm the Shias' image in the West.

"We Shia have a saying," the Hajj adds. "'Don't deal with a crazy person, because he hurts you when he really wants to help you.'"

His words remind me of something Hamza told me. In addition to his insistence that he didn't hurt any of his passengers, Hamza also claimed that as an Amal leader, he helped negotiate the release of those on the TWA flight the Islamic Jihad hijacked in 1985, shortly after my father was taken. One of the passengers, a navy diver named Robert Stethem, was killed during the hijacking, and some of them were held for two weeks until complex negotiations, in which Amal did play a role, convinced the hijackers to free them. Again, Hezbollah was blamed; again, they deny responsibility to this day. The four primary hijackers were Mohammed Ali Hammadi, Ali Atwa, Hassan Izz-al-Din, and of course, Imad Mughniyeh. All four were known to be members of the IJO.

According to Hamza, after he helped secure the passengers' release, some of them wrote him thank-you notes. He proudly informed me that he still has these letters of gratitude.

"In principle, we are completely against kidnapping," said Hamza seriously. "Because we had our imam Musa al-Sadr kidnapped, we don't approve of this tactic. How can we condemn an act and legitimize it for ourselves? But there were those of us who believed they had to protect their people and their country, in any way possible. They thought, 'I don't have the means to make the enemy desist in what he is doing to my family and country.'

"'I don't have a tank to fight their tanks,'" he continued. "'I have a person who can get into a car and blow up their tanks and kill their soldiers. These soldiers have families and their families will start demanding that their sons would no longer be sent to war' . . . but killing and kidnapping civilians for years is another thing."

"So who were the people who committed these acts?" I asked.

"They indirectly knew that one day, the men they kidnapped would be freed and would tell about their barbarity," Hamza said. "Who benefited from this? Where is this barbarism emanating from? Are they claiming faith? In this case, their faith was flawed. Whoever was behind the [Islamic] Jihad wanted to give a distorted view of the faith, just as *daesh* [ISIS] is doing now."

Like the Hajj, he seems genuinely concerned that I understand he was not a part of what happened to my father.

"Please give your father my regards," Hamza said to me. "If he ever comes to Lebanon again, tell him he's welcome in my house. Say to him that the Shia are not monsters."

It's an odd feeling, hearing this from a terrorist. But it's even stranger that I find myself seeing a terrorist as a human being.

THEN
October 2003

I OD'd for the first time not long after I started at NYU. It wasn't serious enough to get me sent to the hospital. I just remember being in the middle of one of those meaningless, teeth-grinding coke conversations and coming to on the floor of my dorm room, with my boyfriend yelling and shaking me. Apparently, I had gone into convulsions. I got up, drank some water, waited a half hour, and did another line.

College was one long party—not the fun kind, but the kind where you wake up the next day feeling like shit and swear never to do that again. In many ways, I never got to the waking-up part.

My parents divorced the year I began college, which infuriated me, because I had been begging them to split up since I was eight or nine. They seemed quite incompatible to me. But they had inexplicably stayed together "for my sake." The divorce was vicious, and since I was older, each of them used me as a sounding board for their anger and frustration with the other. Dad would tell me my cold, heartless mother was taking all his money in the divorce settlement; Mama would say my father had ruined both our lives.

Without any understanding of what a healthy relationship is supposed to look like, I quickly found all the wrong men. I dumped my first boyfriend, a loser with an inferiority complex, after he tried to choke me and my neighbors had to call the cops. I dated a lot after that. People tell me I have an air of sexuality about me, even now, when I'm trying my best to forget that phase of my life. I don't know how to change that, but apparently, it gives men all kinds of ideas. Like my drug dealer, who held me down and raped me my sophomore year of college. He left three bags of coke on the bed when he was done. I snorted them all, crying the whole time.

Midway through college, I met a sweet English guy named Adam who was as messed up as I was, but in very different ways. He had a difficult childhood—probably more so than mine—and although he didn't seek refuge from his trauma in the oblivion of drugs as I did, the emotional fallout from his past played off my own problems in a way that was intense, intimate, and destructive all at once. We fell in love, got engaged, and for a while, I didn't feel so alone. Mama used to call us her twins, because we were born three hours apart. But we were too young and too damaged, and it didn't last. He was the only man I was with for more than a few months who was kind to me during that time, though, and I'll never forget him.

I was not an easy fiancée. One night, while I was ten tequila shots deep at a club, my guy friend decided to relieve himself against the wall while we were smoking cigarettes outside. Some cops took issue with that and started harassing him, so I stumbled over to defuse the situation.

"Officers," I slurred. "It's a Saturday night. Can't we all just chill and go our separate ways?"

One of the cops, an unfortunate-looking fellow with not a hair on his shiny little head, squinted at me appraisingly. "We'll go away if you give us your phone number," he said, leering. "I get off at four."

Normally, I'd have giggled and deflected such an offer, but that night I was in rare form.

"Maybe if you weren't five feet tall and bald," I replied. "Go fuck yourself."

He gaped at me. "What did you just say?"

"Go. Fuck. Yourself. Did I stutter?" I flounced off, swaying.

"Get back here!" he yelled, to which I gave him the finger, not looking back.

Next thing I knew, I was slammed up against the wall of the club and handcuffed. They had to cuff my ankles too, after I started kicking him in the shins. I ran my mouth all the way to the police station.

"Hey, fuckheads, you know you're the bottom two percent of our school system, right?" I spat. "A monkey could do your job. Go back to your studio apartment in Queens." Charming.

After we got to the precinct, they cuffed me to a pipe outside a cell full of guys for eighteen hours, but made the mistake of leaving me too close to the fingerprint machine, which I covertly unplugged, giggling hysterically as I watched the cops try unsuccessfully to fingerprint a suspect. By the end of the night, every man in that cell had asked me for my phone number.

I woke the next morning with a sore arm and an aching head. When I realized where I was, the waterworks began with a vengeance. "I'm a good girl!" I wailed. "I go to NYU! I shouldn't be here. This is a mistake."

My protestations went nowhere, and at some point, they drove me to Central Booking.

"What's Central Booking?" I asked one of the female cops.

"Oh, you'll see," she said, grinning.

As soon as we entered the building, an overpowering stench rolled down the hall and hit me in the face, and I immediately realized what Central Booking was—the place where they put all the criminals. Not wanting to become somebody's bitch, I flattened myself against the wall.

"I am *not* going in there," I shrieked, hysterical.

"You don't go in there, we're labeling you an emotionally disturbed person and sending you to the psych ward," the lady cop warned, unimpressed by my performance.

"I don't care! Take me to the fucking psych ward. I'm not going in there."

So we went to the Bellevue psych ward, where I cried next to a trans woman for three hours until a bored-looking shrink ushered me into a room, asked me some questions, and said I was fine.

Two days had gone by at this point. It was Monday morning, and I could finally be booked. I was originally charged with resisting arrest and assaulting a police officer, both felonies. I told my court-appointed lawyer I was a victim of sexual harassment, and he looked over the report.

"Really?" he asked. "That's not what the police say. They claim you walked up to them and told them you had methamphetamine on you."

Fucking NYPD.

"Sir," I yelled. "If I were doing meth, do you really think I'd waste it by telling two cops?"

"Good point." He sighed.

I tottered into the courtroom on my stilettos, still wearing my skanky Saturday-night dress, rings of mascara decorating my face. Adam, who had been my one phone call, was sitting in the front row, arms crossed, shaking his head and glaring at me. Two of my friends sat beside him, looking worried. I don't remember much of the arraignment, except that at one point, the judge read out the incident report.

"And then the defendant said, 'Expletive, you fascist pigs.'"

Everyone in the room (except me) stifled a giggle. I was eventually let off with a drunk and disorderly and given three days of community service.

A couple of weeks later, after a fight with Adam, I ran out of our apartment and checked myself into a very nice hotel. I asked the doorman where I could get some blow, and spent the next two days holed up in my room doing coke and taking Xanax to come down. Adam must have eventually called my parents, because my dad had the concierge let him in and found me passed out in a nest of plastic baggies and prescription bottles. He dumped a bucket of water on me and sat on the bed with his head in his hands. It was the first time I ever saw him cry. I looked at him in openmouthed astonishment. I wasn't aware I had the power to do that.

I was packed off to my first rehab in Arizona. I phoned in my entire experience there, until I tore the cartilage in my knee playing volleyball, ending my stint at rehab in a wheelchair on Vicodin. I had surgery right after I got out, and all the Percocet the doctors threw at me kick-started a three-year opiate addiction.

———

Despite all this, I managed to graduate NYU with a 3.7 GPA. Don't ask me how. The best explanation I have is that my education was the only thing holding me together. Learning had been my lifeline throughout the destruction of my childhood and adolescence, and old habits die hard. I took a couple of political science classes, one of which focused on Middle Eastern politics. I excelled in that course, mostly because I'd watch the news almost every day, and as high as I usually was, something deep inside me held on to my connection to that part of the world. So I had lots to say in that class, and I actually devoted a fair amount of time to studying for all my classes. But doing well in school was also my excuse for fucking up so badly—I got good grades, I would tell myself. Things weren't all that terrible.

In the meantime, my relationship with my father continued to deteriorate. Every time we interacted, I felt frustrated and dissatisfied, unable to form a meaningful connection with him.

Dad began dating a woman less than half his age. I couldn't stand her. When I would visit, I'd blast the song "Gold Digger" in my room in passive-aggressive protest. I once scrubbed a toilet with her toothbrush and put it back for her to use. He was deeply in love, though, and wouldn't hear a word against her. I tried to tell him I thought she was using him, and was reprimanded for my efforts.

Knowing I despised her, she would smile at me, smug as a cat, and adjust the diamond bracelet he had given her.

My father often seemed to confuse gifts for love. At my graduation, he pulled me aside and said casually, "I know I haven't always been a good father to you," then handed me a Rolex.

I pawned it for drugs within a month.

5. THE RABBIT HOLE

On puppet strings, a nation swings.
—MEGADETH

NOW

I'm on the phone with Oliver North, the man who may have indirectly cost my father an additional four years in captivity. He doesn't seem sorry.

"There are a lot of conspiracy theories, Sulome, and most of them are baloney," he tells me, mispronouncing my name. "There was a lot more incompetence than there was malevolence, and misfeasance rather than malfeasance . . . I was just the guy told to carry things out."

I am talking to North because of two notorious words inextricably linked to the hostage crisis: Iran-Contra, the scandal that almost brought down the Reagan administration.

From the moment I began my own investigation into the circumstances surrounding my father's captivity, I have been immersed in a quagmire of spooks, shady middlemen, and covert arms deals. I find it nearly impossible not to follow the billion or so leads I keep running into "down the rabbit hole," as one of the people I interview puts it. Chasing down obscure information, trying to find the piece that explains it all—that's what reporters do.

But it soon became obvious that Iran-Contra was a mess of epic proportions, and my father and the other hostages had been unfortunate enough to be at its center. North is right about one thing: conspiracy theories accumulate around this event, and it's incredibly difficult to separate fact from fiction.

Iran-Contra is a Gordian knot compounded by the difficulty of getting government officials and politicians involved to talk about it with any sort of transparency. The debacle left egg on the faces of dozens of established figures, many of whom still hold influential positions in Washington.

The scandal shaped the way Americans viewed my father's captivity. It was part of the reason he was front-page news for so long, but as I discover, the publicity surrounding my father may have been some of the impetus for the affair in the first place.

I can't stay away from Iran-Contra; I'm drawn to it inexorably. I start at the very beginning—with the facts, which I get from the findings of the Tower Commission, assembled by Reagan as soon as the scandal erupted: in November 1986, *Ash-Shiraa*, a small newspaper in Lebanon, broke a huge story. It revealed that the United States had been trading military equipment with Iran in an attempt to obtain the release of U.S. hostages held in Lebanon by the Islamic Jihad, a terrorist group believed to have close ties to the Iranian regime. After some digging by the U.S. attorney general, it became apparent that proceeds from the arms transfers were being diverted to assist the Contras, U.S.-backed rebel forces in Nicaragua. Since the Contras were controversial and notoriously ruthless in their methods, this compounded the scandal and exposed those involved in Iran-Contra not only for breaking the laws of their government, but for going against the policies they had always publicly espoused.

That's what everyone already knows, though, and just the bare facts aren't going to cut it. I need to talk to people who were there. I spend months investigating, traveling to Washington and talking to dozens of people, some of whom were at the center of Iran-Contra. I learn quite a bit, and even begin to wonder if the U.S. government's actions during the scandal might have contributed to the length of my father's captivity.

————

Digging around for information on people who were directly involved in Iran-Contra, I focus on the first one I can find who seems to have had strong opinions on the situation as it was unfolding. Robert Oakley was the State Department's head of counterterrorism when my father was abducted. I interview Oakley, now well into his eighties, in D.C., where he lives with his wife, Phyllis, herself a former assistant secretary of state, in a sweet, tidy little apartment at the end of a cul-de-sac. Every now and then, she interjects to clarify a point.

Oakley says that at the time he believed the arms deals had ceased soon after they started, and that when he found out they hadn't, he resigned his position in objection to what he saw as a dishonest and illegal practice.

"We were told it would stop until we realized it was still going on," he tells me in his soft voice. "Then I had enough. If it couldn't be stopped, I wasn't going to be a party to it, even an unwilling one."

"So you knew about it while it was happening?" I ask.

"Bob said he smelled it," says Phyllis.

"They were pretending to do it so we could spot the good guys in Tehran and use them against the 'Communist takeover.'" Oakley sounds bitter. The United States always had a preoccupation with combating the Soviet Union's influence in the Middle East. There were rumors that Iran might have been displaying Communist sympathies at the time, although it seems to me that the religious nature of the Islamic revolution makes that scenario unlikely.

"I heard that," I muse. "That the Soviets might have been gaining influence over Iran. I don't know how true that was—"

"Bullshit, is what it was," Oakley interrupts me. "But that was the lie they were feeding the president."

The fear of Soviet influence was still very real in the 1980s, but it's also true that the timing of the hostage abductions posed a problem for the United States. The pro-Western shah of Iran had been deposed in 1979, replaced by a theocratic Islamic regime with the Ayatollah Ruhollah Khomeini at its head. The new government's violent anti-Western rhetoric, as well as its capture and imprisonment of sixty Americans who worked at the U.S. embassy in Tehran, resulted in escalating tension between the two countries. The hostages were released in 1981, just minutes after Reagan was sworn into office, and it gave the new president a boost in prestige and a reputation for freeing hostages.

Things were different back then. The strategy of kidnapping Americans wasn't as commonplace as it's now become, and the idea of U.S. citizens being held by terrorists shocked the public. In the year before my father was abducted, a number of other Westerners had been taken hostage in Lebanon. Supposedly, Reagan was extremely affected by the plight of my father and the other captives. Their family members, most notably my aunt Peggy Say, were publicly calling for something to be done for their loved ones.

"Your aunt was the political glue that made it happen," a journalist who worked at the AP at the time tells me. "She was the one who provided the political energy for Reagan. He wanted to do something for the hostages. The hostages were personified by Terry Anderson, aka Peggy Say."

I'm startled to hear it.

"Cameras followed Peggy around," he goes on. "The media loved her because she was very articulate, she was very calm, she looked into the cameras and she pleaded for President Reagan to do something."

Growing up, I barely had any interaction with my aunt Peggy, who remained a distant figure to me until quite recently. She and my mother had fought; I was never quite sure over what, although now I realize at least some of their conflict must have revolved around Peggy's penchant for publicity. My mother would often say Peggy was addicted to attention—a sentiment echoed by many of our family friends and my father's colleagues, who worried her public appeals would endanger my father by making him more valuable to his kidnappers.

A few years ago, I visited her in Tennessee a couple of times. She wasn't the coldhearted bitch my mother had always made her out to be. In fact, she seemed kindly, even grandmotherly, although I could sense the steel beneath her smile.

"Difficult" was how my father described her, usually with some fondness.

But my mother's disdain for Peggy meant my father kept her at arm's length after he was released, which I believe wounded her deeply. She also wrote a book, *Forgotten,* about her efforts to free her brother, which provoked a sigh from most of the AP men I interviewed. "Self-glorification" was how one of them put it. Sadly, I will never learn the truth about my aunt, at least not from her, because she just died of lung cancer brought on by years of chain-smoking. It's my personal belief, though, that Peggy was a complex person, as many brave, "difficult" women are. Much like the bravest, most difficult woman I know: my mother, with whom she had always been at odds.

In any case, Peggy posed a problem for Reagan, who had been publicly emphasizing that the United States did not, under any circumstances, negotiate with terrorists. But during the summer of 1985, a few months after my father was taken, Israel entered into the mix and changed the approach. David Kimche, director general of the Israeli Foreign Ministry, met with Robert McFarlane, Reagan's national security adviser, at the White House a number of times. He suggested a convenient tit-for-tat deal, with Israel as intermediary. If the United States agreed to replace them, Israel would sell Iran one hundred TOW missiles, and all the American hostages in Lebanon would be freed. Improbable as it may seem now, in those days Israel was, if not exactly chummy with the new Islamic Republic, certainly an ally of convenience. At the time, the Israelis, led by then–prime minister Yitzhak Shamir, viewed Iraq as a more dangerous enemy, and the Iran-Iraq War gave the two future nemeses some common ground. Israel had also been trying to develop a "periphery policy" by strengthening ties to non-Arab Islamic states almost since it was founded.

When Kimche approached McFarlane, he had a go-between in mind, an Iranian they claimed was well connected there: Manucher Ghorbanifar, who would become notorious as the quintessential double dealer in Iran-Contra. Having had previous dealings with Ghorbanifar, the CIA considered him "untrustworthy," according to the Tower Commission's report, and had blacklisted him.

Don Mell, the former AP photographer who was in the car with my father when he was kidnapped, has a more colorful way of describing Ghorbanifar. He laughs when I bring up the mysterious middleman in the arms transfers. "The guy was a creep show. It's like you're using the Kardashians to do diplomacy, so they got what they paid for."

For whatever reason, McFarlane agreed to work with Ghorbanifar. And to run point on the operation McFarlane picked Lieutenant Colonel Oliver North, a member of the National Security Council. At the time, North was also involved in providing covert assistance to the Contra rebels in Nicaragua. Congress had tried to limit U.S. support of the Contras, but the Reagan administration saw them as an ally in the fight against communism in Latin America.

I won't get into the complex, insider-baseball details of the subsequent arms deals. The end result was the release of three hostages in 1985 and '86: Reverend Benjamin Weir, Father Martin Jenco, and David Jacobsen, all of whom were held with my father at one point. The Iranians were pissed off by the quality of the Israeli weapons they received, and wouldn't—or couldn't—free the rest.

"The Iranians were complaining they didn't get as much weaponry as they were promised, and the Americans were complaining they weren't getting hostages at the rate that they were promised, so nobody was really happy in this," Mell tells me. "We were resupplying the Israelis, and the Israelis were giving them these shitty weapons. It's like going into Costco and buying peanut butter past its expiration date and selling it to someone else."

Iran was also fresh off a revolution, so it was divided into competing factions. It wasn't clear which faction had influence over the Shia Lebanese kidnappers, or indeed, if any of them had had much influence to begin with. Furthermore, the U.S. officials made some spectacular blunders—there's an unconfirmed anecdote that, on one trip to Tehran, McFarlane and North brought the Iranians a Bible inscribed by Reagan, for instance. Allegedly it was also North who decided proceeds from the Iranian arms deals should be funneled to the Contras.

Finally, the shit hit the fan. In November 1986, someone in Iran leaked information about the arms deals to a small newspaper in Beirut, *Ash-Shiraa,* a publication said to have ties to certain factions in the Islamic Republic as well as the IJO. *Ash-Shiraa* is still around, and has been accused of being everything from a mouthpiece for Syria to a Mossad asset. I track down the contact information for its editor. He's still in Beirut, and I plan to get in touch with him when I go back.

———

At the time he was taken, my father was still married to his first wife, Mickey, with whom he had a daughter—my half sister, Gabrielle, who lived with her mother in Tokyo. According to what I've been told, Dad and Mickey's marriage was troubled and he was trying to convince her to get a divorce when he met my mother, fell in love, and she became pregnant with me.

I never learned much about Mickey growing up, although Gabrielle would sometimes come visit us after my father was released. Now in her late thirties, she's a lawyer—intelligent, sweet, but still highly reserved in a very Japanese way. Her fury at my father was always extremely palpable to me, though, beneath her good manners. I always wanted to tell her how sorry I was that he had abandoned her, and how guilty I felt because I was the daughter he chose to have near him, but I could never find the words. I sensed that we shared the same angry befuddlement at Dad's actions and behavior, but I can only imagine what it feels like to know your father cast you and your mother aside for a new wife and daughter. The last time I saw her was during Hurricane Sandy, which happened to coincide with one of my less successful medication changes. We were stuck in my apartment in Tribeca with no electricity for a week, during which I sobbed uncontrollably for pretty much her entire stay, the poor woman.

At some point, I told her through my tears how sorry I was that my father had been so dismissive toward her growing up, and how guilty I felt that I had been the one to take her place.

"Sulome," she said with a sigh, her own eyes filling up with tears—something I had never thought I'd see from someone so obviously uncomfortable with public displays of emotion. "I used to think I was the unlucky one, because he didn't want me. Now I see you, and I think you had it worse."

In any case, Dad's marital situation did pose a problem for the AP, not just because of the publicity surrounding his kidnapping but because they had to figure out how to take care of both families. I believe what the company ended up deciding was to split Dad's salary in half between my mother and Mickey, thus ensuring that we'd all be able to get by in his absence.

"You know, I can just see Lou Boccardi [president and CEO of the AP at the time] sitting there, saying, 'Okay, this happened to my guy in Beirut,'" Don Mell tells me, laughing. "'Oh, and there's this other problem, you know, the other problem is that his real wife is in Japan with his daughter, but there's this other woman who's pregnant with his other daughter, oh jeez.' I mean, they basically tried to cover up your existence for a while."

"Wait . . . what?" I'm shocked to hear this.

"Well, don't you remember there was this thing in the news where you were like two or three years old and you were lighting your father's birthday cake? There was so much discussion about whether they were even going to allow that to happen."

"Huh," I respond after a minute. "Actually, I don't remember ever seeing a camera before I was three. That makes sense."

"You know, they were always trying to shut down everybody. So they tried to shut down your mom. And Mickey, they had to shut her down. So some Japanese guy went to her family and said 'be quiet,' and that was the end of that . . . then all of a sudden Peggy comes out of nowhere."

It's pretty jarring to hear that my father's former colleagues might have tried to pretend I didn't exist when I was a baby. These are the men I grew up around, practically my uncles, and I had always believed them to be champions of my family's cause. It hurts to learn this particular detail, but I try to be objective and consider the difficult position they must have been in. I still believe they sincerely did everything they could to free my father.

At a conference room at the AP office in New York, Lou Boccardi explains that they were faced with a difficult situation when my father was taken.

"We tried to the best of our ability to do the right thing in three directions," Boccardi explains. "One was obvious—you and your mother. You know, the focus was on Madeleine and Sulome, but there was another family, and we felt that was an enormous obligation. Even from the perspective of thirty years ago, or twenty-five years ago, I think we did that right. In a painful situation like that, there was just no way to relieve the pain and the suffering . . . but that was one direction. Terry himself was another, and what we could do about that. Then sort of the AP staff, the public, and the rest of the world, it was kind of a third piece."

"What about the government?" I ask.

"The government was an interesting experience for us," he replies. "I was in places I never thought I'd be . . . We found some people who seemed to be very conscientious and as concerned as we were. We've found some others who I wouldn't apply those words to. We did what we thought was right. There wasn't a class about this at Columbia when I was there . . . you know, this was a new kind of challenge. Unhappily, since then these kinds of horrors have become more familiar, but at the time, there was no place to turn except to the AP's own conscience."

And the AP thought it was best not to publicize my father's captivity. But they couldn't stop the media feeding frenzy that surrounded him, and apparently, both he and the press chose my mother and me over Mickey and Gabrielle. We became the media family; they were the family that didn't exist. I haven't thought about that aspect of their experience before: the news treatment must have made things that much more painful for them. But learning these details about how the press and the government handled the situation also makes me somewhat proud of my aunt, who by all accounts was a dynamo in an otherwise sluggish process.

When Iran-Contra finally broke, the public went wild. Not only was the American government illegally aiding a rebel group, it was doing so with money generated from illicit arms deals with a known sponsor of terrorism, against all previously stated U.S. policy. Stories were aired, investigative commissions were formed, indictments were sought . . . and in the end, no one involved had to do an hour of jail time. Some were presidentially pardoned, others just weren't prosecuted, and Reagan was largely absolved of responsibility. According to Oakley, that's because many in the government didn't want to see another president brought down so soon after Richard Nixon.

"Congress was aggrieved, but everybody else quietly said, 'Okay, let's get this out, but let's do it in such a way that we don't have to see Reagan go through the same thing that happened to Nixon,'" Oakley says.

"Didn't all this have an adverse effect on the subsequent nego-tiations to get my father and the others out?" I ask him.

"Absolutely. We had stopped paying. So he was stuck."

Oakley is my first reliable source to confirm my suspicion that the government's actions actually may have prevented my father from being released for several more years. And as I continue to talk to people in D.C., many of them tell me the same thing: the arms-for-hostages deals probably prolonged his hell.

It's a sickening thought, and it angers me. It was one thing for people in the government to make such a colossal miscalcula-tion out of the humanitarian desire to free its citizens. But if the arms deals were more calculated—and politicians as well as the people around them aren't generally known for the purity of their motives—that will be difficult to understand, or forgive.

From what I've been told, Reagan at least genuinely cared about the hostages' fate. Whether that was out of concern for the hostages themselves or anxiety over the political fallout their con-tinued captivity was having on his administration, I can't say. But there is significant evidence indicating that the neoconservatives in his administration who engineered Iran-Contra had been nurtur-ing secret arms deals to Iran via Israel way before my father was taken, and it wasn't out of the goodness of their hearts.

The most famous conspiracy theory regarding pre-Iran-Contra dealings between the neocons, the Israelis, and Iran has become known as the October Surprise narrative. Its proponents claim that just before Reagan became president, some who were lined up to be in his administration used nearly the same cast of characters that they later employed in the arms-for-hostages scandal to achieve a seriously disturbing goal. According to this version of events, of-ficials like McFarlane and Michael Ledeen—another neocon Iran-Contra figure—wanted to ensure that the Americans taken captive in Tehran when the Iranians took over the U.S. embassy during the 1980 presidential race between Carter and Reagan (the Ben Affleck movie *Argo* recounts events surrounding this episode) would not be released until after Reagan was inaugurated. The hostages were actually freed twenty minutes after the conclusion of his inaugural address.

I won't get into the whole thing too much, other than to say that while it is largely dismissed today, players such as Yitzhak Shamir and former Iranian president Abolhassan Banisadr continue to insist that it happened. Supposedly the Reagan administration, with the help of then–Israeli prime minister Menachem Begin and the Iran-Contra arms dealers and middlemen, supplied people in the Iranian regime with arms shipments from the United States in exchange for a promise not to release the hostages to the Carter administration, which was suffering the intense political fallout of not being able to free them. Carter—never a friend to the Israelis regarding their Palestinian policies—was replaced by a significantly more pliable Reagan, who received a huge boost in popularity and a reputation as a hostage-freer.

The October Surprise narrative appears to have been debunked by a number of influential people, so it's been labeled a conspiracy theory, and it does seem farfetched on the surface. There is other evidence to suggest that U.S. arms deals with Iran predated Iran-Contra, though. In a 1991 PBS *Frontline* interview, Nicholas Veliotes, assistant secretary of state for the Middle East at the time, described his investigation of an Argentinian plane that crashed in the Soviet Union in July 1981. Several newspapers, including the *Sunday Times,* reported on the mysterious plane crash. To make a long story short, Veliotes maintains that Israel had chartered the plane and it was carrying U.S. weapons to Iran. According to declassified government documents, McFarlane and his cronies had been pushing for permission to use Israel as a channel for weapons deals with Iran for some time, and when their proposal was dismissed, it seems they went ahead and did it anyway.

But why would they have taken such a risk? Fear of Soviet influence in Iran was very real then, so that might have been part of the impetus—the neocons wanted to signal to Iran that it had no need to break bread with the USSR because there were friendly faces in Washington. But it's probable that they were highly encouraged by the Israeli government to maintain this weapons pipeline. Israel was in the midst of establishing its "periphery policy" at the time and wanted to strengthen ties with Iran to thwart its greater enemy, Iraq. Israeli politicians may have wanted to make certain their Iraqi nemesis didn't gain the upper hand, so they channeled weapons to Iran, knowing that Iran would be using them against their foe. Also, I imagine quite a bit of money changed hands along the way as a result of these arms deals, and much of it likely ended up in Tel Aviv. Israel was and still is a cornerstone of the global arms trade.

As for the Iranians, they may not have changed their angry rhetoric toward Israel, but Iran was in a viciously even-matched war with Iraq and needed weapons, so it couldn't afford to be choosy as to where they came from. We know from Iran-Contra that the U.S.-Israel-Iran weapons pipeline was fully functional, so it's not that much of a stretch to consider that it may have been in place before the leaked arms deals. In any case, there's an argument to be made that McFarlane and his neoconservatives had another agenda in mind when they triggered Iran-Contra, and it had nothing to do with saving Dad or the other hostages. To some of the more unscrupulous actors in Iran-Contra, my father and the others may have just been an excuse they needed to continue pursuing whatever political agenda led them to nurture the idea of using Israel as a go-between for weapons deals with Iran.

There's another factor that contradicts the notion that every American involved in Iran-Contra was just a naive bumbler trying to do what was best for all the hostages. One of the first men to be kidnapped was William Buckley, the CIA station chief in Beirut. He was taken hostage in March 1984, a year before my father. This posed a major problem for the U.S. government and, of course, the agency.

I meet with an ex-C.I.A. chief active at the time of my father's abduction. He asks to remain anonymous, and is about as evasive as I expected him to be. But he does have a few things to say about Buckley.

"We were dealing with the Buckley abduction quite a lot," he tells me. "[William J.] Casey [director of the CIA at the time] was very concerned about Buckley, who was asked to go to Beirut; he didn't volunteer. He seemed like a good choice because he had a military background. He wasn't your ordinary liberal arts case officer . . . he wasn't delighted at the idea of going, but he was a good soldier, and he went. We would be getting reports that he was being tortured. This really set Casey on edge . . . Buckley was sort of a tragic figure."

A *Washington Post* story by Bob Woodward and Charles Babcock, published not long after Iran-Contra broke, went as far as to say that rescuing Buckley "became a CIA crusade and a personal preoccupation of William J. Casey . . . For at least a year, the CIA undertook extraordinary measures—spending a 'small fortune' on informants, according to one source—intercepting communications and enhancing satellite photographs in hopes of determining where Buckley and other U.S. hostages might be held."

That might explain why Casey threw his lot in with the neocons despite the fact that his own agency had blacklisted the shady Ghorbanifar. Their plan seemed like the best way to get his man out.

So it was likely a convergence of political interests, not simple altruism, that spurred the Iran-Contra arms deals. I'm sure some of the people involved had the best of intentions, but no country wants a man who has all its secrets in the hands of people who hate it.

Whatever the motivations, the scandal that ensued after Iran-Contra was leaked to *Ash-Shiraa* ensured that the U.S. government essentially had its hands tied from that point forward. No one wanted to be caught negotiating with terrorists again. The government had undermined its own famously stern assertion once, and after that, it was unable to negotiate effectively, for fear of public outcry.

That lesson has not been forgotten, even thirty years later. Iran-Contra forever changed the way the United States interacted with hostage-takers and shaped the government's approach to the many fanatics who continue to take up the cause of the IJO and other militant groups—such as the Islamic State. The scandal also dictated the way the media treated kidnappings thereafter. As Americans continued to disappear across the Middle East, "quiet diplomacy" and silence in the press became the accepted tactic; at least until IS began its social media campaign of videotaped beheadings in 2013. After that, kidnappings became front-page news again; another headline I end up in, against my will—but we'll get to that.

As for the American government, "We do not negotiate with terrorists" has become "We don't talk to terrorists who kidnap people," which in my opinion isn't a helpful policy, especially from the perspective of anyone unlucky enough to be taken hostage.

By this point in my investigation, I'm starting to seriously consider the idea that the U.S. government not only bungled the negotiation attempts, but directly extended my father's captivity, most likely by four to five years. Everything I've learned about the Middle

East has made me question the idea that America has ever been the "good guy" in the region, but this is personal, and after what I've been learning, it's difficult for me to contain my anger with the country I've always been taught to honor and respect.

Despite my misgivings, during my interview with Oliver North, I treat him like I would any other subject, with courtesy. North has managed to turn his reputation around since he was implicated in Iran-Contra: he's the author of several bestselling books and, currently, the host of his own show on Fox News. During our phone call, he blames a lot of what happened on other people: a liberal Congress that wanted to take Reagan down, a media eagerly reporting information that would endanger Americans overseas.

I ask him why so many of the men involved in Iran-Contra, including himself, managed to escape the scandal with minimal repercussions. He seems a little bit outraged at the suggestion.

"We were all subjected to a very rigorous ordeal because of politics in Washington," he tells me. "We had a liberal Congress, and they were adamant that there would be repercussions for the president. The special prosecutor offered me a deal: if I would accuse the president of lying, he would drop all charges against me. That's how blatant it was. It was an effort to get Ronald Reagan and it didn't work."

"I've heard from a number of sources that this scandal had an extremely adverse effect on the government's ability to negotiate [with the terrorists], because it was under so much scrutiny after the affair broke," I say. Then I ask him, "Do you in any way feel like your actions or the actions of those senior to you contributed to the length of my father's captivity?"

"I have no doubt that all the public disclosures, beginning with the congressional investigations and consummated by the special prosecutor, were responsible for your dad, Terry Waite, and others, some of whom died . . . being held for so long," North counters. "I told them at the time, 'If you hold public hearings on this, people are going to die.' And they did, both in the Middle East and in Latin America."

"And you feel that was a result not of your actions, but the public reaction."

"There are covert operations being conducted right this second in various places around the world, any one of which could end up with people getting killed," he replies. "Congress has lots of different ways of investigating things, but . . . they decided to bring it out in the open . . . thousands of classified documents, many of which I wrote or crossed my desk, were all declassified, and the result was that Americans were put at risk. Some, like your dad, were held longer; others, such as Terry Waite, who had tried simply to be an intermediary, were captured and taken. Others were killed. And that will happen every time classified information of that nature is declassified. I didn't make that call. Ronald Reagan didn't make that call. Congress did."

Ultimately, our conversation is frustrating. I am angry afterward, but not surprised; North just repeated to me the same things he's been saying all along.

But bringing up Terry Waite seems pretty ballsy, considering North has been accused of indirectly causing his kidnapping. Waite was working for the archbishop of Canterbury at the time. Before the scandal broke, he was recruited to negotiate the release of the Western hostages in Lebanon because he had previously been successful with similar negotiations in Libya. Apparently, North and the other Iran-Contra players wanted a cover story for why hostages were being released; since they couldn't very well say it was happening because of illegal arms deals.

The only problem was, after the real story came out, Waite

elected to go back to Lebanon and continue negotiating. As a result, he was kidnapped himself, and held for more than four years, some of which he spent in a cell with my father.

———

I Skype Waite from my apartment in New York City. I've always had enormous admiration for this man, who shares a lot more with my father than just a first name. Waite operates numerous charitable ventures, including Y Care International, the YMCA's international relief agency, and Emmaus UK, an organization devoted to helping formerly homeless people. He tells me a bit about the charity work he's done in Lebanon too. Like my father, since his release Waite has actually been back to meet with Hezbollah members, something I find astonishing.

"I believe that in the Middle East, there's no way there can be any resolution to the problems . . . unless people can put the past behind them and engage with groups like Hezbollah," he says in his thick British accent. "I told them as far as I was concerned, let's make a new beginning. I asked them for heating oil for Syrian refugees, and they gave it to me."

Waite tells me his kidnapping was an example of the dangers posed by negotiating with hostage-takers without solid protection from a government.

"The real problem facing an independent negotiator such as myself is . . . if you're able to make contact successfully, you can guarantee that every other country that has an interest in that situation will want to know you through their intelligence agents," Waite says. "And you have to be careful, because on the one hand, you want to give aid and support to those who are trying to seek the release of innocent people. On the other hand, if you have any political savvy at all, you will recognize that governments often play out other political agendas around hostage cases. So you're in a dangerous position, because you have to cooperate to some extent, but you can never cooperate fully, because you know there's a chance that political activities will be taking place about which you know nothing. And that's how I got caught out by Iran-Contra."

Waite recounts being encouraged by the U.S. government, and especially by North.

"After Ben Weir and Martin Jenco were released, I was told it was a sign for me to keep up my efforts," he says. "I was the only negotiator at that point to have face-to-face contact with the captors, as far as I know." His efforts, as well as the deceptions of U.S. intelligence agencies, would eventually cost Waite his freedom.

I ask Waite whether he believes the U.S. government was truly driven by concern for my father and the other hostages, or whether there was a more cynical reason for their actions.

"I think there were two motivations," he replies. "I won't say there was no humanitarian motive. I believe there was a desire to get the hostages released. But it was all mixed up with seeking political advantage. Precisely what they were seeking and why, I haven't explored, but almost always, where governments are concerned, it's a blend of humanitarian concerns and broader political dealings . . . as a humanitarian negotiator, you have to take note of the political factors, but that isn't your primary motive . . . and you try to maintain a strict boundary, but you have to tread in those waters, and sometimes you get caught by a wave, as I did."

In his book *Decoy in a Deadly Game: Terry Waite and Ollie North: The Untold Story of the Kidnapping—and the Release*, British journalist Gavin Hewitt wrote North had been heard bragging that Waite made an excellent cover for the arms deals. But when I ask Waite if he's angry that his role as "cover" resulted in four years of captivity,

he says he holds no grudges. My dad has always said he feels simi-
larly about the men who kidnapped him—something I have trouble
wrapping my mind around. It's a noble thing, to bear no bitterness
toward the people who caused you so much pain and took years of
your life. I'm not sure if I'd be able to do the same, in their situation.

"That's politics, and that's the way people operate," Waite says.
"They'll have to live with their own consciences, as I will mine."

Right before we say good-bye, Waite stops me. "There is one
thing I'd like to say about your father, if I may. I owe Terry a very
great debt of gratitude, because for most of my time I was in extreme solitary . . . it was very difficult to come out of that and
back into the company of other people, particularly at a time
when I was severely ill with a bronchial infection. I couldn't lie
down at night; I had to sit with my back against the wall gasping
for breath, and your father would reach across and put his hand
on mine. He was remarkably compassionate, and he didn't say
anything at all . . . he was a great support, and I'd just like you to
know that. I know Terry's had his ups and downs, but he is an
extraordinarily good man."

This floors me. I've always been so angry with Dad for his
inability to be a good father; I failed to consider whether he is a
good man. I'm somewhat surprised to realize that despite his difficulty in building a bond with me, all evidence points to the fact
that he is. Maybe sometimes, good men make bad fathers, especially when they've been robbed of as much as Dad has. As far as I
know, he never had a particularly inspiring model for good parent-
ing to begin with. An unhappy childhood, two tours in Vietnam,
reporting on war, and then being kidnapped and brutalized for
seven years would emotionally cripple anyone. Maybe—and this is
a thought that hasn't occurred to me before, although perhaps it

should have—my dad tried his best to love me the way I needed him to. Maybe he just wasn't equipped to do so.

I have to hold back tears at the thought of my father and this man, chained and blindfolded in a Lebanese basement, and how much that small touch must have meant in those circumstances. I don't think I've ever been prouder of Dad than I am in this moment. I might never get to the bottom of Iran-Contra, but I've gained a better understanding of our government's role in this event, and hearing Waite's anecdote about my father makes all the convoluted politics seem even more soulless and empty. Two men, their chains, and the pain they shared. That's what matters, in the end.

"Thank you, sir," I reply. "I can't tell you how much that means to me."

THEN
December 2007

The years I was doped up blend together in my mind. Now, when I look at pictures of myself from back then, I don't recognize the glassy-eyed girl in them. I was locked into a downward spiral of self-hatred and hopelessness, and at the time it felt bottomless. I remember bumming around Europe for a summer, then coming back to New York and babysitting for a while, which ended rather abruptly when one of the mothers caught me nodding off while I was taking care of her kid. Because of the lawsuits my family won against Iran, I had all the money in the world to spend on drugs, and I made some dealers a lot of money.

When I was twenty-three, I met Michael, a forty-year-old ex-army ranger. I was out at a bar one night and took him home. He had a girlfriend at the time, which I didn't find out about until later. But he must have seen me and thought: *Jackpot.*

I've read up a lot on sociopathy since I got Michael out of my life. It all fits—the lack of remorse, the stone-cold manipulation. Sometimes I'd look into his eyes and they'd be as black and dead as a shark's. Pretty early on in our relationship, I wrote a letter and gave it to a friend of mine. It said if anything happened to me, the cops should knock on Michael's door.

He was good at what he did, though. He would call me a junkie whore, then cry and tell me I was the best thing that had ever happened to him. He told me he understood me, that he saw the parts of me I was most ashamed of and loved me in spite of them. Starved for unconditional love, I drank it up. He eventually broke up with his other girlfriend, moved in with me, and started spending all my money. Then the real abuse started. He never completely beat me up; I think he knew I wasn't far gone enough to stand for that. But he did smack me around quite a bit, and I did my best to hide it from everyone I knew. He once dragged me across a room by my hair. Another time, my neighbors called the cops when I screamed that he was going to kill me because he was trying to wrap his hands around my throat. I broke up with him for a week, then took him back, only half believing his tearful apologies. But he had me convinced I was so disgusting no one else would ever want to be with me. We were together for almost two years. Every single meaningful person in my life despised him. My mother practically spat when his name was mentioned.

At that point, my father married the horse trainer, who had just turned thirty-two, six years older than me. At their wedding, I took three Xanax with my champagne and missed most of the reception, held at the house my parents had built together, because I passed out in the basement. Dad and I wouldn't speak for weeks, sometimes months, and when we did, it seemed like he couldn't wait to get me off the phone. Now I imagine he must have been at a loss as to how he should react to my downward spiral. Looking back, I can see that he just didn't know what to do, and I suppose he tried to be there for me sometimes, in his clumsy way. But he was so infatuated with his new wife that I felt like an afterthought. On the rare occasions when I'd visit him in Athens, I was barely home, spending every second I could getting fucked up with the few friends I had from high school. I realize now how much that must have hurt him, but all I could understand at the time was my own pain and anger at his seeming unconcern for me. For the remainder of their marriage, I despaired at ever having a relationship with my father, who grew ever more remote as I became more damaged.

As my relationship with Michael—and my drug abuse—progressed, it seemed like there would be no limit to my self-destruction. My parents and friends were at a loss, and even my mother seemed to have come to terms with the fact that she'd probably pick up the phone one day and hear that her only child had died of a drug overdose. I lost track of the times I made her cry; she told me once she had to stay away from me because she couldn't watch her daughter disappear anymore. Sometimes, she said, there were flashes of my real self—the girl who could connect with people of every social status, from sex workers to politicians, and charm them into revealing the parts of themselves they normally kept close. But then I'd retreat into oblivion, becoming alien once again. The shame of what I was putting my loved ones through consumed me, but I didn't know how to stop. I became so hopeless one night that I swallowed half a bottle of antianxiety meds. Immediately regretting it, I took myself to the emergency room. It was the second of three times in my life I'd make a halfhearted attempt at suicide.

An answer to the painful question of my life appeared one day while I was browsing the Internet and came upon the term *borderline personality disorder* (BPD). It piqued my interest, so I started researching it. I learned that, evidently, it's the most lethal psychiatric illness because of the high suicide rate associated with it. I found the criteria in the *Diagnostic and Statistical Manual of Mental Disorders*. They are as follows:

1. Frantic efforts to avoid real or imagined abandonment.

2. A pattern of unstable and intense interpersonal relationships characterized by alternating between extremes of idealization and devaluation. This is called "splitting."

3. Identity disturbance: markedly and persistently unstable self-image or sense of self.

4. Impulsivity in at least two areas that are potentially self-damaging (e.g., spending, sex, substance abuse, reckless driving, binge eating).

5. Recurrent suicidal behavior, gestures, or threats, or self-mutilating behavior.

6. Affective instability due to a marked reactivity of mood (e.g., intense episodic dysphoria, irritability, or anxiety usually lasting a few hours and only rarely more than a few days).

7. Chronic feelings of emptiness.

8. Inappropriate, intense anger or difficulty controlling anger (e.g., frequent displays of temper, constant anger, recurrent physical fights).

9. Transient, stress-related paranoid ideation or severe dissociative symptoms.

You have to exhibit five of the nine criteria to qualify for a diagnosis. I had all nine. I also read that some of the risk factors for BPD include abandonment in childhood or adolescence, disrupted family life, poor communication in the family, and emotional abuse.

I looked at my computer screen and burst into tears. It was

like the missing piece to the fucked-up puzzle of my life. I had always known there was something wrong with me, something in my
mind that made me play out these destructive cycles ad infinitum.
The circumstances of my childhood were extreme; it was a revelation to learn they must have had an extreme effect on my psyche,
although I probably should have realized that by now. But I always
avoided thinking about my past with every ounce of my being and
every drug I could get my hands on, so I had never made the connection before.

The next day, I marched into my shrink's office waving a sheaf
of papers at him in agitation, babbling, "Doctor, I think I have this.
Borderline personality disorder. It all fits. Look!"

He took the papers from me and frowned at them uncomfortably through his glasses. I'd been seeing him for about a year at
this point, and although he was nice enough, I never felt as though
anything had changed as a result of our therapy. A quiet, awkward
man, he'd listen politely to my sobbing and ask me questions like
"Do you think the OxyContin has anything to do with how you're
feeling?" To which I would practically tear my hair out in frustration. *No shit, doc. Drugs = bad.* But without them, I knew I'd implode
into a supernova of inexplicable shame at my very existence, and
anything was better than that.

"Erm, well, Sulome," he said hesitatingly. "I think the rehab
you went to in 2007 might, well, they might have mentioned something like this."

I was flabbergasted.

"Wait," I hissed. "Are you telling me I was diagnosed with this
years ago, and no one told me?"

"Well, you were on so many substances at the time, it was hard
to tell what was the drugs and what wasn't. You still haven't passed
a urine test in months."

"That is *not* the point. Drugs or no drugs, you knew I might have a mental illness and you didn't tell me?"

"I didn't think it would be helpful. But since this diagnosis seems to resonate with you, let's talk about where we can go from here."

"Seriously, Doctor? *You* can go to hell."

Let's just say that was not a productive session. I left fuming, but by the next week, I had calmed down and was ready to discuss options. I researched possible treatments for BPD and saw that mood stabilizers were often helpful, so I got past my anger at my psychiatrist and he agreed to put me on one.

In hindsight, that was the first step I took toward sanity, although it didn't feel like it at the time. There would still be plenty of crazy to come, but learning of my diagnosis gave me some hope that if I was sick, I could get better someday. For a long time, I thought I'd wake up one day and be "cured." I would then take my place among the sane, well-adjusted people who made living look so easy. I've since learned that's not how it works. But looking back—that was when I at least started trying to halt the self-destruction.

A few weeks later, while Michael was out of town, I locked myself in my room and quit OxyContin cold turkey. My shrink offered to give me Suboxone, which would help with the withdrawal, but I said no. I wanted to feel every second of the dope sickness, so the next time I thought about taking a pill I would remember that terrible, aching pain. I was tired of watching my life drift by me in an apathetic haze. I couldn't hear the word *potential* applied to me one more time with a tone of wistful regret.

After I stopped puking and shaking, I started asking myself why I was letting a scumbag twice my age treat me like shit. I wish I had immediately cut Michael loose at that moment, but it took another month or two. The last straw came while we were leaving a bar, and he grabbed me by the throat and threw me into some empty outdoor tables. I landed on the cold concrete and thought, *Enough*. I pretended to ask for his forgiveness like I always did, then called 911 the second I was alone.

That night, Michael was cooling his heels in jail. I got a restraining order, which he would constantly break with calls, e-mails, and texts, sometimes calling me names, sometimes begging me to take him back. For months, I would lie awake at night imagining how he was going to kill me. I still think were it not for the fact that he would have been suspect number one in any murder investigation, he would have happily done so. I don't believe he has a conscience, and people without consciences are capable of almost anything. To him, killing me would have been like taking out the trash.

But thankfully, the calls and texts became less frequent, then finally stopped. Once they did, I was left trying to figure out what the hell I wanted to do with my life.

———

One day while watching the news, I suddenly came to terms with something that had always been in the back of my mind: I wanted to be a reporter.

I grew up around journalists, so I knew that world pretty intimately, which was of course the reason I used to want no part of it. Obviously, my father's experience colored the way I viewed the profession, but the damage I saw in his friends and colleagues also made me reluctant to join their ranks. Alcoholism, emotional numbness, inability to hold down a relationship . . . many of them had the whole potpourri of fun PTSD symptoms.

People used to ask me when I was little if I wanted to be a journalist, and I'd always laugh and say no, thank you very much. Journalism didn't have a single positive connotation to me, growing up. My parents' footsteps trailed through some pretty miserable terrain, and I had no desire to follow in them. As far as I was concerned, that job had wrecked my life.

But reporting had been stitched into the fabric of my life from the moment I was born, and finally embracing it, however reluctantly, felt right, somehow. I loved talking to people, and getting them to open up to me. I was concerned with shitty corners of the globe where terrible things were happening to people no one knew or cared about. Be that as it may, I had no desire to save the world—I think my lifelong exposure to journalism saved me from that delusion, common among many aspiring reporters. But I felt passionately that reporting should be accurate and true. I despised the oversimplified sensationalism I saw in so much of the news, and I wanted to write honestly about things I knew to be messy and real—the normal people trying, and the world that made it so hard for them. Growing up in a hugely publicized situation that was, in actuality, very different from the media portrayal gave me an intense belief that the world should be told the truth about things, and I wanted to tell it.

In 2009, at age twenty-four, I started interning at the Committee to Protect Journalists, and I won't lie and say I didn't get that job because of my father, who was on the board of directors. When my dad learned of my newfound interest in reporting, he smiled vaguely and said, "I had a feeling this would happen. I'll see what I can do." I was still drinking too much and dabbling in drugs, so I dressed inappropriately, showed up late, and was frequently reprimanded by my boss. But when I was asked to write blog posts, I always did a good job, and the looks of surprised respect from my coworkers were enough to give me some faith in my ability.

I applied to Columbia University's graduate school of journalism, and got in, probably also partly because of my father and the fact that he used to teach there. This was something I felt self-conscious about for a long time—I longed for the day when I had built up enough credibility to escape from under the umbrella of his name and reputation. But for the moment, his name, and my talent, seemed like all the support I had on my fragile new path.

I loved police reporting, and writing about international affairs. My Covering Conflicts teacher despised me, but I learned things from her about being a foreign correspondent that I haven't forgotten to this day. On my final evaluation, she wrote that no news organization would put up with me. She was probably right. To get through the long hours and heaps of work, and to counteract the sedative effects of the mood stabilizer I was on, I started abusing my ADD medications. That soon turned into buying Adderal from dealers, and I shed weight until I was stick-thin and scary-looking. I was always late and unprepared for class, and my fellow students would sneer at me behind my back for my short skirts. But I worked hard, had clean copy, and wrote good stories, to the frustration of my professors, who would sigh and say I had plenty of skill but no discipline.

The most valuable thing I learned in journalism school was the term *joyful entitlement,* which basically means marching into a place you have no business being, walking up to a person who has no reason to talk to you, and getting a story simply because you act like you should. Being joyfully entitled is one of the most important qualities a journalist can possess, in my opinion. For a girl who felt undeserving of even small kindnesses, it was a difficult concept to grasp. But the more I watched my journalism improve, the more I began to believe I might be able to hack it as a foreign correspondent, which I had by that point chosen as a career path.

I left Columbia a reporter, albeit a crazy one. After graduation, I went to the only place that made sense to me: the country I had grown up loving, my mother's homeland and my father's prison. I moved to Lebanon.

6. THE SPOOKS

He who controls the past controls the future. He who
controls the present controls the past.
—GEORGE ORWELL

NOW

Hassan Sabra is not an easy man to track down.

It should be simple to set up an interview with the editor of *Ash-Shiraa*, the newspaper that broke Iran-Contra. Editors of publications that break momentous, history-making events aren't usually recluses. I manage to find a number for the *Ash-Shiraa* office online, but it looks like the newspaper hasn't been in the news-breaking business for some time. Through some deep Googling, I unearth an article mentioning some conflict with a former Lebanese president in the nineties over something Sabra wrote. Strange, for an outlet that was so prominent during the civil war to have faded from view like this. It's still listed as a functioning business in Lebanon, though, so I call the office number.

The secretary who picks up seems extremely wary when I ask to speak with Sabra.

"He's not in town," she says to me in Arabic.

"Okay, well, will you please give him my number and tell him I want to interview him about Irangate?" That's what the Lebanese call Iran-Contra.

"Of course," she says politely.

I'm not particularly optimistic that he'll call me back. Honestly, I'm a little perplexed that his secretary was so guarded with me. I decide to just go to the office in person. It's a lot harder to duck someone when they're standing in front of you.

But as with the Hezbollah press office, deciphering the written address for the *Ash-Shiraa* headquarters is no small feat. It's somewhere in Hamra, a big, bustling area of Beirut. After a lot of misunderstandings and misdirection from well-meaning passersby, one of whom points me to another neighborhood, I accidentally end up at the office of *An-Nahar*, a different newspaper entirely. Once I realize my mistake, I ask one of the reporters there if he knows anything about Hassan Sabra and *Ash-Shiraa*. He laughs.

"I worked in the archives there for a little while," he tells me. "The man's got intelligence agent written all over him. He actually has warrants against him in Lebanon and I'm pretty sure he's on the run. I doubt you'll be able to sit down with him."

I nod, unsurprised. The Iran-Contra leak had smelled fishy to me since I learned about it. Sabra clearly had been furthering somebody's agenda by publishing that story, and Lebanon's local media is for the most part a collection of competing propaganda outlets. Each major political party has its own newspapers and TV stations, so unbiased journalism is generally a rare commodity in Beirut. Also, the country has always been notoriously easy for intelligence agencies to penetrate, and no more so than during the war. But for whom would Sabra allegedly be spying? The reporter seems to think it's Syria, and I'd read quite a bit about *Ash-Shiraa*'s supposed ties to the Syrian regime.

After some more searching, I finally give up and go home. A few days later, my cell phone rings. I pick it up and a man asks for me in Arabic. "Yes, I'm Sulome," I reply. "Who may I ask is speaking?"

"This is Hassan Sabra," the man replies. "My secretary said you wanted to interview me about Irangate."

Taken aback, I schedule a meeting with him for the following week. I hire a translator because Sabra speaks very little English, and I don't trust my Arabic for an in-depth political interview. I had asked Sabra for detailed directions to the *Ash-Shiraa* office in Hamra, so we make it on time. The building is one of the shadiest setups I have ever seen. Thuggish young men loiter around the entrance, which is unmarked. The whole place has an air of menace about it.

"What a creepy establishment," I murmur under my breath.

"Oh, don't be scared," the translator tells me with concern, thinking I was anxious about going inside.

I burst out laughing. "Don't worry about me," I reply. I've made an effort to look respectable but super feminine to catch Sabra off guard with my questions. I guess my ploy is working, because the translator obviously seems to think I'm an idiot.

When we ask which floor is the *Ash-Shiraa* office, one of the sinister-looking young men barks at me suspiciously: "Who are you looking for?"

"Mr. Hassan Sabra," I reply. He confers with his cohorts while we wait, makes a phone call, and finally we're allowed upstairs, where the secretary greets us cheerfully and ushers us in to see the boss. Sabra is a round, soft-spoken man in his fifties or early sixties. He politely serves us coffee as we settle in. I'm doing my best little-girl-lost routine, and I even catch the translator rolling her eyes at my cluelessness.

"What is your book about?" Sabra asks.

"I'm studying the civil war, and I found your name while

researching Irangate," I reply through the translator. "My first question is about being a Lebanese journalist during the war. What was it like? It must have been very difficult."

"I went through very hard circumstances, and almost died many times," Sabra says somberly. "I was shot twice. You can see here, where one bullet went in, and here, where it came out the other side. Here is where the other one went in." He shows me some vicious-looking scars.

"Why did someone try to kill you?" I ask. "Was it because of something you wrote?"

"It was because I've always been against the Syrian regime, and particularly Iran," Sabra responds. "But I was with Khomeini during his trip from Paris to Tehran, in the same plane. Back then, Khomeini didn't have the policy against Lebanon yet, and he was just supposed to have a revolution in Iran against the shah. I was supportive of this until the Iran-Iraq War, when Iran started interfering in the politics in Lebanon. Their slogans and speeches were not Arab at all. They were trying to take the Shia out of the Lebanese context. I'm Shia and I'm Lebanese, but I'm Lebanese before being Shia. So why would I be under the umbrella of Iran? I have my own identity. That was when they tried to assassinate me."

Hezbollah is often accused of placing Iran's interests over those of Lebanon. Today, the group's involvement in the Syrian civil war—most likely at the behest of Iran—demonstrates that the argument is not without merit. Hezbollah officially entered the war on Bashar al-Assad's side in May 2013. By all accounts, they've aided him in decimating his own country and slaughtering the Syrian people, thus seriously damaging Hezbollah's credibility as a resistance movement. Following the group's decision to publicly announce their involvement, Hezbollah's popularity in Lebanon took a huge hit.

Although the rise of the Islamic State has since helped boost public opinion of Hezbollah's efforts in Syria—because ISIS is seen by many Lebanese as a more immediate threat to their country than Assad's regime, and Hezbollah the country's primary defender against the violent jihadi group—there is truth to the accusation that Hezbollah answers to Iran, not the Lebanese people.

But Sabra's insistence that he was motivated by patriotism and refused to throw in his lot with Iranian radicalism makes about zero sense to me. Sabra claimed in that crucial Iran-Contra story that the people who leaked the information about the arms deals to him were his close friends and associates of Mehdi Hashemi, a Shia cleric and former official in the Iranian Revolutionary Guard Council (IRGC), Iran's elite fighting force. Sabra also discussed his connections with Hashemi in a *Washington Post* article shortly after the story broke.

Hashemi was reportedly a maniacal fundamentalist committed to exporting the Islamic revolution to other nations through terrorism, and has been cited as the founder and sponsor of the Islamic Jihad Organization, the group that kidnapped my father. He was a protégé of Hussein-Ali Montazeri, at the time widely viewed as Khomeini's likely successor. Hashemi was once an influential member of the IRGC and for a time headed its Office of Liberation Movements (OLM), which was tasked with nurturing Iran's relationship with Shia in other Middle Eastern countries, including Lebanon.

As such, Hashemi would have been involved with helping to mobilize Lebanese Shia. It's also quite clear that Hezbollah was an IRGC project from the outset. A contingent of the Revolutionary Guard was dispatched to Lebanon's Beqaa Valley in the early eighties, where it set about training the discontented Shia to fight against the Israelis.

But a U.S. Library of Congress report I found online explains that while Hashemi was with the IRGC's Office of Liberation Movements, he was constantly at odds with Iran's Ministry of Foreign Affairs, which preferred that the Islamic revolution be exported to Lebanon through education and example rather than terrorism. The OLM was removed from the IRGC's jurisdiction in 1984 and absorbed by the Ministry of Foreign Affairs. Apparently frustrated by the Iranian government's lack of zeal, Hashemi resigned his position and formed his own enterprise, the Office for Global Revolution (OGR), which was nominally part of Montazeri's staff but acted independently in what appears to have been at least somewhat of a rogue operation.

Everything I can find about Hashemi indicates that he formed the Islamic Jihad sometime during the early eighties. This most likely occurred around the same time that the IRGC came to Lebanon with the mission of training the future Hezbollah fighters. Hashemi's point man with the IJO was Ali-Reza Asgari, an IRGC brigadier general also involved in training Hezbollah. Before arriving in Lebanon, though, Asgari traveled to Syria in July 1982, where he requested the help of Bashar al-Assad's father and predecessor, Hafez al-Assad, with establishing a "network" in Lebanon. It's widely assumed that the network he referred to was Hezbollah, but considering the ongoing conflict between Hashemi and the Foreign Ministry, it makes sense that Hashemi would have seized an opportunity to nurture his own group—one with which he was free to play out his fantasy of exporting the revolution through terrorism.

I'd say there's a good chance the IJO was a pet project of Hashemi's—one that wasn't well received by others in the Iranian government. Regardless, Hashemi seems to have continued pursuing his own agenda until he was actually arrested by Khomeini in October 1986, just before the Iran-Contra story was leaked to

Sabra. His alleged crimes included treason and a number of other offenses that were made public before his death, including setting up secret networks in Iran and founding extremist terrorist groups.

But it's also likely Hashemi was arrested because he had been voicing his displeasure with the arms-for-hostages deals, which were being negotiated by moderates like Akbar Rafsanjani, speaker of Parliament at the time. Since Hashemi had most likely ordered that the hostages be taken in the first place, he probably didn't appreciate seeing his plan hijacked (no pun intended) and turned into leverage with which to normalize relations with America. He'd supposedly been threatening to go public with the arms deals before he was imprisoned. We know that Hashemi's cohorts leaked Iran-Contra to Sabra following the arrest, and the rest is history.

This appears to offer a solution to the puzzle of whether the Iranian government had much influence over the kidnappers. At the time, Iran was plagued by factionalism—rival groups were all jockeying to lead the direction of the still-new Islamic republic. It makes sense that one of these factions, led by Hashemi, would have engineered the kidnappings and bombings to further its own radical interests, while others in the government, led by Rafsanjani, were trying to change Iran's relationship with the West.

A *Los Angeles Times* story from November 14, 1986, reports that the hostages were believed to have been taken by Hashemi's group of radicals, against the wishes of moderates like Rafsanjani, who had promised the U.S. government he would put an end to the kidnappings. As the *L.A. Times* put it, "The hostages have become pawns in Iran's tortuous political infighting between Islamic radicals and moderates." Following the Iran-Contra leak, Hashemi was executed in September 1987; soon after, Montazeri lost favor with Khomeini.

In any case, Hashemi is literally the last person you'd expect a supposedly moderate Lebanese nationalist and opposer of Iranian meddling to ally himself with. I need to unravel this.

"Why was Hashemi arrested?" I ask.

"They don't need that much information in Iran," Sabra says evasively. "If you say hello in the wrong way, they arrest you for betrayal."

I'm trying to find a way to ask about the allegations that Sabra is foreign intelligence. "I know at this point, nobody knew who was working for whom, and a lot of journalists were being accused of spying," I venture. "This was a big problem for everyone who was working here at the time, and after Irangate, it must have been a problem for you. I imagine that was difficult. How did you handle it?"

"No one else in Lebanon published the Irangate story because they didn't want trouble with Iran," Sabra replies. "I was the only one who published it. The Iranians accused me of being a spy for the U.S. The day that Mehdi Hashemi was sentenced to death, they tried to assassinate me."

I nod, looking impressed. "Another thing," I interject, dropping the innocent act. I'm looking forward to seeing his reaction to this. "I know *Ash-Shiraa* received many videos and pictures of the hostages. My father is Terry Anderson, and that's why I'm writing this book."

Sabra gives a little jump, then collects himself. "Please, send him my regards," he says hesitatingly. "I'm sorry if what I wrote made him be imprisoned longer . . . Reagan said several times that they were very close to sealing a deal to release all the hostages, but because *Ash-Shiraa* would write about these deals before they happened, they had to cancel them at the last minute.

"I would always think to myself that these people, it's not their fault," Sabra continues, all kindly concern. "They're only innocent people. They just happen to be hostages, and they are the victims of American and Iranian politics. I felt really sorry, but sometimes when you do your job, some people have to get hurt."

Bullshit, I think. News articles from the eighties citing *Ash-Shiraa* referred to it as a publication with ties to radical elements in Iran and Hashemi in particular. *Ash-Shiraa* also seems to have been the source of much inside information regarding the hostages; it's quoted constantly throughout the crisis. If Sabra was allied with Hashemi, the man who founded the Islamic Jihad, and he essentially served as the IJO's media mouthpiece, he bears a lot more responsibility for my father's captivity than he's admitting.

"I'm a journalist, don't worry," I respond sweetly. "I understand. But you obviously had some sort of channel to the Islamic Jihad. Why did you receive all those photos and videos?"

"I had a good relationship with Hashemi, Montazeri, and other people in Iran," Sabra replies, fumbling. "Also with Hezbollah at the time, and they were behind this. Actually all of Iran was behind this. I used to have a good relationship with Hezbollah. It doesn't exist anymore, but back then I had a good relationship with them. They all wanted to give a good picture against extremism to the world. I'm a very moderate man, and against extremism as well. But in reality, Hezbollah is a very extremist party."

This is becoming more and more nonsensical. Why would Hezbollah, an Iranian-sponsored operation, trust this man, who outspokenly hated the Iranian government and dealt it a severe political blow by leaking Iran-Contra? And if Sabra is so moderate, why was he working with Hashemi, by all accounts a foaming-at-the-mouth radical?

It's beginning to look like the Iranians who sponsored Hezbollah may not have been the same people who created the Islamic Jihad. That would make sense, given the postrevolutionary factionalism of Iranian politics at the time. It would also explain why the

Rafsanjani-led Iranians who participated in Iran-Contra with the approval of Khomeini had so much trouble convincing the IJO to release all the hostages. In an old *New York Times* interview with the enigmatic Ghorbanifar, he claimed that Iranian officials actually had to seize Reverend Weir from his captors by force. Of course, Ghorbanifar is not necessarily a reliable source, but that would explain all the analytic speculation by historians and journalists over why the official, government-sanctioned Iranians working with the United States on the arms deals had so little power over the hostage-takers.

It's an interesting prospect: Could Hezbollah and the Iranian government be telling part of the truth when they say they weren't morally responsible for the IJO's terrorism? I remember something Naim Qassem, now deputy secretary-general of Hezbollah, said to journalist Hala Jaber during an interview for her book *Hezbollah: Born with a Vengeance*. She asked him if they were behind the kidnappings and bombings, and Qassem told her no. But Jaber pointed out that Hezbollah was powerful and influential enough at the time to have stopped the kidnappings whenever they chose. Instead, the militia allowed the IJO to operate in their neighborhoods freely.

"Should we have started a conflict with these groups for the sake of the Americans?" Qassem asked.

Harsh as that may be, it's a valid point. If this theory is correct, Hezbollah—only just beginning to coalesce into a coherent movement itself—probably wasn't privy to every detail of the political wrangling going on in Iran. Some Hezbollah leaders may have found the IJO's methods distasteful, but they did share a religious ideology and a hatred of the West. So the Hezbollah leadership looked the other way and let the IJO continue its terror spree. They may even have aided or joined in the IJO's efforts when they appeared to serve Hezbollah's interests. There's a possibility that Hezbollah may not have originally been taking direct orders to kidnap and kill civilians; but even if that's so, I wouldn't consider them entirely innocent either.

I'm losing patience with Sabra's weaseling, and I have leads to follow up on.

"I'm really sorry to have to ask you this, because you've been so kind and welcoming, but to be frank, you've been accused of being intelligence," I say flatly. "All kinds: Syrian, Israeli—every kind under the sun. What's your reaction to these allegations?"

The translator is looking at me with her mouth open. I congratulate myself on that NYU acting degree.

"The conflict in the Arab world is not merciful, it's very unethical," Sabra complains, looking more and more cornered. "You can be a friend in the morning and then you become a secret agent for the enemy in the afternoon. It's not merciful. Where's the proof? These are just rumors and sayings of the people . . . I don't live here anymore. I come here secretly. I've been living in Cairo since 2005. Until now, I receive threats and calls for murder."

"Of course, that's terrible, but I had to ask," I say. "Thank you so much for speaking with me, Mr. Sabra. I'll be in touch."

"Wait, before you leave, can I please take a photograph with you?" Sabra asks hurriedly. "I always take pictures with my guests."

Could this be any fucking weirder? But hey, it's not like I've made a secret of my investigation; quite the opposite, in fact. I'm not certain how things like this work, but I have a feeling no one meets with ex-CIA agents in Washington and Hezbollah members in Lebanon without being noticed by spy agencies. I flash a cheesy grin at the camera while his secretary takes a photo of us, then leave with the translator, who respectfully whispers, "Well done," in the elevator.

Two days later, the evening before I'm set to leave for New York, Sabra calls me and invites me to lunch. I imagine he wants to pump me for information and perhaps convince me of the purity of his motives, although who knows. He might have more sinister intentions, and I'm certainly not eager to find out.

"Thanks, Mr. Sabra, but I'm going home tomorrow," I say politely.

———

I need to learn how the United States understood the relationship between Hezbollah and the Islamic Jihad at the time my father was kidnapped. The American narrative that's taken shape over time is that the Islamic Jihad was just a cover Hezbollah used to distance itself from the bombings and kidnappings. But my reporting is leading me to believe things may have been more complicated than that. Most importantly, there's the question of Mehdi Hashemi and the clusterfuck of Iranian politics during the eighties. Was the Islamic Jihad spawned from a rogue operation within the still-fractious Iranian government, led by Hashemi? Did Hezbollah's orders and the IJO's instructions in fact come from different places? Is anyone in D.C. aware of this line of inquiry?

First, I try asking Bilal Saab, another D.C. think-tanker and senior fellow at the Atlantic Council. Saab's analysis on Lebanon is respected in Washington, and I've quoted him for a story before, so he's a good place for me to start. His opinion is mostly in line with what I've always been taught, although he does acknowledge that Hezbollah's current identity is very different from what he believes was its previous incarnation as a terrorist group.

"I think there was strategic benefit during the early phases of

Hezbollah to keep it as confusing as possible and not to have it all under one organizational structure," says Saab. "That's pre-1985; 1985 was when they publicly came out with that statement saying, 'This is who we are, deal with it.' There was value in keeping it very decentralized because you can maintain plausible deniability and everybody will be confused about what's going on."

Plausible deniability. I keep hearing that glib phrase, and I guess that would explain why people like Mughniyeh ended up rising so high in Hezbollah's ranks. But if everyone still thinks Hezbollah was responsible for the IJO's actions, well, their denials don't seem very plausible, do they?

Moreover, if the IJO was originally getting its orders from Hashemi, who was running the IJO's operations following his execution in 1987? Could leadership have passed to his point man, Ali-Reza Asgari? At some point, though, Hezbollah leaders would have had to step in and take the helm, because it eventually became clear that the IJO was damaging their interests as well as those of their patrons in Iran—at a time when Hezbollah wanted to establish itself as a legitimate political entity in Lebanon.

So let's say Hezbollah leaders realized the IJO was not helping their cause. Is it possible that Hezbollah eventually took control of the IJO, dismantled the terrorist group, and absorbed some of its more valuable members? Like Mughniyeh, for instance, who was certainly a strategic mastermind despite the probability that he was also a psychopath. If that's the case, then Hezbollah's role in my father's kidnapping was far more nuanced than anyone understands. Assuming the Hezbollah takeover of the IJO occurred sometime in the late eighties, when it became a truly cohesive, structured organization, then Hezbollah certainly held on to Dad for a while after that would have taken place. Perhaps the group and its Iranian sponsors were trying to leverage their newly acquired hostages into some type of political gain for themselves—making Hezbollah's claims of innocence ring false.

But I'm getting ahead of myself. First, I have to find out if anyone in D.C. actually believes that there was a difference between Hezbollah and the IJO. Barbara Bodine is one of the first to entertain that hypothesis, and as the former U.S. State Department's acting coordinator for counterterrorism, she's a pretty reliable source.

"You're quite right to make the distinction between the mainline Hezbollah as a resistance operation taking place in response to an actual occupation, versus the guys who [kidnapped] your father and his fellow hostages," Bodine tells me.

I'm a little surprised at her candor. Everyone involved with this work in Washington is extremely careful about how far they'll go down roads like this one. It's not an easy thing, stepping outside of the indelible black circle that's been drawn around a historical event by your own government. Perhaps that's why we have so much difficulty learning from history: half the time, we're not even allowed to fully explore its possibilities. There's a subtle, unspoken tendency in D.C. to marginalize every scholar, historian, journalist, or politician who dares to question what we've been told about our role in world events. All too many "experts" sit waiting in the wings to ridicule and snipe at those who don't toe the line.

This subtext lingers in the background of every conversation I have in D.C. about the unexplored theories I've come across during my reporting, and my talk with Randa Slim of the Middle East Institute is no exception. But she does seem to seriously consider my questions, and concedes that the conventional understanding of Hezbollah's role in the terror attacks is probably oversimplified given the complexity of the environment at the time.

"The whole thing was so murky," Slim murmurs. "One day this faction was in; another day this faction was out. It was very hard to say, 'This is Hezbollah, this is not Hezbollah.' It was a situation that was so dynamic, so in flux. People in, people out. Groups in, groups out. You have to take that into consideration. There was not the kind of central command over Hezbollah that Nasrallah has now."

"It was more fractured," I offer.

"Yeah, it was," Slim responds. "Also, in Iran, you had this play that was going on between different centers of power. It was the Youthful Revolution at the time. Khomeini did not consolidate that revolution for some time. It took the regime a while to really take control of it and for it to become what it is today. During that time, you had many Iranian groups also trying to play out the domestic politics of Iran through Lebanon, getting the revolutionary fervor going."

Which is exactly my way of thinking. Lebanon has always been used as a stage for other countries to act out their bitter little proxy wars against each other. Is it so unimaginable that opposing factions in Iran after the revolution would use proxy actors as tools during their period of political infighting? In a postrevolutionary environment, it's generally a free-for-all to see which group can consolidate the most power and influence the fastest. People bet on different horses. Hezbollah may have been one horse, the IJO another. It's an interesting scenario, and others seem to find it plausible as well.

When asked during a Skype conversation, my dad's fellow hostage Terry Waite agrees that it makes sense to separate the Islamic Jihad from Hezbollah when discussing the IJO's acts of terrorism—at least to some extent.

"I think it's very plausible that each unit, like Hezbollah on the one hand, and this splinter group [the IJO] on the other, had their own modus operandi, and therefore they didn't necessarily overinterfere with each other," Waite tells me via Skype. "It could well be that what Hezbollah says is true, and they didn't have direct responsibility for the abductions, but didn't do a whole lot to prevent them."

Ex-diplomatic spook and private intelligence analyst Fred Burton has some insights into the American intelligence community at the time that seem to line up with what I've been considering. During our phone call, I ask him whether it's possible to distinguish between Hezbollah and the IJO.

"Why do you think all the hostages were finally released?" I ask Burton. "What Hezbollah guys have told me is that the IJO turned out not to be helpful to their cause at all. It tarnished their image, especially when they wanted to become more legitimate. It also tarnished the image of their Iranian sponsors at a time when there was at least an effort on the part of Iran and Syria to achieve some sort of dialogue with the West. Now this is all speculation, of course, but could it be that Hezbollah decided to change their image and approach, which is when they dismantled the IJO and absorbed people like Mughniyeh? This would have been around the same time they started releasing most of the hostages. Do you think that's a fair assessment?"

"I think so," says Burton. "I can tell you that at that time period, we really didn't know. To be candid, you probably have much more clarity into that than we ever did in the fog of the terror wars at that period of time, when we didn't know who the IJO was. We were trying to identify personalities and arguing back and forth: Is this Hezbollah? Is this Iran? Is this Iranian controlled? Who are these guys? I think your point is very well taken, and that's as good an explanation as any.

"We in the intelligence services [often] pigeonhole certain groups and people," Burton continues. "It's simple to have a menu item of these groups and place people in there without thinking much into the motivation. You look at the individual and say, Hassan Izz-al-Din [one of the IJO members] is associating with Hezbollah, therefore these things must all have been carried out by Hezbollah . . . I think that goes back to the lack of [insight] into the failure of human intelligence."

It's far from an ironclad confirmation, but Burton's observations do lend some credibility to the theory that Hezbollah and the IJO may have been operating separately. Then another source—a journalist whom I approach—tells me a story that sounds pretty firmly situated within Crazytown. He's asked me to refrain from revealing his name; let's just say his reporting on these subjects is respected, although his work is not without controversy. He says that during a 2006 trip to Lebanon, he interviewed a top Hezbollah member who said the group hadn't kidnapped anybody. Like me, he became curious and started poking around to see if there was any truth to this claim.

"I was talking to people who might know about this stuff," he says. "Then one day I was sitting in my hotel in August 2006 and a guy came up to me. A nasty guy. He sat down and he said, 'You're inquiring about the kidnappings.' I said, 'Who are you?' He replied, 'Are you inquiring about the kidnappings or not?' I said, 'Yeah.' He said, 'Well, stop inquiring.' I told him, 'I don't know who you are; I don't feel threatened. I'm sitting in my hotel, so why don't you stop threatening me and have a cup of coffee.' He said, 'You know who did the kidnappings. We don't want the light shined there.' Then he left."

This reporter tells me he has excellent U.S. intelligence contacts, and having read his work, I believe that to be true. He reached out to some of them and managed to set up a debriefing session with four CIA representatives.

"I told them the story about how I began to have doubts that Hezbollah were the kidnappers, at least the original ones," he recounts.

"These are smart people, and they didn't say a word. They just sat there and listened to me and then a young guy in glasses says, 'Well, thanks for coming in; we'll get back to you.' I said, 'Well, what are you going to do?' He says, 'We're going to do some homework and some checking, go back and talk to people.'

"A month later, I get called back in," the journalist continues. "There were the same four people and the guy who was the talker looked at me and said, 'Well, we want to thank you for coming in and giving us that briefing two months ago. I want you to know that we've done a very thorough investigation because this is a very interesting case and it has implications for our foreign policy. So, I'm going to tell you that what your Hezbollah source said may in fact have some truth to it . . . there is reason to believe that what you were told is correct.'"

"Wow," I say to the journalist. I imagine myself in that room, with those four spooks telling me that with a straight face. I would have lost my shit.

"I said, 'You're fucking kidding me.'" The reporter laughs. "He kind of smiled and said no. They sat there and looked at me. I said, 'Who the hell is the Islamic Jihad?' One of them just replied, 'You said you had one question. We answered it.'"

What a story. This reporter could be bullshitting me, of course, but I don't see what purpose that would possibly serve and he's a legitimate journalist who's been published by many reputable outlets. Plus, Bodine and Burton have already intimated that there might be some truth to this theory, so it's not out of the realm of possibility that other government sources would have told this guy the same thing.

I remember something Timur Goksel, the former UNIFIL spokesman, said to me in regard to the respective ways in which Hezbollah and the Islamic Jihad used suicide bombings.

"Hezbollah sponsored suicide bombings," Goksel reminded me as we ate our *manakeesh*. "But they were not haphazard. They were very well planned and the martyrs were handpicked by a committee."

"These were suicide bombings in the south against Israeli convoys?" I asked.

"Yes."

"That's different from going and blowing up an embassy, though, right?"

"They are different," Goksel agreed. "Hezbollah used a military tactic, but very well regulated. I know there was a long list of people who wanted to do it, but this committee, mostly clergy, they said, 'If he is newly married, he has children, he is out. He cannot do it. He has a family to take care of.' They had rules like this. It's very interesting. In the south, what I've also been told is that the men they chose were medically not very well."

"Sick," I muse. "It makes sense."

"As I said, you are right," Goksel told me. "It's different from the ones in Beirut."

Tactical differences in the way Hezbollah and the IJO carried out suicide bombings would seem to line up with the idea that the groups were operating with different agendas. But not every ex–U.S. official is on board with this line of reporting. Ryan Crocker, former U.S. ambassador to Lebanon, for one, says he doesn't think it's wise to seriously distinguish between Hezbollah and the IJO.

"I've always had the feeling that while there might have been different nodes out there, they coalesced fairly rapidly into a single entity," he tells me. "I think it was the Iranians who were pushing that. You remember, of course, this is just a few years after the Islamic revolution. They were trying to figure out how to project power outside of Iran . . . Imad Mughniyeh showed up if not right

at the beginning, pretty early on. His linkages to the Revolutionary Guard were there from the beginning, obviously on the military side of Hezbollah. Tufayli was a politician, Mughniyeh was a
killer . . . and none of them really carried membership cards."

Fair point. But Sobhi Tufayli was secretary-general of Hezbollah while Mughniyeh headed the IJO. That doesn't necessarily contradict the theory I'm following up on. I would still like to
know when it was concluded that Hezbollah was responsible for
the IJO's terrorism. Tufayli was eventually kicked out of Hezbollah, for reasons that are still somewhat unclear. He's supposed to
be living in exile in Brital, a town in the Beqaa Valley. I add his
name to the list of people I should try to track down on my next
trip to Lebanon.

———

In October 2014, another ex-spook I approach, whom I'll keep
anonymous, agrees to be interviewed by me in New York. Since he
didn't join the CIA until the late nineties, he wasn't active in the
agency at the time of my father's captivity, so I almost don't bother
reaching out to him. But I decide it can't hurt to learn more about
the way the agency operates in the Middle East, and we meet for
lunch in Hell's Kitchen.

Soon after we sit down, he launches into a long bout of mans-
plaining when the topic of female CIA agents casually comes up in
conversation.

"Let me say this," he booms, articulating his words as though
I were a mentally challenged four-year-old. "Over the course of my
career I had a number of women who worked for me as case officers.
The good ones all came in older. None of them in their twenties
were worth anything. They were useless in their twenties. They were

young; they were pretty. Every guy they went out with wanted to sleep with them and they couldn't get anywhere. The better looking they were, the more difficult it was . . . the girls were a big problem. I didn't want to see them, didn't want them within twenty miles of me. Useless, totally."

Being a woman in my twenties, I take serious issue with this assessment. But I nod, smile demurely, and listen as he presents his "analysis" of my father's captivity. I happen to love mansplainers. They underestimate women so much it's embarrassingly easy to play into their fantasy of a quiet, innocent young girl captivated by their genius and get them to say really stupid things, which I can then write about.

"Let me just walk you into this slowly," he begins. "Have you heard of Imad Mughniyeh?"

I've been reporting on this for almost two years, and the man kidnapped my father, I think. *But no, tell me about Imad Mughniyeh, because my tiny little female brain can't have possibly grasped that kind of complex information.*

I nod, wide-eyed.

"Well, there were times that Mughniyeh wouldn't listen to the Iranians at all. He did whatever he wanted and they would complain about him too . . . remember something, the Iranians had different political objectives than Hezbollah. Hezbollah was all about taking out the Israelis and trying to create an Islamic state in Lebanon."

"But then how did you know from the beginning that the IJO was part of Hezbollah?" I ask. "It's all so confusing to me."

"We knew it was Hezbollah holding the hostages," he says flatly. "Very early on. Amal was talking to us. Amal said, 'It's not us, it's them.'"

That's like saying an IRA member would be credible if they

blamed a Protestant militant for a crime at the peak of the Irish troubles. "But there was a lot of fighting between Amal and Hezbollah then," I point out.

"Well, yes," he responds without missing a beat. "They were at war."

Okay. Logic doesn't seem to derail this man, but what about emotion? I'm curious to know how much effort he's put into truly understanding the minds of the people he was meant to be protecting us from.

"Would you have any empathy or understanding at all for what it's like being Shia and having someone invade your land?" I ask. "Do you think there's any truth to the idea that to really understand your enemy—"

"I understand my enemy quite well," he interrupts. I speak over him.

"—you have to sort of put yourself in their shoes?"

"No, not at all," he huffs. "Look, would you like me to recite the history of Islam? I know quite a bit about Islam. I took Arabic for years . . . I've spent a lifetime doing this and the problem is that these people are so gleeful in their delivery of pain that I've lost any sympathy for them . . . Americans are not out there gleefully killing Muslims."

"So, but . . . please don't be offended by this." I hesitate, so overwhelmed by his superior intelligence that I hardly know what to say. "I'm playing devil's advocate here, but do you . . . don't you think that . . . are we in any way responsible for backlash against us in terms of our policies?"

"How do you mean?" he barks. "What are you talking about?"

"I mean our policies in the Middle East going back decades."

"Look, the United States has made mistakes, but we are the single greatest force for good on the planet," he tells me with utter sincerity. "No country has given as much aid and protected and helped so many people . . . we are actually the greatest country on the planet. You have no idea how many countries' democracies we saved over the course of my career . . . nobody gives us credit for that, the American people."

His words aren't surprising. Early in our conversation, it became clear that he's a die-hard neocon. He talked about President Barack Obama as if he were the Antichrist.

"So you don't hold with the whole idea that we install and help keep dictators in power?" I ask. Saddam Hussein, the Taliban, Egypt's President Mubarak . . . those are just a few of the questionable leaders and groups we've sponsored and protected over the years. One might even say the United States' oil-hungry meddling in Iranian politics—including a CIA-staged coup against one of Iran's only secular, democratically elected leaders, Mohammad Mosaddegh, in the fifties—as well as our support of the autocratic shah, helped bring about the revolution. It's probable that Iranians turned to radical Islamism in response to the continued brutality of the shah's secular regime. I want to say, *Hey, douchebag, there's a reason these people hate us.* But I continue to bite my tongue.

"Not every country is organized for democracy," the ex-spook fires back at me. "Look at Afghanistan. You know what, I tell you the best thing they could have had? A benevolent dictator . . . we don't run around trying to set up dictatorships. We are trying to set up stability and create the grounds for democracy."

Fucking hell. If this is the best and brightest the Central Intelligence Agency has to offer, then our nation is totally and completely screwed. I didn't get much from this interview, but it's a solid reminder that I don't need to religiously adhere to the government's official version of events.

———

As a CIA field officer stationed in Beirut during the eighties, Bob Baer is a natural source for me to approach. He's most famous for writing the books that inspired the George Clooney movie *Syriana*, and has made quite a career as a media source on American foreign policy since he left the agency, so I'm pretty sure he'll talk to me. He agrees to an interview, which we do over Skype.

Baer is likable: blunt, humorous, and disarmingly honest—at least, that's the impression he gives. I remind myself that no one ever really leaves the agency, as they say, but I'm encouraged by his frankness.

I begin by asking him about the Boogeyman. "I keep hearing that Mughniyeh's motivation [for the kidnappings] was his brother-in-law being taken in Kuwait," I say. "It seems kind of a simplistic reason. What do you think was his motivation?"

"I think there were multiple factors at play," Baer responds. "He wanted to drive the French and the United States out. It was the middle of the Iranian revolution. They wanted to drive out Western culture and influence. They wanted to close down the CIA and French intelligence. They wanted the marines to leave. They wanted the Israelis, of course, to leave. It's hard to sort things out with this type of movement, but he also wanted his brother-in-law out. And, at some point, I'm sure there was a lot of personal ambition on the part of Mughniyeh."

"Right, that makes sense," I respond. "He wanted to work his way into some power."

"Exactly, but when does personal ambition bleed into nationalism?" Baer asks rhetorically. "I just don't know. Somewhere there's a line there, but I don't know. I've never met the guy. I just know that he fought and was involved in the Islamic resistance."

"I've heard that the Islamic Jihad was being directly sponsored by a [faction] that separated from the Revolutionary Guard, while Hezbollah was this larger, monolithic organization," I say. "Not that Hezbollah can't necessarily be held accountable, but I've been told they were two different animals."

"They were two entities," Baer agrees. "They operated separately. Their money was separate. Sometimes [the IJO] took orders from Iran, sometimes they didn't . . . Hezbollah had a different agenda. They were building hospitals and fighting Israelis."

This is pretty solid testimony to back up the theory I've been investigating. And my growing respect, if you can call it that, for Hezbollah's strategic maneuvering is apparently shared by Baer.

"I mean, this is the most effective resistance in modern times," he tells me. "Who predicted in 1982 that [Hezbollah] would be a Shia problem? I never saw it predicted. I think it's phenomenal, I mean, their technical abilities, their ability to keep secrets, take on the Israeli army, and beat it effectively or fight it to withdraw."

This seems like an eminently useful attitude for an intelligence agent to have toward an enemy. You don't approve of what they do, you're still going to fight them, but you respect your opponent, you grasp how their mind works and what path brought them to where they are now. How can you possibly effectively combat something you don't understand?

It makes me think of something that Aurélie Daher, a French scholar, said to me. She recently published a book called *Hezbollah: Mobilization and Power*, which I came across during my research. Daher quoted numerous Hezbollah sources and seemed to be well connected with members of the organization, so I reached out to her and we had a lively and fascinating conversation at a café in D.C.

"When you ask Hezbollah about the hostages, bombings, et cetera, they say, 'It's not us who did it, we didn't do it,'" Daher explained as we sipped our coffees. "So a lot of people would say, 'Oh, they're lying.' Well, even if they are lying, I think there's something interesting about the fact that they're denying this. It's like they don't want to be looked at as people who abduct other people, which means that morally speaking, they know that it's wrong."

This jibes with the Hajj and Hamza's almost conciliatory attitude toward me when they found out who my father was. Even if everyone in Hezbollah is lying and they personally gave the orders to kidnap Dad, it's clear that on a psychological level, they understand that it was wrong. That's not something most American analysts take into account when they publish books and papers about this "terrorist organization." These people are human beings, whether they are right, wrong, innocent, or guilty. Acting like they're not human doesn't help anyone, least of all us Americans, if we hope for our government to resolve this conflict—whether through violence or diplomacy.

Before I end the Skype call with Baer, I ask if he knows anyone else I should speak with regarding my investigation. "You should talk to this guy in Amman, Mustafa Zein," Baer tells me. "He was with Mughniyeh in the old days, at the time your father was kidnapped. Zein is no bullshit. Now, he may tell you some crazy things, so beware, but you should speak with him."

I jot down Zein's number. I probably won't be in Jordan anytime soon—but it might be worth following up on.

THEN
December 2011

My Palestinian guide was looking at me like I was crazy. Which at that moment, I sort of was.

I had been in Lebanon for about eight months, working as a

feature writer with the *Daily Star*, an English-language newspaper. I was in Ain el-Hilweh—arguably the most dangerous refugee camp in the country, with almost weekly car bombs and gunfights—for a story on foreign intelligence agents rumored to be operating in the camp.

Ain el-Hilweh is a heartbreaking place, full of big-eyed children in rags. The Lebanese government prohibits Palestinians from owning property or working in most occupations, mostly because xenophobia is something of a national trait and Lebanese fear that the Palestinians will assimilate into their society, flooding the job market with cheap labor and becoming a burden to the state. Today, Syrian refugees in Lebanon are faced with similar hostility from their host country.

There's a long-standing ban on construction in the Palestinian camps, where refugees live in increasingly overcrowded, squalid conditions. The ban is frequently ignored, so poorly constructed upper floors are regularly built and collapse, resulting in dozens of fatalities a year. Tangled wires carrying stolen electricity stretch from one rickety building to the next, another potentially lethal consequence of camp life. On a later visit to the camp, I'd speak to a seventeen-year-old Palestinian girl whose mother had been electrocuted by one of these faulty wires. She lived in a tiny room with her two younger sisters and brother, all of whom she supported financially.

That day, I was there to talk to a prominent member of Fatah—a militant branch of the Palestinian Liberation Organization—known as Lino. We were in a room full of men brandishing machine guns, his entourage heavily armed because he had narrowly escaped two assassination attempts in the last month. I was interviewing him about a series of bombings and sabotage incidents in and around Ain el-Hilweh, which he blamed on foreign covert agents. The room was stuffy and thick with cigarette smoke, and I made an effort, as I often do in those situations, to pretend I spoke no Arabic, in case they would think I was *mukhabarat,* or secret police. Most nervous militants are suspicious of journalists, even petite female ones.

It was an uncomfortable and somewhat dangerous situation that wasn't helped by the fact that earlier in the day, I'd taken about five times the dose of Ritalin I was prescribed.

The prior week was a blur. A month before, I had stopped taking one of my medications because it made me gain twenty pounds and was so sedating I felt like I was trudging through glue most of the time. It's a mood stabilizer, but also an antipsychotic; my previous bouts of abusing ADD meds had never resulted in psychosis, so I wasn't prepared for the result of this particular binge, which was what I can only describe as a psychotic break.

I was barely making it to the office, and my mind was swirling with conspiracy theories—my paranoia went through the roof. I sent a number of extremely embarrassing e-mails detailing my suspicions to some very important people, who thankfully did not answer. I somehow convinced Fadi, my editor at the *Daily Star,* to let me come to Ain el-Hilweh in search of a story on foreign intelligence assets in the camps. No matter how bizarre my behavior or disheveled my appearance, I consistently turned out stories that generated page hits, so I had earned his trust. Every time I tried to stop taking so much Ritalin, I'd crash and fall into a yawning pit of depression, so I decided I just wouldn't stop until I ran out, hoping to avoid the jagged despair that consumed me when I wasn't high. But I had built up a tolerance to the drug by then, and kept having to increase my dose in order to achieve the same rush of energy and sensation of controlled competence. Taking large amounts of an amphetamine-based medication without an antipsychotic to balance it out can easily lead to a psychotic break, so when the mood stabilizer left my system, I lost my mind a little.

———

I had chosen to work in Lebanon for a number of reasons—I spoke some Arabic and had traveled to Beirut almost every year since I was born. As a result, I was very close to my mother's family. Lebanon meant summers in my aunt's tiny, crowded apartment in one of the poorer Christian neighborhoods of Beirut. It was the smell of the Marlboro Reds my grandmother compulsively smoked; lazy days on the beach and dinners at a tiny restaurant by the sea—fresh fish piled high with fried pita bread, endless plates of hummus, and the burst of watermelon for dessert. My aunts would gossip constantly with my mother about the neighbors; my cousins and I would fight viciously and laugh uncontrollably. They were the best friends I had growing up, the next best thing to the brothers and sisters I wanted so desperately. Lebanon was one of the only places I felt at home, surrounded by people who loved and accepted me.

But I was also familiar with the country's sociopolitical landscape. Just as I remembered the comfort of my family, I never forgot the bullet holes pockmarking almost every wall in Beirut. Or the time Israel shelled the city when I was twelve—how my mother screamed at me to get away from the windows as the night boomed and cracked. The country is still haunted by the everyday violence and lawlessness of its fifteen-year civil war, though that war ended nearly a quarter century ago. I was always aware of Lebanon's volatile politics, and of how strained and fragile the postwar peace really was.

In fact, it was partly my frustration with that environment that drove me to leave the United States and live in a place that was in many ways still quite foreign to me. I didn't go back to Lebanon to confront my past or anything profound like that (although I should probably have foreseen that that would inevitably happen, with or without my efforts). I did it at the time because I loved that beautiful, fucked-up place, and was tired of seeing it quietly tear itself apart. I thought people should know about this gorgeous, war-weary country full of ruthless warlords posing as politicians, pitting segments of the population against each other in their battle to control the government. And about the opportunistic governments of other countries who were also shitting all over it. In his book *Beware of Small States,* David Hirst illuminated how Lebanon has been used as a forum for the proxy wars of other nations since its creation in 1920.

It's a place with abundant history, culture, and potential, and yet the Lebanese, despite being so proud of their starkly beautiful mountains and lush valleys, their beaches and Roman ruins, can't seem to love their country enough to reach across the vast divide of sectarianism and stop hating one another. I found it infuriating, fascinating, and heartbreaking all at once, and I needed to be in the middle of it.

It also seemed clear that Lebanon was, in many ways, crucial in maintaining the precarious balance of power in the Middle East, and I believed it was an important time to be a reporter there.

———

At that point, after I'd been lost in a drugged haze for so many years, reporting was the only thing keeping me going. Getting on meds had changed my life—I went from cokehead to nonfunctional opiate junkie to at least some semblance of competence. My head wasn't always the hellish swamp of pain and self-hatred it used to be, and going to journalism school had taught me I had something to hold on to, something I loved. But I carried my amphetamine addiction with me when I moved to Lebanon in 2011. I felt like my life was an endless game of Whac-A-Mole: every time I beat one demon down, another popped up, cackling.

I was also still mentally ill, although at the time, not self-aware enough to realize it. Every time I went on a new medication, I felt better. I'd think I had kicked this borderline thing for good. I'd take them for a while, then party too much and forget. My mood swings and unhealthy interactions with the people around me would get worse, along with the only thing of value I thought I had—my overt sexuality. Promiscuity, however, is generally not a good look, and even less so in conflict situations, with the threat of rape constantly hanging over you.

So I started living for the job. I quickly realized being borderline had its benefits, in the right circumstances. My talent for empathizing was incredibly useful during interviews. Everyone has a story, and whether they're aware of it or not, most people want to be understood—they crave talking to someone who can slip into their skin for a moment and share in their experience. I've found that this applies even to the most hardened of killers.

My first few stories bought me some measure of respect from my coworkers, who had at first probably assumed I was a spoiled wannabe riding her dad's coattails. I started by covering subjects like transgender Lebanese and child beggars, but I was soon assigned meatier and more dangerous pieces. I went to Roumieh, the most notorious prison in Lebanon, to speak with mentally ill inmates, and to a Palestinian refugee camp to interview drug addicts about substance abuse there. I loved my work.

But I would soon discover the job has even more pitfalls than

I'd been aware of growing up. For instance, there is a kind of workaday machismo, paired with the numbness of PTSD, that characterizes the approach of a lot of conflict journalists, and it's insidious. When I was just starting to freelance in Lebanon, a well-known TV reporter asked me why I got into journalism.

"You know, you can't become a war reporter just because you have a nice rack," he said to me in a tone obviously meant to be playful.

Humiliated, I started trying to explain my reasons to him, and he stopped me with a smile. "Sulome," he said, "when you see little dead children all piled up on top of each other, it stops being about giving voice to the voiceless. I do this because I'm good at it, and because I like to fuck the competition." People like him, who need to hide behind a brittle veneer of inhumanity in order to escape the weight of what they've seen, are a cautionary tale to me.

A close friend I would meet in Lebanon has been covering war for more than five years. He drinks himself to sleep most nights to avoid night terrors. He visited me in New York not long ago, and on the subway ride from the airport to my house, he saw a homeless man begging for money, saying he had once been shot in the face. My friend and I were at a restaurant when he told me this story, and he looked at me across the table with haunted eyes. "I saw his scar, and I knew the caliber of the bullet that shot him. No one should know a thing like that."

I'm not fearful of my own death; when you've sat up with a knife to your wrist, praying for the strength to press a little harder, death doesn't seem all that scary. But I am afraid of the horrors I would suffer if I were taken like my father. I'm also terrified of the possibility of seeing other people dying in front of me.

Nonetheless, despite my understanding the emotional trauma that comes with conflict reporting, the adrenaline called me, even back then. I would never do the hard-core bang-bang, bullet-dodging kind of journalism, not even later, but it always beckoned me; it still does. That hit of knowing you can die at any moment is better than any drug I've ever taken. But I also knew the price this job can exact. Growing up, I lived it every day. The sacrifice my father made for his career was etched into my psyche, impossible to forget. I know now that I need to be very careful, and remain vigilantly aware of the impact this work has on me. The lesson came hard that night in Ain-el-Hilweh.

———

It was well past dark in the camp. I was in the Palestinian NGO worker's car, shaking like a leaf while I watched the seemingly endless line of cars in front of us as we waited to leave. When we'd arrived at the camp, I had flounced up to the Lebanese soldiers guarding the entrance and handed them my U.S. passport as well as my entrance pass, provided by the NGO. They had gaped at the stupid American girl insane enough to march into this place without any sort of protection, then allowed me to enter. It only occurred to me later that the Lebanese army, being the airtight institution it is, every terrorist and potential kidnapper in Ain el-Hilweh probably knew I was there.

My guide was watching me tremble with mounting concern. "Are you okay, Miss Anderson?"

"I need to get out of here," I said in a whisper. In conjunction with the dangerous, desperate environment of the camp, my Ritalin-induced paranoia was overwhelming me.

"What's the matter? It's just a little traffic. The roads here are very narrow and this often happens."

"No," I replied, almost shouting. "I need to get out of this place. Now."

I got out of the car and started walking, though I had no idea how far it was to the gate. My driver called after me, then pulled the car over and ran to my side.

"It's okay, Miss Anderson! I'll take you to the gate. Just calm down."

"My father was kidnapped," I blurted out. "I have money. I'm afraid they'll take me too."

He put a hand on my heaving shoulder and whispered to me, as one would calm a frightened animal. "It's fine. You're with us; no one will touch you here."

But he was beginning to look increasingly suspicious to me, and I flinched from him.

"Just get me out of here. Please."

As soon as we exited the camp, I leaped into the car my newspaper had provided and told the driver to take me home to my apartment in the Hamra neighborhood of Beirut, about an hour away.

That drive was the most terrifying of my life. I was convinced that every car behind us was a villain intent on snatching me and condemning me to a hell of captivity and rape. After a while, the puzzled looks my driver was shooting me in the rearview mirror became sinister, and I was convinced he was in on the plot. When we arrived at my apartment, I scrambled out of the car without saying good-bye and fit my key into the lock with shaking hands.

I spent the night squirreling around my apartment, peering out windows, taking more Ritalin to ward off the yawning chasm of misery I knew awaited me when I crashed, and Googling conspiracy theories to feed my fevered brain. At about 4 A.M., I think I tried to go to sleep so I could make it to the office the next day. Needless to say, that was a futile effort. Instead, I lay in my bed, staring at the ceiling and muttering to myself in a voice that was increasingly unrecognizable. The empty place below my rib cage yawned endlessly. Insanity unfurled, stretched lazily, and grinned at me. *This is your life,* it whispered. *This is forever.*

After a while, the call to prayer drifted through my open window: *"Allah w Akhbar . . ."* The muezzin's voice was thick and rich; and although I didn't speak enough classical Arabic to understand everything he was saying, I had grown up hearing the *adhan,* and I knew some phrases by heart.

"There is no god but Allah," he chanted. "Hasten to success."

An admonition, or maybe a promise of redemption, just out of reach. I saw it then, the choice I had to make, and began to cry silently. There was oblivion, and there was survival. I knew the road I was traveling by heart, and what it would bring me—pain, pain, and more pain. That was the path I'd been on for years, and it represented a life I often considered ending, a chaotic, substance-fueled existence pocked with endless chasms of self-loathing. But for the first time in my life, I noticed there might be another way. I barely recognized it, and I knew immediately it wasn't going to be natural for me, or easy—but in that moment, I decided I was going to get better. I also realized there would be no cure, no pill to make the crazy disappear. If I chose that way, it was going to be a long, hard slog, and my soul sagged with exhaustion. It was the closest I've ever come to suicide. It was also the moment I decided I was going to live.

The next day, I called my mother and asked for a plane ticket back to the States. A week later, I was hospitalized for the second time.

7. THE CONSPIRACY THEORY

He who lives by fighting with an enemy has an interest
in the preservation of the enemy's life.
—FRIEDRICH NIETZSCHE

NOW

I'm beginning to think this trip was a mistake.

Mustafa Zein and I are sitting in a room at the Four Seasons Hotel in Amman, Jordan. I treated myself to the room because this whole investigation is starting to get to me. Hours spent peering blearily at Google search results, trying to follow up on the hundreds of frustrating, tantalizing leads I keep stumbling upon, are taking their toll. I knew I should follow Baer's suggestion to speak with Zein, since he was supposed to have participated in the hostage negotiations. So I reached out to him, booked my ticket from Beirut to Amman, and was thoroughly enjoying the lavish hotel.

Until our meeting. Now I'm looking at Zein with mounting concern for his sanity and wondering how to get through this craziness as fast as possible so I can go check out the hotel swimming pool.

"Let me tell you what I have." Zein is chattering rapidly at me. "I brought you this as a gift." He hands me a thin, bound booklet with the words *Summary of Science and Faith* on them. I place it in my lap.

"I'm the only game in town," Zein continues. "The politicization of Islam is anti-Koranic, anti-Islamic, through and through, and the so-called Islamic religious state is anti-Koranic. This is a summary of mine. You have never seen anything like it, because I put the Koran under the scientific test."

"Hmm," I respond, thinking, *What the fuck has Baer gotten me into?*

"What did I prove?" Zein asks rhetorically. "That there is a hereafter cosmologically. That there is God scientifically. And that there is an accounting to the soul, and where the soul is positioned in your body. This spark of divinity from paradise, which is antimatter. How do you keep antimatter in a laboratory?"

"Um . . . suspend it?" I offer. Glad I recently watched that episode on Discovery Science.

"Within a magnetic field!" he crows. "What is that magnetic field within your body? The solar plexus! That's the scientific proof. I know it's there. The instantaneous human combustion."

"When people just go up in flames?"

"The antimatter soul should go out before the heart stops and the field vanishes," Zein explains. "But if it touches the cells, it turns—and this is a scientific discovery I copyrighted in the United States—it turns the water into its basic elements: hydrogen, oxygen, electricity, fire. Hydrogen: fuel. Oxygen . . . so you will have burning from the cellular level."

"Amazing," I murmur, looking at the door. "Fascinating."

"Yes!" Zein says, laughing. "You are getting my full story, political and spiritual."

I see an opportunity. "Right, your political story," I interject.

"Can you tell me how you became involved in the hostage negotiations?"

I know Zein was used as a crucial source by the CIA because I just finished reading Kai Bird's moving, well-sourced book *The Good Spy,* about the life and death of Robert Ames, the CIA agent who was killed in the 1983 Beirut embassy bombing. The attack was carried out by the Islamic Jihad.

Zein plays a pivotal role in the book. His long-term friendship with Ames and recruitment as an unpaid CIA source—the unpaid part is something Zein heavily emphasizes to me—led to the establishment of an intelligence-gathering and personal relationship among Ames, Zein, and Ali Hassan Salameh, a high-ranking member of the PLO.

The book describes how Ames, by all accounts an intelligent, empathetic, and sincere man, essentially went somewhat "off the reservation" as a result of his relationship with Zein and Salameh. According to Bird's reporting, Ames always displayed Arabist tendencies and seemed sympathetic to the Palestinian cause, but with Zein and Salameh's influence, he began working quite hard to bring the U.S. government around to the idea of resolving the Israeli-Palestinian issue through negotiations with the PLO. Because Salameh came to trust Ames so deeply, their unusual friendship—unusual in the sense that it was not a typical agent-source dynamic; there was real mutual respect and admiration between the two men—led to some extremely valuable information being shared. In fact, it looked like the Zein-Salameh-Ames team was making real headway in getting Yasser Arafat, then–chairman of the PLO, to compromise on some major points regarding a potential peace agreement with Israel.

Then, in 1979, the Mossad assassinated Salameh. Don't get me wrong, they had their reasons—for one, the suspicion (now widely held as fact, although Bird's book raises questions on this point) that Salameh masterminded the 1972 Munich massacre in which eleven Israeli athletes and a German police officer were killed by Black September, an armed wing of the PLO. Certainly Salameh was known to have been chief of operations for Black September, and that group is believed to have committed some significant acts of violence, including hijackings and bombings. So it makes sense that the Mossad would want him out of the picture.

What makes less sense from a purely psychological perspective is why Ames would have become so close to Salameh. The man was known as a terrorist. How could a high-ranking CIA agent allow himself to intimately, personally invest in someone like that?

All I can offer by way of explanation is this: some people might look at the casualty statistics from the most recent 2014 Gaza war and ask an important question. Were the 2,251 Palestinians who met their deaths via Israeli military action (according to the UN, almost 70 percent were civilians) any less victims of terrorism than the 71 Israelis (5 were civilians, the rest soldiers) who died under Hamas rocket fire? What exactly is terrorism?

Strictly defined, *terrorism* is "the use of violence and intimidation in the pursuit of political aims." I, for one, can imagine few things more intimidating than the enormous stockpile of U.S.-donated arms, defense technology, wealth, and political influence wielded by Benjamin Netanyahu's Likud government today. Certainly any real examination of casualty estimates from the Arab-Israeli conflict will demonstrate that while both sides are willing to act violently to achieve their political aims, the Israelis do so much more effectively. Palestinian dead make up 87 percent of the total number of people killed as a result of this conflict since 2000.

One could argue that things were different when Bob Ames was alive. While it would defy credibility to ever have called this conflict equally matched, there seemed to be slightly less of a David-and-Goliath feel to the whole dynamic. The Palestinians had been invaded and displaced, they were fighting back (with the limited help of other Arab nations), and so a war was taking place in which one party hurt the other and vice versa. Also, targeting enemy combatants is quite different from terrorizing and killing civilians. As the leader of Black September, Salameh would have ostensibly been responsible for the deaths of civilians.

And yet, Ames might have looked at this man and thought, *Well, we don't shirk at dealing with governments that have massacred millions of innocents. Why should I refrain from associating with someone who may be responsible for a fraction of that?* Especially if that relationship could have helped bring about the end of a conflict that was already proving significant in both its destabilization of the Middle East and its devastating impact on American foreign policy. I wasn't in Bob Ames's head, so this is pure speculation—but I think it's as good an explanation as any.

In any case, Zein and Ames's efforts in this direction were largely stalled when Salameh was assassinated—until the Israeli invasion of Lebanon in 1982 and worldwide outrage generated by the Sabra and Shatila massacres. In that political environment, it seemed more likely that Ames, with Zein's help, might be able to convince his superiors in the agency and their bosses in the Reagan administration to consider establishing a friendlier dialogue with the Palestinians. So they continued to collaborate on a possible resolution to the conflict that would involve active negotiations with the PLO.

Then the embassy was bombed by the IJO, Ames was killed, and it looked like that dream was well and truly put to rest. I believe I understand Zein's role as middleman between the CIA and the Palestinians. But how did he come to play a part in the hostage negotiations?

"My plan was to exchange the American hostages with the seventeen in Kuwait," Zein tells me. "I was dealing with Imad Mughniyeh."

"Directly?" I ask.

"Directly!" He laughs. "I knew him when he was sixteen years old and working with the Palestinians. I knew him intimately because, you see, I'm Shia from the northeast, I was Shia in a Palestinian organization, and my name was at the top. I was the one who sent him at seventeen years old for special training in Algeria."

"Okay."

"Who recruited Imad?" Zein asks. "General Ali-Reza Asgari, who was the second in command of the Revolutionary Guard in Iran . . . Ali-Reza Asgari gave Imad the job to record the names and the addresses of foreign patriots, Western patriots in Beirut."

"Okay," I encourage him. This bolsters my theory regarding Asgari's role as point man with the IJO.

"See, all this information would hurt Israel because now you have the culprit, a general from the Revolutionary Guard, being guided by his master, the Mossad, so the liability was placed on Iran and the Mossad got a free pass."

I take this in for a moment, blinking.

"I knew from Imad when Imad was alive," Zein continues. "He told me the car that hit the embassy in Beirut was supposed to go to the marine barracks first. The last minute, it changed course and came to the embassy. The one who changed the course of that car was a Mossad agent . . . Asgari was a former SAVAK officer working for the shah and was trained twice by the Mossad in the early 1970s. He became a Mossad agent in 1980."

SAVAK was the shah's notoriously brutal secret service, sort of the Iranian KGB. The Mossad and the CIA helped the Pahlavi regime establish the organization in 1957. It became Iran's most hated and feared institution because of the gruesome torture methods it would use on opponents of the shah.

"I don't understand," I interrupt. "You think Imad Mughniyeh was working for Israel?" This seems odd, considering the Mossad and CIA were widely blamed for Mughniyeh's assassination in 2008. I can't say I shed tears when he died—whatever faction in Iran pulled his strings, there's no doubt the Boogeyman engineered my father's kidnapping with enthusiasm.

"Without [his] knowing," Zein corrects me. "He was working for the Revolutionary Guard. There was this separatist group—"

"So the orders were coming from this unit, he thought it was Iran, but in actuality it was the Mossad? Is that what you're saying?"

"Through Ali-Reza Asgari. And where were they meeting? In the Iranian embassy in Damascus to separate themselves from Hezbollah in Beirut . . . Imad was not a member of Hezbollah at the time, and the group that was doing jihad work was not a part of Hezbollah. They had a special unit that they were within . . . it was a purely Iranian Revolutionary Guard operation through Ali-Reza Asgari, who was working with the Mossad, and I've got the proof, because who marketed Iran-Contra to the United States? The Mossad."

Well, documented history proves he's right about that last part. In many ways, Zein's allegations would explain so much—but no, every journalist I know would roll their eyes at this. Yet I find myself continuing to nod along with Zein as he speaks. Have I completely lost it? At this point, I'm exhausted and I need to do some thinking, so I end the interview. Just after I turn off my recorder, Zein looks at me.

"How did you get your name?" he asks suddenly.

I get this question a lot. Normally I just laugh and say my

mother made it up, because the real story is so strange. But for some reason, I decide to tell Zein the truth.

"My mother says she saw it in a dream," I say.

"Does she remember the dream?" Zein asks. "Did she tell you what it was?"

"Yes, she did," I answer. "It was a couple of months before they took my father. My mother had just found out she was pregnant with me and they were going to call me Daniel if I was a boy or Danielle if I was a girl. One night my mother dreamed she was walking in a desert. She came to a large, black stone building. She says it looked like a church but it wasn't a church. She went to the back of the building and there was a graveyard, and the first tombstone she saw had the word 'Sulome' carved on it in big letters and the word 'Anderson' in small letters. She put her hand on the stone and says she felt this woman was significant to American culture and politics. Then she looked to see when this woman was born and when she died, but the dream went all blurry before she could read it. My father was waking her up to go to his tennis game. The first thing she said to him when she opened her eyes was 'We're having a daughter and her name is going to be Sulome.'"

Zein nods thoughtfully. "Some people are like the hub of a wheel," he tells me. "Things happen around them. They have a very strong purpose in this material life. You must be one of these people."

Well, I don't know about all that. What I do know is that in June of 1985, my birth was reported by most major news agencies in the hope that Dad would hear he had a new daughter, and that's how my father learned of my existence. Recently, I found a letter he wrote Mama from captivity.

"Madeleine, my love, my heart, I saw our daughter on TV the other night and I cried for joy," my father wrote thirty years ago from his prison. "I only saw her for two or three seconds, enough to notice your black hair and beautiful, bright eyes. But I can't describe how it felt to end months of not knowing. Our guards had seen the piece in the early news and brought in the TV for the late-night cast—all in Arabic, but at least I saw my family and the pictures. Is it Danielle? Or Sulome? No matter, I only wish you had been in the film."

I saw that letter and cried because my father loved me before he knew my name.

———

I actually end up reading the self-authored pamphlet Mustafa Zein gave me, *A Summary of Science and Faith*. I can't decide whether it's a revolutionary interpretation of Islam or just plain crazy. Something about its message moves me, though. I remember what Zein told me during our interview that summarized my beliefs more articulately than I could.

"Religiosity is the greatest crime man has committed against God," he said.

In that respect, I think he seems saner than most.

Philosophy aside, I'm curious about his claims that Ali-Reza Asgari was a Mossad asset, so I start researching again.

After reading *The Good Spy*, I know that Asgari is indeed believed to be the architect of all the Islamic Jihad's terrorism. From the limited information I can find online about his time in Lebanon, he appears to have been working for Mehdi Hashemi, who my reporting leads me to believe may have been operating separately from the IRGC members training Hezbollah.

What makes Asgari interesting is that in 2007, he disappeared while in Turkey. Because he was a brigadier general of the Iranian Revolutionary Guard and former deputy defense minister, his disappearance did not go unnoticed. At first, the Iranians were saying he had been kidnapped by a Western intelligence agency—high irony, if that were the case—but as news reports unfolded, most observers seemed to believe he had defected to either Israel or the United States. Zein told me Asgari had originally defected to the United States but ended up in Israel.

"The Mossad sold Asgari to the Bush White House as another person than the one who had commanded the Iranian guards in Lebanon," he writes in an e-mail. "It is I who went to Damascus to bring evidence that Asgari was and is the degenerate who commanded the Iranian Guards in Lebanon from 1982–1992 and now no one in Washington wants to hear his toxic name . . . he lives in Israel now."

Zein's testimony aside, it was clear from the moment Asgari disappeared that he was probably a mole. A 2007 article in the *Sunday Times* quoted multiple sources as saying Asgari was a high-level mole and his defection had been orchestrated by the Mossad. The *Washington Post* reported that he was in the United States providing the CIA with a treasure trove of valuable intelligence on Iran and Hezbollah, and reports surfaced for months about Israeli and U.S. actions supposedly triggered by information he provided. The Iranians insisted that Asgari had been kidnapped by the CIA and Mossad. An alternate narrative appeared that included Asgari's death in an Israeli prison, but Western media coverage seemed to take it for granted that he had been a mole.

I find a 2012 report from the Library of Congress called *Iran's Ministry of Intelligence and Security: A Profile* and read this passage: "Asgari's defection was significant because he was deeply engaged in establishing Iranian links to Hezbollah. Asgari seems to have provided intelligence to the Israelis and may have been the source of the intelligence they used in Operation Orchard to strike Syria's nuclear reactor."

With this in mind, Mustafa Zein's claim that Asgari was supplying information to the Mossad during the eighties is sounding a little more plausible. If he later became an Israeli mole, would it be such a stretch to consider that he may have been cooperating with the Israelis earlier on? The scenario wouldn't be completely out of place in the vicious, backbiting atmosphere of covert ops in Lebanon during the war. I feel the idea twisting its roots into my mind, trying to take hold of my perspective. But I must battle the urge to swallow this entirely. Even if there is some truth to Zein's claims, there are infinite ways this scenario could have played out and no way to prove any of them now. So while I resolve to follow up about this during interviews, I know I need to double my focus on finding out more about the men who kidnapped my father.

THEN
March 2012

After I got back to New York and spent a couple of days cringing in my bed, detoxing from Ritalin, my mother and I researched possible treatment centers where I might be able to get my head together. We landed upon a dual-diagnosis inpatient facility in Connecticut that treated both substance abuse and mental illness. It cost a small fortune and boasted a number of celebrity alumni.

I was there for two months. No need to go into detail about that time, except to say that the facility was more a drug rehab than a psychiatric hospital—they were well equipped to deal with addicts; less so crazy people. Their curriculum was based heavily on the twelve-step model, so by the time I got out, I had two months clean, one shiny Narcotics Anonymous chip, and a list of meetings in the city. I also started at a dialectical behavioral therapy outpatient center, which again, cost an absurd amount of money. That wasn't counting my $300-an-hour psychiatrist. The expense made me painfully aware of how lucky I was to be able to afford that kind of care. I knew so many others didn't have the same privilege, and I found that incredibly unfair.

So I hit the ground running. I went to a meeting a day, stood up, announced countless times to everyone that I was an addict, and watched my clean time mount with some satisfaction. But after a month or so, that shiny sober feeling began to melt away, only to be replaced by something darker, a familiar swirling sadness I had thought I'd put behind me. I watched my friends in the program get their shit together, start jobs, and feel better. But I would sit in a room full of people who were supposed to be like me and feel completely alone.

When I shared in meetings, I'd cry to my fellow addicts about how I heard a voice in my head most of the time telling me I was worthless and disgusting; but the voice wasn't anyone else's. It was mine, so I simultaneously believed it utterly and knew it was whispering lies to me. Desperately seeking understanding, I'd tell the room that I was in constant, bone-breaking battle with myself, and without drugs to numb the pain, I'd often end up on my couch or in my bed, hugging my knees to my chest and sobbing from the depths of my soul. I'd say I thought about killing myself all the time, just to make the pain go away. But apart from one or two people who nodded, I was generally met with blank stares. I began hearing the word *crazy* muttered behind my back.

The therapy was going significantly better. DBT was developed by a psychologist who knew what it was like to feel empty and alone. She compiled a thick volume of life skills that seem pretty commonsensical on the surface, but like many borderline patients, I was accustomed to unhealthy coping mechanisms and it gave me some tools to work with when I was feeling terrible. My therapist was a kind, encouraging man who was usually available outside of sessions to listen to me when I felt like I was falling apart. The meds were helping a little, but I was still struggling with impulsivity, and trying to find solace in men who weren't particularly nice to me.

I was also bored stiff. I had a degree from Columbia and some experience working at the *Daily Star,* but when I would apply for journalism jobs in New York, they couldn't give less of a shit about a little paper in Lebanon, so I was told I didn't have enough experience. Besides, since the advent of the Internet, journalism was and is still becoming a ruthless, thankless profession. I knew competition was fierce, and I needed a leg up at a well-known U.S. publication.

So I gritted my teeth and applied for internships, knowing I was overqualified for them. In the summer of 2012, I managed to land an unpaid position at a major magazine in D.C. Ignoring the advice of everyone in NA who said moving in my first year of sobriety was a recipe for disaster, I picked up and left for Washington.

Let's just say the six months I spent in D.C. were not the best of my life. The magazine internship was brutal. Aside from the icily professional female editor in chief, it was an almost exclusively male newsroom, and from what I understood, the crop of interns before me had been mostly quiet girls, fresh from college. I was loud, pushy, still somewhat unbalanced, and I knew the long hours of free bitchwork the magazine was getting from me were more than they deserved. The newsroom was quiet as a graveyard—not a sound but the clitter-clatter of keyboards. Every now and then, someone would make a snarky comment, people would snicker, and then it would go back to silence.

I made a few friends, and my fellow interns helped keep me sane, but I'd cry in the ladies' room at least once a week after being snubbed by another staff member. My condition often made me behave inappropriately or laugh too loudly at odd things. I went back to New York almost every weekend, desperate for the refreshing, in-your-face rudeness of my city. At least there, people have the decency to tell you to fuck off to your face.

And there was the fact that I had fallen off the wagon. Shortly after I celebrated six months clean, I started drinking and smoking pot again. It seemed fine at first, but as I grew more and more miserable, I started to drink too much, and ended more than one night with my face in the toilet. But something really wonderful happened toward the end of my time in D.C. About a month before I left, the doctor I had been seeing put me on a new mood stabilizer, and with the new med in conjunction with the one I was already on, I started feeling the anxious self-loathing lift. I stopped drinking as much, thought before I spoke or acted, and learned how to turn down men I wasn't actually interested in. I felt calmer, more balanced, better than I ever had before, actually. I started looking forward to the next chapter in my life with a little more hope.

It was with great relief that I finished my internship and started trying to figure out my next step. I applied for jobs again, with no success. But a year of following car bombs in Beirut and rocket attacks into Israel on Twitter had frustrated me beyond belief. I had been convinced there was going to be a war at least three times while I was interning, and my mother had to talk me out of buying a one-way plane ticket to Beirut.

So I finally succumbed to the conflict bug I'd been infected with since birth. In many ways, it felt quietly inevitable. I desperately missed the life-or-death stakes in Lebanon, the rush of adrenaline, and most of all, the feeling that I was doing something that mattered. So I talked my panicked mother down, bought the plane ticket, and landed in Beirut just as the Mediterranean winter was starting to wrap its damp tendrils around the city.

———

Not long after I arrived, I realized I hadn't ever bothered to make friends with other journalists in Beirut. I mostly socialized with my cousins and their friends when I was living there, too mired in misery to really care much about schmoozing with anyone. I felt certain my erratic behavior had, as always, made me the target of much mean-spirited gossip among my coworkers and the few other reporters I had met.

But now I felt the need to be around people with similar concerns and interests. I felt mentally stable enough to handle the Beirut journo scene. So I e-mailed Josh Wood, a stringer with the *International Herald Tribune* whose work I had admired for some time. I felt self-conscious approaching someone I had never met to hang out, nervous I would come off like some opportunist or sycophantic amateur. But he seemed nice enough, and we made an appointment to meet at a local bar.

It was a bit awkward at first, but after a couple of drinks, we were both laughing our asses off. His cynical humor appealed to me, and I think my brassy bravado amused him. There was nothing romantic about the interaction; he had a serious girlfriend back in the States and I was dating someone in New York. But when the bar looked like it was going to close, Josh invited me back to his place to hang out with his friend.

And that was the night I met Peter Kassig, a former army ranger who couldn't have been more different from the asshole who abused me for two years. Pete grew up in Indianapolis and served in Iraq during the "liberation" of the country from Saddam Hussein and his "weapons of mass destruction." It soon became clear to him that the invasion was nothing more than rich men exploiting the tragedy of 9/11 to become wealthier; at the expense of many innocent lives. He was ashamed of what he watched his country do to the Middle East.

So Pete came to Beirut, armed only with his hopeful idealism and the need to heal instead of hurt. He had been a medic in the army and soon cofounded an NGO that provided medical aid to civilians in war-ravaged Syria, risking his life to help people the world had all but abandoned. It was the kind of sacrifice I could barely wrap my head around, and he talked about it without any air of martyrdom. But as I would come to learn, that was Pete.

He was a good-looking guy, with an infectious laugh and a sweet innocence that belied his ranger tattoos and tough talk. But he was five years younger than me and I was absorbed with the guy I was seeing back home. Pete was definitely flirting with me that night, but I just laughed it off and the three of us stayed up until dawn talking about everything under the sun.

We discussed my father at length. They were very curious about my family's experience, so I told them about the tinfoil game pieces and how Dad's kidnappers broke his glasses. I shared with Josh and Pete things about my fucked-up life I had never said to anyone else. I could tell they understood the consequences we all risk in this kind of work, and most of all, they were familiar with trauma.

We would end up talking about Dad many times throughout our friendship, but I'll never forget something Pete said that night.

"Jesus," he muttered in awe after I finished one of the stories about my father. "I don't know what I would do if that happened to me. I think I'd probably go out of my mind."

8. THE WARLORDS

Demoralize the enemy from within by surprise, terror, sabotage,
assassination. This is the war of the future.
—ADOLF HITLER

NOW

Sobhi al-Tufayli has seen better days.

Josh and I roll up to his bunker in Brital, a town in the Beqaa
Valley. Our fixer is driving, and as usual, I'm about to fall out of the
car and kiss the ground in relief that I survived the trip. He is highly
skilled behind the wheel, but in typical Lebanese style, he drives at
heart-stopping speed, and I've left nail marks on Josh's arm from
clutching him in panic.

The first thing we notice as we arrive is an octogenarian militiaman brandishing an ancient machine gun, accompanied by a couple of unarmed teenagers. Not exactly an intimidating entourage
of bodyguards, but luckily for Tufayli, we aren't there to harm him.
We both want to interview the former secretary-general of Hezbollah, Josh for a story and I for my investigation. One of the teenagers ushers us into the receiving room while the elderly militiaman
glares at us threateningly.

"Not sure if that gun will even fire," Josh murmurs to me when we sit down. "It looks like it should be in a museum." I stifle a giggle as we're served bitter black coffee in small china cups.

Finally, Tufayli makes his entrance and we greet him politely. I'm wearing a hijab out of respect for his position as sheikh, to Josh's endless amusement. We're all seriousness now, though, as Tufayli holds court.

Tufayli's relationship with Hezbollah is complicated. He was replaced as secretary-general by Abbas al-Musawi in 1991, but the reasons for his ouster remain unclear. Some say he opposed the establishment of Hezbollah as a political entity in the Lebanese government because it "moderated" the organization and opened it up to the corruption of the state. Since he left, he's become an outspoken critic of Hezbollah and Iran, and generally seizes most opportunities to make his opinions clear, which is how we managed to secure an interview with him.

I don't know whether Tufayli's grievances are legitimate or he's just bitter about his ouster, but I'm curious to see how the sheikh responds to the allegations that he was involved in terrorism. As always, I don't bring up my father right away. Instead I listen as Josh asks Tufayli about the situation in Syria and Hezbollah's role in the conflict next door.

Tufayli is quite dismissive and rude to Josh, so I'm nervous when it seems like it's my turn to ask questions.

"Sheikh, this might take longer because Miss Anderson is writing a book," our fixer tells him in Arabic.

"What book?" Tufayli asks.

"What should I say the book is about?" the fixer asks me in English.

"Just tell him it's about Lebanon during the war."

"She should send us a copy as a gift," the sheikh pronounces, which I promise to do without meaning a word of it.

"I know Hezbollah started as a resistance movement," I begin. I want to warm up to my important questions. "The Israelis invaded Lebanon five times, but are you saying the resistance aspect isn't legitimate anymore? What should Hezbollah do now? Should they disarm and become purely political? What's the best course of action for them?"

"What's best for Hezbollah, for the Lebanese people and the region always, is the right path," Tufayli tells me through our fixer. "What I mean by the right path is the path of justice, the path of the will of the people . . . The regime in Lebanon is corrupt, and Lebanese officials are corrupt to the highest degree. The body of the regime is in decay. Hezbollah did not contribute to this in the past. If Hezbollah came and said, 'We would like to build a state free of corruption, with clean officials, and would like for the rule of law to be respected in earnest, and not to interpret the law in a different way on a daily basis through personal whims' . . . if the instruments of the government are purged of their many impurities, I believe that the Lebanese people would have stood behind [Hezbollah], and no saboteur would be able to impose himself, no matter how much wealth or influence he has—especially those with known profiles. Moreover, no one whom Hezbollah has deemed corrupt will ever be able to get into power. This means that all officials need the consent, approval, and judicial records from Hezbollah for the people to accept them as public servants in the Lebanese government."

Not a succinct man. Also, I'm willing to bet that the Lebanese people wouldn't stand behind Hezbollah if the group tried to exert that much control over the government. Tufayli seems pretty radical, and I know around the time he was booted out, Hezbollah decided to take a different, more diplomatic political approach, so it makes sense that he would have clashed with the rest of the leadership. But wait . . . the sheikh isn't done yet.

"Unfortunately, Hezbollah went and split the country into two camps, with people taking sectarian sides; Sunni and Shia," he continues. "They recruited Shia under the banner of fearing the Sunni and vice versa . . . and that's how we came to struggle with ourselves; we eat each other when we fight against our neighbors and brothers and countrymen and relatives . . . the path of corruption always leads to destruction. This is not exclusive to us. The Americans; why are they hated in the world? It's because they're instruments of corruption everywhere they go. If they had really been champions of freedom, people would have nothing but fondness for them. Instead, they are hated because they are liars."

Tufayli has a way with words. But unless we want to be there all day listening to his pronouncements, I think I should move on to more pertinent questions.

"I'm going to go into the past a little bit," I tell the fixer. "Tell him I don't want to dredge anything up—but the terrorist attacks that were blamed on Hezbollah in the eighties, does he feel any responsibility for them? Does he think that this legacy is haunting the Shia?"

"The value of nations and their respect, their legacy, depends on the extent to which they adhere to their principles," Tufayli replies. "Their waning and destruction depends, on the other hand, on the extent of their lies and hypocrisy in applying their principles. I'm Sobhi Tufayli, an imam in a mosque. I'm not a general and have no ties to the military. But when an enemy inexcusably occupies my country, and when the major powers in the world assist and share in this occupation, I would become a traitor, lacking in honor and respect to myself and others, if I didn't resist this occupation.

"In reality, if we want to label anything as terrorist, it should be the unjustified political crime," he continues. "We here in Lebanon today have the right to defend ourselves. But there are those who

would come here from the ends of the earth, not to defend themselves but defend their interests . . . and what are their interests?
Their interest is to put their hand in my pocket to steal. And if I
object, I am a terrorist. The truth is that American and Western
policies are terrorist policies . . . *daesh* are the result of Western policies in the region. Madmen, deranged people, idiots . . . but this evil
is the result of a great injustice . . . our problem here is not with
the small-scale murderers. It is with the large-scale murderers, and
those who create them."

I'm actually shortening his quotes quite a bit.

Our fixer translates for me. "Blah blah blah, you get the point,"
he finishes with an eye roll that the sheikh can't see.

I lean forward and look Tufayli square in the eye, speaking to
him directly in Arabic.

"*Sheikhna* [our sheikh, an honorific], I speak some Arabic because my mother is Lebanese," I begin.

Tufayli smiles. "Where is your mother from?" he asks me.

"Originally from Smar Jbeil," I answer. It's the name of the village where my grandfather's family used to live. Then I go for it.

"What I want to ask is this: there were people caught up in the
war who had nothing to do with it, especially those who came from
America and Europe," I say. "One of these people was my father,
Terry Anderson. And I'm with you one hundred percent about the
wrongs committed politically by the Americans here, as well as
their wrongs in the past . . . but what's important is that my father
was innocent. He was working as a journalist."

Tufayli leans back. His eyes widen just a little at this information, but he's too much of a pro to show more of a reaction.

"Who is your father?" he asks.

"Terry Anderson, one of the hostages taken in Lebanon," I
reply.

"I'm against this filthy act perpetrated by known entities," the sheikh says. He's holding my gaze now, the first time he's really engaged with either Josh or me during the interview. "We in Hezbollah were against kidnapping, and we still are. This is not an honorable act and it harms us, our movement, our honor, and our values.

"After the Iran-Iraq War, the Iranians sent me a message telling me to take the hostages and do with them as I pleased," Tufayli continues. "I told them this is a stain and I refuse to soil Hezbollah with it. Of course this does not mean there weren't any Lebanese working with the Iranians. But this was done at a distance from our leadership."

"Ask him about the office in Iran that was running the Islamic Jihad," I tell our fixer. "Was it run by Mehdi Hashemi, separately from the mainstream Iranian government?"

Tufayli dodges the question. "I'm in solidarity with you and your father," he tells me. "And I believe he was unjustly treated, the way we all were, by this insane policy. Of course I am not saying this to defend or advocate any position. I say this out of fairness."

"Was the Islamic Jihad separate from Hezbollah?" I ask, persistent.

"There were security groups," Tufayli says. "So if I'm an Iranian official and I have one or more cells in Lebanon, I use them to kidnap and exchange hostages. Clear?"

"Yes, *sheikhna*," I tell him. This seems to fit with what I've heard about Asgari nurturing the IJO as his own private terror cell, unconnected to the Hezbollah leadership—which somewhat bolsters Zein's narrative. If Tufayli isn't lying—and he very well might be—then perhaps Hezbollah's claims of innocence have some merit.

I notice our fixer gesturing at me to wrap it up. I'm surprised

Tufayli has been this frank with me and I can sense him getting edgy. Time to go. "Thank you so much for your hospitality."

———

Penetrating even the very outer circle of Hezbollah by getting some of its followers and fighters to trust me has been no easy feat. This is a group that exists in a state of constant paranoia. Lebanon is a major hub for espionage in the region and Hezbollah is still considered by the United States to be a terrorist organization. In 2009, Hezbollah and the Lebanese authorities busted a large Israeli spy ring, reportedly by turning a Mossad operative into a Hezbollah double agent. The group took down a CIA ring in 2011—and those are just the incidents that were made public. All this means Hezbollah members are immediately suspicious of an American girl— even a half-Lebanese one speaking decent Arabic—who shows up in Dahiyeh asking questions about a thirty-year-old terrorist act the world considers them responsible for.

My fixer, who has asked that I not use his name because he fears Hezbollah leadership will take action against him, is a large part of the reason I was put in the same room with them. He's a Dahiyeh boy, through and through. The men from that neighborhood— almost exclusively Hezbollah fighters and party supporters—all know and trust him, so they are willing to speak with me out of respect for him. But once I'm in that room, it's my job to get them to trust me. Part of that is just establishing a rapport with them, as I would try to do with any other source, but I am uniquely positioned to reach Hezbollah in a way others cannot.

I find that revealing my father's identity almost always works out for me in these situations. For one, it's completely obvious that many people associated with Hezbollah feel a collective sense of shame for what happened to Dad, which was clear from my interactions with the Hajj and Hamza. They also seem to respect me for being Terry Anderson's daughter and still sitting in a room with them, unafraid, treating them like human beings. I think they can see that I just want to understand how this could have happened. As a result, they are generally more forthright with me after discovering who I am.

This gives me rare journalistic access to their world, which I do my best to respect by reporting on them with as little bias as possible. I'm not Hezbollah's PR rep, so not every story I write is going to make them happy, but I think it's clear that I'm not pursuing a vendetta—just doing my job. I believe a few of them have come to trust me, in a strange way. Not because I think they're just the cat's pajamas—they're religious fundamentalists, and I'm no fan of those, no matter which book they pray from—but I've come to reluctantly admire their sense of honor. Say what you like about Hezbollah; the men I meet who identify as such all share a sort of code. Are they saints? Would I even call most of them good? Not a chance. But they've become people in my mind, and something about their identity makes sense to me—the resistance part, I suppose.

Also, it must be said: there are a different set of political circumstances here in Lebanon, where most of the party leaders and politicians have blood on them up to their elbows. The country is run by former warlords, many of whom were known to commit the odd atrocity or two in wartime. Samir Geagea, current executive chairman of the Lebanese Forces, the largest Christian political party in the country, actually spent eleven years in solitary confinement for his war crimes—until he was pardoned in 2005. Geagea now lives in luxury, enjoying his political comeback.

Every powerful figure in Lebanon has a cemetery in the closet. Case in point: Walid Jumblatt, the Druze tribal chief and head of the Progressive Socialist Party (PSP), a leftist political organization, is having coffee with me at his gorgeous home in the Clémenceau neighborhood of Beirut. Jumblatt is something of an enigma. His heavily armed Druze militia, which was responsible for its share of violence during the civil war, earns him the title of warlord. He's been dubbed "the Weathervane" because of his political tendency to abruptly shift sides and ally himself with opposing factions. His reputation as a calculating, highly intelligent man is widespread, and even the Lebanese who hate him seem to display a grudging respect for his intellect.

As a major player in the war, Jumblatt concerned himself with the kidnappings, mostly because he assumed personal responsibility for Terry Waite's safety on the negotiator's fateful trip to Lebanon. When Waite was captured, Jumblatt reportedly tried everything to find and free him, so I decide to see if the tribal chief would tell me something about what went on behind the scenes. Jumblatt is considered royalty by the Druze, and servants hover in the background as we speak, kowtowing to him like a king when they refill the coffee.

"This is quite a complicated issue," Jumblatt tells me. "As for the Islamic Jihad, it was a small organization. We heard about it after the 1983 attempt on the marines and the French, but we didn't know who was behind it . . . I believe it was the Iranians and the Syrians under Hafez al-Assad."

Jumblatt has a strange relationship with the Syrian regime. Once close to the Assads despite the fact that the Syrians likely killed his father, Kamal Jumblatt, in 1977, he's changed his tune since the start of the Syrian civil war. The PSP is increasingly vocal in its condemnation of Bashar al-Assad's war crimes.

It doesn't seem that Jumblatt will tell me much about the hostage crisis. For whatever reason, it's clear he doesn't want to go there. But we start talking about the current situation in Lebanon, and I have more luck with that line of questioning.

"The *daesh* kidnappings are really for shock value in a lot of ways, right?" I ask Jumblatt. "Especially the Westerners. ISIS doesn't kidnap to bargain; they kidnap to make a statement."

"Yes, they don't kidnap to negotiate," Jumblatt agrees. "They kidnap, then later on, they kill. Now they have killed Americans, British, French, but also *daesh* and Jabhat al-Nusra [another Islamist group] are fighting. It's a mess in Syria. A total mess."

"This is a frightening state of affairs," I remark. "For Westerners in Lebanon especially. Do you think that hostage-taking could become a problem in Lebanon again?"

"With the decay in the situation nowadays, it might be again, yes," Jumblatt says darkly. "We are living in total uncertainty."

As I'm about to end the interview, he asks me why I'm writing this book.

"I'll be honest with you," I say, surprising myself by confiding in this highly intimidating man. "What happened to my father completely destroyed me for a long time. He came home really messed up. Until I was seven, I thought he was going to be a superhero, and it wasn't like that at all. So on this very personal level, I want to know what happened, and it's not about the book or about anything else, not really. I just want to know."

Jumblatt looks at me with his sharp gray eyes. "Maybe your father being kidnapped was even more difficult than my father being killed," he tells me. "I shook hands with the man who killed my father, who was responsible for his death, and I didn't feel any need for revenge. Sometimes you just have to move on."

I now have a warlord for a life coach. It's quite a funny moment, but as I'm trying not to giggle, I suddenly realize something I had been unaware of. I'm being carried by a winding, inexorable current, and I can see all that raw, raging pain from a growing distance as I float past. I imagine watching it slowly recede behind me until it's very small and far away.

THEN
May 2013

I could feel the ring of prisoners closing around me, their eyes burning holes into my tensed back. It was time to get the fuck out of Roumieh.

I had come to the most dangerous prison in Lebanon for a story, but also because I had access. In the spring of 2013, very few journalists were allowed in. This was partly because the press had not been kind to the place, which was an overcrowded den of broken lives and human rights abuses, but mostly the Lebanese government's aversion to exposure was due to a rapidly deteriorating security situation inside the jail.

Two years after the Syrian civil war started scratching at Lebanon's door, rebels fighting Syrian president Bashar al-Assad were already well into the process of Islamization that would eventually culminate in the dramatic seizure of power by the Islamic State a couple of years later. At this point, IS, then known as ISIS (the Islamic State of Iraq and Syria) had just begun consolidating and controlling certain areas within the ravaged country, and they were still just a whispered name to me, another boogeyman in the dark.

One thing was certain: Roumieh showed signs of being completely overwhelmed by the jihadi brand of crazy that was bleeding into Lebanon from Syria. The Islamist prisoners segregated in the infamous Block B had formed a kind of mafia, and their power was growing. Rumor had it many of these inmates enjoyed *khaleeji* (Gulf) patronage as well as support from certain local politicians, and just like outside the prison walls, money and influence bought quite a lot of clout in there. It was said the Islamists basically had the run of the place. South Asian and African migrant workers, who made up the lowest rung on the prison ladder, would work as their maids, and as one ex-resident of Block B would tell me, "People gave us things—microwaves, MP3 players, fridges, things like that." He declined to share whom he meant by "people."

The immediate result of the jihadis' monopoly on power was a surge in violent incidents within the prison. Riots became an almost weekly occurrence, and prison guards were routinely held hostage until the Islamists' demands were met or a truce negotiated. Many of them, I learned, were foreign militants caught crossing the border from Syria or men accused of carrying out terrorist activities in Lebanon. In short, they were exceptionally dangerous people—a kind of precursor to the *daesh* incursion into the country that would eventually result in murmurs about the infamous black IS flag in Tripoli and battles between the hated group and the Lebanese army along the Syrian border, which continue to this day.

I had managed to gain access through a rather pervy priest who ran an NGO staffed almost exclusively by attractive young women. He never outright made a pass at me, but he certainly slimed his hand onto my leg a few times, and while I immediately shifted away from his touch, I tolerated his greasy stare because I knew he was my best shot at getting into Roumieh to write about the Islamist takeover.

The prison was as depressing as one would expect. Stained clothes hung from every barred window, and the whole place smelled like unwashed armpits and feces. When we arrived, the sun had just crept up over the horizon, and the courtyard was empty.

The prisoners were allowed to mingle in public areas of the jail for most of the day, but it was too early for many of them to make an appearance. True to Lebanese form, Roumieh was divided along sectarian lines, and the priest and I first met with inmates in the Christian wing. They had been expecting us, and were polite and relatively respectful, probably because the priest was highly regarded among that population as a result of the charitable work his organization did inside the jail.

When one of them asked if he could show me around, I didn't want to reveal my trepidation, so I glanced meaningfully at the priest to see if I should go or not. He gestured for me to follow the inmate, who was heartbreakingly eager to show me the art room, where he proudly displayed some of his woodcarvings. After I had oohed and aahed enough to prompt a wide yellow grin from him, he told me I should see the kitchen, which had been rebuilt after some inmates had burned it down a couple of years previously to protest the terrible prison food.

The kitchen was located on the other side of the courtyard, which we crossed as I took in the situation with mounting panic. A couple of hours had passed by now, so it was about midday and the prisoners from other blocks were all too awake, and all too interested in a female wandering around unguarded. I was in the midst of a throng of rapists and murderers who hadn't seen a woman in God knows how long.

I will not *be gang-raped in a Lebanese jail,* I thought fiercely as I felt them pressing closer. No one, certainly not the guards, would have been able to pull them off me.

So I closed my eyes for a minute, took a deep breath of ripe prison air, and focused on projecting the fuck-off-or-I-will-shank-you-in-the-dick attitude I generally adopt in situations where being a woman means risking one of the worst potential consequences of this job. I pictured the hell I would experience if one of them decided to lunge at me, and tried not to scream.

I pulled it together, followed the rather sweet convicted murderer to the kitchen, peered in and said hello to the surprised, sweaty Bangladeshis and Ethiopians slaving away in there, and then practically ran back to the Christian wing with a mob of leering criminals in my wake.

"*Yalla, abouna,*" I hissed at the priest through my brightest smile. "Time to go."

As soon as the prison doors clanged shut behind me, I felt my knees turn into liquid, and I had to fight the urge to collapse in a shaking heap on the ground.

To my mother's distress, by the time I went on my jaunt to Roumieh, I was beginning to feel comfortable freelancing in the Middle East. I worked in Cairo on an episode of a TV show and reported a handful of stories in Lebanon for *The Atlantic, Foreign Policy,* and *Vice.*

For one piece, I went to Tripoli, already quite a dangerous part of Lebanon. It was at the time plagued by frequent violence between the Alawite population in Jabal Mohsen and Sunni residents in the adjacent neighborhood of Bab al-Tabbaneh. There, I spoke to a nine-year-old child soldier who proudly showed off his machine gun. Soon after, I drove up to Arsal, a northern town on the Syrian border now completely off-limits to Western journalists because it's been heavily infiltrated by IS militants. The assholes have settled right in, even instituting sharia law in the areas they control. Hezbollah and the LAF are still fighting to regain control of the area around Arsal, but at this moment, *daesh* seems to be firmly entrenched.

When I visited, though, the town was heavily populated by the thousands of desperately impoverished Syrian refugees fleeing the devastation of the war. Mostly children, the elderly, and women bereft of their men, who were probably dead or still fighting in Syria, they settled in horrifyingly bleak camps in and around Arsal. Rebel forces hadn't been completely hijacked by jihadis yet, and there was still much support inside Lebanon for the Free Syrian Army's revolution against Assad.

The refugees didn't benefit from any of this revolutionary zeal, though. Instead they were treated as an unwanted burden and plagued by the xenophobia and racism of their Lebanese hosts. Some of the women informed me that the men of Arsal had been kidnapping young Syrian girls, raping them, and throwing them—their marriage prospects ruined—near the camps for their parents to find. As a result, mothers were marrying their teenage and sometimes prepubescent daughters off to much older Lebanese men, both to preserve their honor and because each girl was simply one less mouth to worry about feeding. I spoke to a thirteen-year-old with ice-blue eyes who sobbed hysterically as she told me about the forty-year-old groom she was about to wed.

"I'm disgusted by him, but I'm doing this for my family, so we can live in security," she told me in the weary voice of a grown woman. "He's the one who feeds us and protects us, and I'd rather be violated by one man than every man in town."

I cried for hours after that interview, though I didn't shed a tear while I spoke to her. I resolved that day never to cry in front of a trauma victim. *Who the fuck am I to cry?* I thought. It's not my suffering. I have no right to weep in their faces when I go home to my family's beautiful home with running water and soft beds, to the millions of dollars sitting in my trust fund.

And my trips back to the States were a complete mind-fuck. I'd sit in a bar or club watching the sleek New Yorkers sip their twenty-dollar cocktails in horror.

This isn't real life, I'd say to myself. *This is Disneyland.*

I went back as often as I could to see my doctors, but a month was about the longest I could stand without going out of my mind with boredom. At this point, I was going long stretches without speaking to my father, who had filed for bankruptcy, moved out of his mansion in Ohio, and was teaching journalism at Syracuse University. He seemed greatly humbled by his losses and would often reach out to me, but I was still quite angry with him and tried to forget about it as I buried myself in my work.

In the summer of 2013, I watched with interest as the Gezi Park protests erupted in Turkey, taking social media by storm. The idea of a bunch of middle-class kids spontaneously deciding to stand up against Turkish president Recep Tayyip Erdoğan's autocratic government intrigued me, especially because the protesters faced brutal retaliation by the police. Also, I was casually dating a Turkish guy at the time. He was completely enthralled by the protests and more than willing to set me up with some of his friends in Istanbul, so I lined up stories, packed my bags, and went to join the fun.

It was an intoxicating experience, and practically every foreign journalist was there covering it. I choked on tear gas and dodged water cannons almost every day and night for two weeks, sometimes barely sleeping for a few days at a time. I felt myself stray closer to the line between "soft conflict" reporting—what I call everything short of outright war journalism—and watching people get grievously hurt. I knew at this point that however grave and terrible these things were, I was also beginning to crave the adrenaline rush. Most of my friends had already worked in Syria, and when I got back to Beirut, I found myself seriously considering taking the leap into actual war journalism.

One of my friends, a much wiser and more experienced journalist named Mitch Prothero, had somewhat taken me under his
wing not long after I'd first arrived in Lebanon all dewy-eyed and
enthusiastic (but mostly clueless). He accompanied me to Tripoli
for the first time and gave me lectures that have proven invaluable
to this day.

Mitch also introduced me to the single most important person in my journalism career: my favorite fixer, Dergham Dergham,
a semigangster who's on friendly terms with practically every
shady character in Lebanon. D, as I've always called him, has had
a long list of questionable career choices, but he's honest, and
when he likes you, he'll go to the ends of the earth to help you get
a story. We hit it off right away, and I've been to many lunches at
his house with his lovely wife and little terrorist of a son. I freely
admit he opened many doors for me, and continues to do so to
this day.

With D's help, I wrote lots of stories, including my first piece
involving my personal experience as Terry Anderson's daughter, as
part of a story on kidnapping in Lebanon for *The Atlantic*. I spoke
to drug lords and kidnappers, former hostages, experts, and others in an attempt to explore the possibility of a resurgence in kidnappings within the country, as incidents of hostage-taking were
already beginning to take place with increasing frequency. I tried
to weave my own story in with the larger issue as best I could. The
most difficult interview for me was with an ancient, bentbacked
woman whose son had been kidnapped and taken to Syria during
the civil war, never to be seen again.

"I know he's dead," she croaked at me, tears streaming down
her wrinkled face. "I just want to bring his bones back to Lebanon."

In that moment, I thought about how lucky I was to get my
father back, to have him in my life at all, despite all the pain of our

complicated relationship. My pledge not to cry in front of a victim forgotten, I held the old woman's hand and wept with her.

—————

There was one problem. Caught up in the Beirut journo party scene—which is thriving, since nothing takes the edge off PTSD like a good bender—I had started drinking too much, smoking pot, and occasionally dabbling in cocaine again. This had an extremely adverse effect on my mood, and a couple of breakups that year left me devastated and bordering on suicidal. I knew I had to figure out why this kept happening to me, and how I could curb my urge to latch on to unsuitable men, then fall apart when they left me. After a hysterical night spent in my bathroom with a knife to my wrist, I decided it was time to address my lingering issues once and for all. I scoured the Internet for the best treatment facilities designed for borderline patients and landed upon one near Boston.

I told my friends in Beirut I would be gone for a while, although I didn't tell all of them why. I did confide in Josh and Pete, though. By coincidence, Pete was about to move to Gaziantep, Turkey, where he would be working full-time with his NGO in Syria. I threw us a joint good-bye party at my house before we both left, and the night before, Pete and I drove around buying booze and snacks.

At one point, we started talking about our childhoods, and Pete gave a big sigh.

"My parents always loved me," he said sadly. "Very much. But it never felt like enough. It's always seemed like I'm desperately alone, and I keep waiting for someone to fill that void inside me."

I looked at him from the passenger seat with surprise. I had no idea he felt this way, under his ranger drawl and good humor. "I know exactly what you're saying," I replied.

The party was a lot of fun. I had never been quite accepted by the foreign journalist clique in Beirut, but I made some friends that night I probably wouldn't have otherwise. We spent most of the night drinking and talking politics, to the dismay of any nonjournalists who happened to be unfortunate enough to find themselves in the room with us.

"Poor things." Pete laughed at one point as someone beat a hasty retreat from a conversation about chemical weapons casualties. "They must think we're nuts."

I soon left Beirut for New York, where I was waiting to be admitted to the treatment center. A month later, in October of 2013, Pete messaged me on Facebook. I hadn't spoken to him since the party.

"Hey girl," he typed. It was kind of late, maybe 11 P.M. I was lying on my couch considering going to bed. "I miss you!"

"I miss you too, Mr. Pete," I replied. "Where are you?"

"I'm in Aleppo, we're being shelled."

"Shit, please be careful."

"Hey," he wrote. "You know I love you, right?"

"I love you too, Pete," I told my friend, a little surprised at this expression of emotion. "Stay safe for me, okay?"

A few days later, Josh happened to be visiting me in the city and was crashing on my couch. One night, before we were about to go out for drinks, he looked up at me from his computer with stunned eyes.

"They took him," Josh said to me unbelievingly. "ISIS has Pete."

9. THE HUMAN INTELLIGENCE

History is a wheel, for the nature of man is fundamentally
unchanging. What has happened before will perforce happen again.
—GEORGE R. R. MARTIN

NOW

There are few heroes in the Holy Land.

The Middle East is known as the cradle of civilization, because
it includes Mesopotamia, widely considered to be the place where
six thousand years ago, a species of nomadic hunter-gatherers decided to stop wandering and root themselves to one area. Once that
occurred, they were free to harness their evolutionary gift of superior intelligence and build cities, farm, develop social systems, and
record their thoughts in writing.

Much of humanity seems to have nurtured a fascination with
the region since. The three major Abrahamic religions—Judaism,
Christianity, and Islam—all originated there. From the Crusades to
twentieth-century neocolonialism to our present-day preoccupation with its affairs, the Middle East has emerged as a focal point
for dramatic conflict. And given the human tendency toward black-
and-white thinking, it makes sense that we often succumb to the
fantasy that a particular side in the struggle is "right." We desper-

ately want to believe that a certain political actor is morally sound and engaging in the good fight against a villainous entity.

I believe this is a fallacy that should be immediately dispensed with. In my experience, with very few exceptions, any heroism that takes place in the region does so on an individual or small-scale level. People like my friend Pete show up there and engage in acts of incredible self-sacrifice. Certain locals give their land to refugees or start philanthropic NGOs with no agenda other than helping those less fortunate—things like that. There are certainly some lovely glints of humanity that polish the darkness. But I've come to understand that any sort of participation in Middle Eastern politics—or politics in general, actually, but especially so in the Middle East—involves a long process of sacrificing morals one by one. This is not to say that some sides aren't simply more cruel and brutal in their tactics than others, because that's quite clear. Bashar al-Assad, for example, or IS.

Contrary to what is overwhelmingly believed in the United States, I think the Israeli-Arab conflict is a solid illustration of this concept. So while I am careful about how far I'll pursue Zein's claim that the Israeli government turned Asgari, who was essentially at the center of the Islamic Jihad's terrorism spree, into a high-level intelligence source, I can't in good conscience abandon the theory altogether. It has just as much circumstantial evidence behind it as other, more widely accepted and established theories surrounding this event—and my experience with Middle Eastern politics has already informed me to ignore what I've heard about there being a "good guy" in this conflict. Plus, I must admit that I feel the pull of the idea strongly. I already dislike the way the Israeli government has behaved in the region. It would be so easy—and certainly tempting—to find that it played a destructive role in my own personal history. But I have to keep reminding myself that it's been thirty years since this happened and there's less than a snowball's chance in hell of my miraculously stumbling upon any incontrovertible proof.

So I take Zein's accusations to my sources. Let's be clear: lots of them don't consider it a possibility. Wright, Goksel, Crocker, even Baer—I bring Zein's allegations to almost all the sources I already interviewed, and most of them say it's crazy talk. I have to give that all the weight it deserves, and I often question whether this was just one of those weird red herrings that pops up in many investigations and I should just keep moving forward. Then I feel the idea pull me back into its grip, and I find myself nursing an obsessive pre-occupation with this version of events, which spurs my reporter's instinct to drop it altogether for fear of sacrificing my perspective to bias. I argue with myself about it constantly and often end these internal dialogues drained, half-convinced I should run screaming from this whole mess.

Somewhat to my surprise, though, not everyone I speak with dismisses the idea so readily, and some of those willing to consider it a possibility are not the types to spout lunatic conspiracy theories. The first person to tell me it's not out of the realm of possibility is David Hirst, former Middle East correspondent for the *Guardian* and author of *Beware of Small States,* the book about Lebanon that captured my interest when I was just starting my career.

"Are you saying the Israelis were engineering some of the kidnappings through agents in Iran?" Hirst asks me when I describe the theory during our interview.

"I'm not saying that I necessarily believe this, but it's something I've been told," I respond.

"Well, it's not inconceivable," he says. "The fact that the Israelis were involved in Irangate, supplying weapons to the Iranians in the way that they did, with American connivance . . . it's not inconceivable, and . . . well, the Israelis are capable of extraordinary things. For example, the bombing of the *Liberty* . . . but something like this would be almost impossible to prove."

He's correct, of course, about it being impossible to prove, but Hirst does bring up two interesting points. The first, regarding the USS *Liberty*, is only relevant insofar as it offers some historical context. During the Six-Day War in 1967 between Israel and Arab nations supporting the Palestinians, an Israeli jet fighter and several of Israel's torpedo boats attacked the *Liberty* in the waters off the Sinai peninsula, killing thirty-four American servicemen and wounding almost two hundred. The Israelis apologized and said they had mistaken the American ship for an Egyptian one, and that's the explanation that's been widely upheld over the years. But many crew members who survived the attack and some educated observers disagreed, saying it had to have been deliberate. In any case, it demonstrates that the "special friendship" between Israel and the United States wasn't without turbulent episodes.

And if one closely examines the relationship between the United States and Israel at the time of my father's abduction, there are some interesting details that provide a bit of fragile contextual support for the idea that Israel wasn't behaving quite like the friendly ally it was supposed to be. While the multinational peacekeeping force that the United States led was seen by many Lebanese as supportive of Israel, it was originally formed with the intention of allowing the Palestinians to evacuate safely, and that was a responsibility it seems that Reagan took seriously. In that capacity, the United States often clashed with Israel, especially after the Sabra and Shatila massacres. When you think about it, the peacekeeping force's objective was to help Lebanon stabilize, and for an enemy nation all too eager to watch Lebanon destabilize, that would have been inconvenient.

For example, the marines stationed in Beirut frequently clashed with Israeli forces, and in March of 1983, the commandant of the marine battalion in Lebanon sent a letter to the secretary of defense charging that Israeli troops were deliberately threatening the lives of marine peacekeepers. My father told me a story, which is also documented in a *New York Times* article from February 1983, about how a marine captain actually climbed into an Israeli tank, drew his gun on an Israeli lieutenant colonel, and said the tanks would pass "over [his] dead body." Apparently, the Israelis were trying to horn in on an area controlled by the peacekeeping force and refused to back down when told it was off-limits to them. The incident resulted in the United States lodging complaints with none other than the Israeli chargé d'affaires, Benjamin Netanyahu, under whose command all this harassment and intimidation of American troops was taking place.

Right around now, I begin to ask myself some very important questions. I'm well aware of what I'm risking by even pursuing the idea that our supposedly closest ally had intelligence regarding terrorism against us, chose not to share it, and even possibly manipulated the circumstances so it would benefit from the violence. This line of reporting would be considered career suicide by 90 percent of established American journalists. That is by no means something I take lightly. I fought hard for this career—I have no wish to see it crumble before my eyes.

Also, I never forget that I have a diagnosed mental illness. In fact, though, borderline personality disorder is nothing like schizophrenia in that it doesn't involve hearing voices or having delusions. While paranoia is associated with BPD, the word is generally understood to describe social paranoia, or the fear that people are saying negative things about you behind your back. But I'm also aware the distinction between social paranoia and delusional paranoia will be lost on most people, given widespread ignorance regarding mental illness. So that leads me to consider my actions more carefully as I proceed.

Years of therapy have trained me in the art of self-awareness, so as the investigation progresses, I often ask myself if I'm letting go of my grip on reality and wonder whether I'm caught up in a paranoid fantasy that happens to exist along somewhat the same lines as my personal political opinions. After all, living with mental illness is a constant struggle, and I will never forget what it felt like to lose my reason, as I did when I had my psychotic break in Ain el-Hilweh. So I spend much time examining my own thought processes as they relate to my reporting on this topic.

The first thing I realize is that try as I might to be objective, this is my father we're talking about, so my attempts to distance myself from the information I gather can only go so far. I make a valiant effort to ignore this at first, insisting to myself that I'm a journalist and therefore must report with complete detachment. But the more I learn, the more I realize I'm lying to myself in regard to my objectivity. Apart from the fact that Dad, whom I've come to love very much despite the complexity of our relationship, was imprisoned and brutalized for years, his kidnapping robbed me of a childhood and poisoned much of my adulthood. I can pretend to myself that my experience as a reporter affords me the ability to examine his captivity with impartiality, but as I find myself vacillating between utter conviction that Zein's statements about Asgari and Israel are gospel truth and anxious self-doubt that my mental condition is causing me to consider a lunatic theory as though it were credible, I increasingly realize the pretense of complete objectivity is pointless. I am personally invested in this investigation. How could I possibly not be?

So I struggle with that for a while, until I finally determine that the best I can do is to try to let my skeptical journalistic perspective inform my reporting as much as possible while also acknowledging the impossibility of that process being complete. Yes, there is a chance that this is all in my head. I know I shouldn't allow myself to get pulled into the appealing trap of certainty, or when I feel it closing around my feet, I have to at least try to yank myself free before I convince myself that I can believe any of these theories to be absolutely true.

These events took place thirty years ago, I remind myself. *Almost nothing I learn will be able to quiet all my doubts.*

Around this time, I begin to experience some serious trouble with my electronics. My brand-new Apple laptop's Internet access becomes increasingly slow, then stops altogether. I call a tech company to look at it, and when they can't find a reason for why it's become so difficult for me to get online, they wipe my hard drive. Less than a day after the company returns the computer to me, the exact same thing occurs again.

Then very strange things start happening. Unfamiliar executable files appear on my computers and devices such as my digital recorder and hard drives. Saved files containing information about my investigation duplicate themselves. Some e-mails I send to sources don't arrive. Warnings about unknown devices on my network and other computers using my IP address pop up on my screen with increasing frequency, both in New York and Beirut.

The next three months are what I can only describe as a nightmare. One after another, six more computers cease to function properly. Two PCs stop powering on altogether. Two smartphones stop accessing the Internet for no apparent reason. I won't go through all the scenarios that run through my head or every security measure I try to take, because they barely make sense to me. As someone who is technologically challenged, to say the least, I have to do much research and beg many people and organizations for help. No one seems to be able to provide much assistance, and I'm quite certain a few of them think I'm just being hysterical. I spend a lot of money and many frustrated tears trying to figure out what's happening, and it isn't long before I'm convinced someone is gaslighting me.

I spend a significant amount of time obsessing over this, and yes: at this point, I somewhat succumb to paranoia. Around this time, the movie *Citizenfour* is released, and as I follow Edward Snowden's exposure of the NSA's surveillance program, it becomes abundantly clear that governments using technology to violate our privacy is a reality of the world we live in. So I'm occupied by that thought for a while until I realize there's no possible way for me to find out whether this is a legitimate effort to stall and intimidate me or just a series of unfortunate electronic malfunctions and an overactive imagination. As soon as I let go of my efforts to discover the reason for my online woes and continue my investigation, for whatever reason, my computer starts functioning normally again. Once in a while, a file will still duplicate or a warning pop up on my screen, but as I've resigned myself to the fact that there's nothing I can do about it, I continue to work without giving these incidents much more thought.

All this might further indicate to some that I'm losing it, and I'll be honest—there are moments during these few months of electronic purgatory in which I question that myself. In my defense, though, catching a glimpse of what goes on under the surface of our understanding and the governmental fuckery that indisputably takes place while we live in blissful ignorance—that is something one can't really un-see. I have a feeling even people with pristine mental health begin to question their sense of reality after encountering that world.

In any case, all this makes me seriously consider abandoning the Asgari line of reporting, as does my immediate impulse to buy into it wholeheartedly. But I can't let go of it until I've been convinced it has no credibility, so I contact someone who was involved, albeit unwittingly, in Iran-Contra and would be well informed about this case from all perspectives, including that of hostage: Dad's old cellmate, Terry Waite.

"I'm going to bring up this claim to you now, and I have difficulty believing it because it just sounds so outlandish, but there's been a claim made that one of the people in the Islamic Jihad was either directly or indirectly allied with the Mossad," I tell Waite. "It seems fantastic, but I just wanted to see what your reaction was to the likelihood of something like that."

"That is a theory one hears," Waite responds calmly, if somewhat carefully. "It's not the first time I've heard that the Mossad were actively involved in promoting that for their own interests' sake, through their intelligence agents. It's a theory that could possibly be true, but I have no evidence for it whatsoever."

"Absolutely, no, I completely understand," I respond. "It's so hard to know what's real."

"It doesn't mean to say that the theory is wrong," Waite interjects, a smile in his voice. "It means to say it's extraordinarily complicated, and I can't see that the CIA, for example, is going to reveal any documentation they have, certainly not within living memory."

It's becoming obvious that I need to talk to some Israelis about this investigation. I reach out to several people who were in the Israeli government or intelligence services at the time, but receive no response. Until I happen upon an article about Victor Ostrovsky while looking through a box of clippings about my father's kidnapping provided to me by the AP.

Ostrovsky wrote a book, *By Way of Deception,* just after he left the Mossad in 1990. The Israeli government tried to prevent it from being published in the United States—and they actually succeeded at first, although the ruling was overturned and the book was released as planned. In its lawsuit, Israel confirmed that Ostrovsky was a Mossad agent, and although much of the criticism leveled at his claims centers around the fact that he was not a high-level agent and couldn't have had access to all this information, Ostrovsky explains that the Mossad at the time was extremely close-knit, and says he heard his superiors discuss these things openly. He also claims to have had access to the Mossad computer database, where he accumulated knowledge of the operations he describes.

Of course, Ostrovsky's claims have been challenged, and I have to take that into account. Then again, when an ex-Mossad *katsa* (case officer) leaves the agency and starts writing highly uncomplimentary books about his former employers, I'd imagine people ideologically aligned with the Israeli government would challenge his credibility. False flags, morally reprehensible covert operations, and professional betrayals do happen in this environment. Spy agencies don't spend their time knitting sweaters.

Yet we continue to dismiss almost all suggestions of covert operations, especially those of Western or Western-allied nations, as conspiracy theories. In fact, it's usually only when a government openly acknowledges these events, leaks information about them, or holds formal investigations, as in Iran-Contra, that people seem to take the possibility seriously. But governments don't generally announce what their spy agencies are doing. That's why these operations are called covert. I'm not suggesting that every crackpot conjecture should be taken seriously; neither am I certain that Ostrovky's version of events is the correct one—but in this case, I find myself believing that it deserves as much time and consideration as other narratives.

One of the major claims Ostrovsky makes in the book is that the Mossad had specific intelligence regarding the car that blew up the marine barracks before the attack took place, but chose to share only very vague information with the United States. I approach Ostrovsky, he agrees to speak with me, and we chat on the phone.

"The thing about Israeli intelligence is that they had more knowledge and access on the ground, because the ground is [geographically] closer," Ostrovsky tells me. "We never shared intelligence. We made it look like we did, but if we ever gave information, it was very vague."

"If that's true, on a personal level, as the daughter of someone involved, it would feel very much like a betrayal to me, you know?" I say.

"And in a way, it is." Ostrovsky sighs. "I'm trying to be balanced in my answer, because you have to consider that your first priority is your own. But then that carries on to . . . well, it's just your own. Everybody else is just a tool to get more information. And allies shouldn't act like that.

"Don't forget, Lebanon was divided into so many groups, and every group had its own agenda," Ostrovsky continues. "We were just hiring everyone we could and recruiting them left, right, and center. We had people on the ground, we had a submarine in Beirut—a submarine was what we called an underground station. We were sitting in Jounieh, we were sitting in the Beqaa, we had the South Lebanon Army that was doing things for us. So we were very well saturated in the area. Very few things could happen without us knowing about it. And there was a huge Palestinian refugee presence, which was very easy to recruit because they had ties to their families in the West Bank or Gaza, and promises can be made. Refugees are the easiest to target, and most of the activity in that area started in the refugee camps or around them. Information was abundant . . . and a lot of the intelligence was coming from civilians we would tap into in various ways, which the Americans were prohibited from doing."

"That's true," I interject. "Several CIA people told me that they were constrained in that way." Burton, Baer, and others had lamented agency regulations regarding the development of civilian sources.

"Let me explain to you a little bit about the journey I've been on," I continue. "The whole idea of—well, it came up as Israeli involvement in the whole thing, which I found extreme. I mean, my first reaction was 'This sounds insane.' But then people who didn't seem nuts started telling me that it might be true but is probably a little more complicated than that—more like the Israelis didn't give the orders but knew what was happening, could have stopped it at any time, and used it to their own advantage instead. That seems more along the lines of what you say in your book."

"Well, here's maybe a comparison," Ostrovsky says. "Let's say you take a city or neighborhood in America that's run-down. The FBI doesn't really know much about it, and they can't. But the local police and the precinct in that area, they know everything that's going on, because they have to. So consider that Lebanon was our precinct. There wasn't terrorism in Syria, we were okay with Jordan, we had an okay situation in Egypt. Really, the only problem areas were the West Bank and Gaza Strip, and of course Lebanon. So we saturated the place . . . there was barely a movement in Lebanon that we didn't know about."

"What about the hostages?" I ask. "Do you think the Israelis had an idea of where they were, who had them, how to get to them, stuff like that?" That is, obviously, the most pressing point to me.

"Well, think about this from an Israeli perspective," Ostrovsky says. "Let's say we know a hostage is being held in this-and-this place. How many people actually know that? Not many. So if the place is attacked and he's released, our sources are burned. Do we let our sources go, or do we see if we can get something for us? Because the same sources that bring you information about where hostages are held are the same sources that give you information about a team of terrorists who are planning to attack one of our bases or something."

That's an explanation I hadn't considered for this type of double-dealing. In a war, every intelligence agency has to look out for their own first. The Israelis may have thought, *Why should we risk the lives of our soldiers by sacrificing these sources to free American hostages?*

"I get where you're coming from," I tell Ostrovsky, somewhat reluctantly. "But it seems like, from what I read in your book, that it went further than that. Instead of saying, 'We're not going to reveal our sources,' it went to 'Let's take advantage of this situation to gain whatever benefits we can.'"

"Well, that is true," Ostrovsky admits. "But consider this: you have to think historically, the way the Mossad thinks. In its infancy, it had people in Egypt who were captured and held in prison for many years. They were sent from Israel to bomb American installations in Cairo to make it look like there was an anti-American movement in Egypt and cause damage to that relationship."

The episode in Egypt that Ostrovsky is referring to is known as the Lavon affair, which took place in 1954. It's a documented false-flag operation in which a group of Egyptian Jews was recruited by the Israeli military to plant bombs inside American and British civilian targets, such as movie theaters and libraries. The attacks were meant to turn the Americans against Egypt and create an environment of instability that would prompt the British to retain their troops in the Suez Canal. Israeli historian Shabtai Teveth wrote in his book *Ben-Gurion's Spy* that the assignment was "to undermine

Western confidence in the existing Egyptian regime by generating public insecurity and actions to bring about arrests, demonstrations, and acts of revenge, while totally concealing the Israeli element. The team was accordingly urged to avoid detection, so that suspicion would fall on the Muslim Brotherhood, the Communists, 'unspecified malcontents,' or 'local nationalists.'"

The Lavon affair led to the arrest of several Mossad agents, both Egyptian and Israeli. Two members of the cell committed suicide and two were executed by the Egyptian government. The Israeli defense minister Pinhas Lavon tried his best to deflect responsibility for the operation but was eventually forced to resign. Israel continued to publicly deny any role in the incident until Israeli president Moshe Katzav awarded the surviving agents with certificates of appreciation in 2005.

"The picture I was trying to portray in the book was: 'anytime my enemy becomes more of your enemy is to my advantage,'" Ostrovsky says. "And the U.S. has a basic policy flaw—it's a flaw, in my opinion, because you can't keep to it—that they kept saying, 'We don't negotiate with terrorists.' So the reliance was completely on the information that Israel would provide."

Hearing this, and being aware of other similar, equally well-documented Israeli covert ops in recent decades, all I can say is "Wow."

"Imagine that all the hostages were released and everything would be nice and dandy," Ostrovsky explains. "American memory is very short. If you take a thorn out of their foot, it heals very shortly and they'll start walking back and forth again."

"But it sounds so crazy," I murmur.

Ostrovsky laughs. "The nice thing about craziness is that time dulls it and makes people understand that it's actually not so crazy, that crazy is the way things work . . . It's the balance of weakness.

Separate and rule. Once one group gets stronger, you help the other group, so they get stronger and the other gets weaker. Just keep everybody down so that no one group can suddenly get up and take over. Because then you have stability."

"Do you think Israeli intelligence went all the way up to the top, or were their sources just people on the ground?" I ask. I'm thinking of Asgari.

"In some areas, the intelligence was going almost to the top," Ostrovsky replies. "If the head of the organization was recruited, I wouldn't have been at a high enough level to know about it. That would have been kept between maybe three people: his handler, the prime minister, and the head of Mossad. That's not the mundane, everyday operation. But yes, we definitely had people who were hearing what the top guy was saying . . . The thing about human intelligence is that the higher you go, the more you understand the intent. The lower you are, the more you have to rely on what you see in the movement and try to analyze the intent."

Well, he's certainly talking like a spy. "Human intelligence." At this moment, as I think about the possibility that my father could have been saved and wasn't, humans seem pretty fucking stupid to me.

THEN
November 2014

I opened my eyes, rolled out of bed half-conscious, and grabbed my phone to check Twitter, as I usually do first thing in the morning. Being a journalist means you have to monitor the news pretty much every waking hour. It was Sunday, November 16, 2014. My boyfriend Jeremy was still sound asleep next to me.

I looked at my phone and immediately burst into tears. Jeremy sat up, alarmed.

"Baby, baby," he said sleepily. "What's wrong? Calm down."

"He's dead," I gasped between sobs. "They killed Pete."

It was a little over a year after ISIS stole my friend from the world. Until October 2014, everyone in his circle, who were mostly journalists, had observed a complete media blackout of his kidnapping; meaning that no reporter with a conscience would have touched the story. We were told that was the best way to make Pete less valuable to his captors, which made sense to me, given that my father was the most-publicized, longest-held U.S. hostage in history. But then ISIS released a video of British aid worker Alan Henning's beheading. After they had killed Henning, they pointed the camera at a slight young man clad in the orange jumpsuit the terrorists used as a cruel mockery of the Guantánamo Bay prison uniforms. They threatened to end Pete's life if the U.S.-led airstrikes against them didn't stop.

I couldn't watch the Henning video. Apart from not wanting to witness poor Alan Henning's life end so brutally, I couldn't see another person I loved thin, wasted, and powerless. Some news outlets published screenshots, though, and those were enough.

Suddenly everyone wanted to know all about Peter Kassig, the new ISIS hostage. A handful of his friends, including me, wrote about our relationship with him in hopes of sending a message to his captors. I published an essay, knowing it would get a lot of publicity because of who my father is. We all called Pete "Abdul-Rahman" in our writing, because we knew he had taken that name when he converted to Islam at some point during his captivity. We were clinging to any reason they might let him live.

The essay did as well as expected, and I got lots of interview requests, which I turned down. As well intentioned as we all were, Pete's family didn't want any of us going on TV and saying something that could upset their efforts to free him. But of course, the second his death was announced, every outlet I had rejected and many more wanted to talk to the daughter of Terry Anderson about her friend who had just been beheaded by ISIS. That's how I found out Pete was dead. I looked at my phone and saw all the e-mail notifications from journalists asking me for interviews. In that moment, I hated us all.

I knew I would only talk to the media about my friend once. Apart from the emotional exhaustion of giving multiple interviews about something like that, I wasn't about to ride Pete's death to publicity as I'd seen other "hostage friends" do. I went on *Anderson Cooper* so that people would know how wonderful Pete was and said no to all the other news organizations.

Josh and I traveled to Indianapolis a few days later for Pete's memorial service. I met his parents at his childhood home. The photographs of a young, grinning Pete all over the house pressed into me like thumbtacks.

As we were preparing dinner after his memorial service, Pete's mother, Paula, told me that while he was in captivity, my friend would make game pieces out of tinfoil and play chess with the other hostages, just like my father did—exactly the way I had described to Pete on the night we first met. Learning that detail broke something inside me. I held on to her and we both cried.

The next couple of months were not easy. Jeremy and I had discovered I was pregnant right before Pete died, which would have been great—unexpected, but great—were it not for the fact that the psych meds I was on pretty much guaranteed the baby would not be in good condition if I carried it to term. I had to have an abortion, and I couldn't get the little phantom image of the child we could have had out of my mind. When my friend died, I melted down a little for a while. No terribly self-destructive behaviors—just a lot of crying and trailing a mental finger across old scars, tracing the outlines of the places that used to hurt.

Obviously, I didn't watch the video of Pete's execution either, but the inevitable media analysis pointed out that he wasn't shown giving one of those scripted speeches before he died, as the other hostages were. Pete's supposed executioner, "Jihadi John," as the media dubbed him, made a comment about how Pete didn't have much to say, and they cut straight to his decapitated head. I read that the other hostages, like James Foley, Steven Sotloff, and Henning, were compliant before their deaths because the murderous bastards who killed them forced them to act out mock executions many times before they died. They had no reason to think the last time would be different from the others, so they didn't resist.

But the general consensus was that Pete had fought back, and he was likely shot in the head before they desecrated his body. I remembered something Josh had told me after Pete was taken; during one of their many conversations about what they would do if they were kidnapped, Pete said something prescient:

"If they take me, I'm going to fuck up their beheading video. I'll punch one of them in the face and yell, 'Obama, legalize it!'"

I knew Pete had lived up to his promise, minus the joke about weed, which I'm including to give a sense of who he was as a whole person, not just the one-dimensional posthumous portrayal you can read in the news. Pete was incredibly noble and self-sacrificing; none of that has been exaggerated in the slightest. He was also hilarious. I thought about him punching one of those disgusting human beings in the face and felt so proud of my friend I could barely hold the feeling inside my body.

———

My year up to that point had been strange, exciting, and painful all at once. The borderline treatment center was a valuable experience, but the best thing that came out of it was the referral they gave me as I was being discharged. I finally found a shrink I couldn't bullshit, and he showed me things about my mind I'd been completely unaware of.

One of the most useful concepts he taught me is called splitting, a common thought pattern among people with BPD. It occurs when one hasn't developed the psychological skills to bring together positive and negative ideas of oneself and other people. It's also known as black-and-white thinking, and it's characterized by conceiving of oneself and others as either good or bad (respectively), with no understanding of nuance. Once he explained it, I realized it was something I had struggled with since before I hit puberty.

For example, in my relationship with my mother, I either thought of myself as worthless, disgusting, and inadequate and of her as a paragon, or I'd despise her as a monster who had ruined my life while I was the perfect child. I couldn't grasp the concept that Mama was a flawed human being who had made many mistakes—including unconsciously raising me with a belief that she was infallible and I was incompetent—but she had in turn been raised with an unhealthy pattern of interacting with the world. She also has many wonderful qualities and adores me past reason. Mama is a complex person; not simply good or bad, but like most of us, a little of both.

The same goes for Dad. I learned to stop vacillating between thinking of him as a hapless victim of circumstance or a terrible father who didn't care about me. I realized Dad was both a good man who loved me and he also hadn't been a particularly effective father. I started to understand that many of my parents' behaviors, which I had always interpreted as responses to my deficiency, were actually a product of their own unhealthy thought patterns.

I saw that I had always engaged in splitting during my relationships with men, which led to an intensity and tumultuousness that alarmed many of the more stable ones and caused things between us to burn out quickly. Those who fed off that dynamic were usually pretty messed up themselves. I had never really dated in a healthy way, with a sense of self that wasn't warped or insubstantial.

My doctor also taught me to critically examine my own role in all my relationships, a process less about blame than about honesty and self-awareness. I learned how to be curious about myself without being judgmental. I saw that I had always held two distinct people inside me: a lonely child of seven desperate to be held and comforted, and an independent, strong woman in her twenties who would constantly berate the little girl. *Shut up, stop whining. You're pathetic, grow up.* As I began to heal, those two parts of myself stopped battling and began to integrate.

I also learned that years of therapy had left me with a sense that I was much more fucked up than I really am. My doctor pointed out that I had managed to get through college and grad school despite everything, build a promising career, and make huge strides, both psychologically and professionally, in the last couple of years. It was a revelation: I wasn't broken. Maybe I had never been more than a bit cracked and chipped. And really, who isn't?

All of these realizations were extremely calming, a new sensation for me. I finally managed to start forgiving my parents as well as myself for the way things turned out with us, and my love for them became less tangled and confusing. I would look at myself in the mirror and see someone worthwhile, capable, and resilient. It felt like coming home to a house I'd only ever been inside while dreaming.

One day I asked my doctor what my exact diagnosis was at that point in my treatment. He looked at me thoughtfully.

"You certainly used to have borderline personality disorder," he told me. "But I wouldn't diagnose you with it now. You don't fit the criteria anymore."

I was stunned. BPD had been such an integral part of my identity for so long; I scarcely knew how to understand myself without it. But I thought about what it was like at the bottom of the endless, light-swallowing cyclone of shame that had trapped me during my worst moments. I remembered how completely devoid of hope I used to be; how impossible this moment had seemed at the time.

I wasn't "cured." That doesn't actually ever happen, to me or to anyone, really. But I knew I was becoming a whole person, and I cried, not out of sadness. My tears were the mountain-scaling, race-finishing kind.

———

I met Jeremy at the end of April 2014, on a dating app, of all places. He told me he had grown up Orthodox Jewish and lived in Israel when he was younger. I said I was half-Lebanese and worked as a journalist in Beirut. His response was all I needed to say yes to a date.

"Hey, that's cool," he sent me in a message. "Let's do it on the Temple Mount."

Our relationship didn't begin without some hitches. I wasn't the only one who had developed ineffective behaviors over the years. Jeremy spent most of his life pretending to be someone else: a devout Orthodox Jew. He was married at twenty, had a child, and suddenly found himself trapped in a world that still felt like an alien planet to him. Although he never stopped being a great dad to his son, he left his wife and the Orthodox community a couple of years before we met—something I felt took an extraordinary amount of bravery. But over many years he had developed two distinct personalities as well, and it made things difficult for a while. He had trouble being honest with me at first, and given my trust issues, that was not easy to overcome.

Nonetheless, by June, we realized we had fallen in love. I could see him changing, becoming more sincere and open. I began to let him in more and more as I learned to believe he would not hurt me. It was the first time I had ever allowed a man to see everything about me instead of just certain aspects of who I was. I was half-stunned to realize my imperfections didn't chase him away, that he loved even the parts of me I was most ashamed of.

But there was also the fact that we'd been raised with two completely different worldviews. My opposition to Israeli policies in the Middle East and his Zionist upbringing caused many clashes at the start of our relationship. But we both felt strongly that what we believed and where we came from didn't change our human connection with each other.

That June, in the midst of the 2014 Gaza War, a friend asked us to take part in a small campaign meant to promote dialogue between both sides of the conflict. We snapped a picture of us kissing while we held a sign that said JEWS AND ARABS REFUSE TO BE ENEMIES, which was the name of the campaign. I posted the photo on Twitter with the caption *He calls me* neshama, *I call him* habibi. *Love doesn't speak the language of occupation. Neshama* means "my soul" in Hebrew; *habibi* means "my darling" in Arabic.

Two days later, my tweet went viral. We were suddenly all over the news and I was drowning in interview requests. The campaign exploded with dozens of other Arab-Jewish couples, families, and friends sending in photos holding the same sign. I wrote about the campaign and gave interviews at first, because I believed strongly that we needed to encourage empathy in the face of such violence and dehumanization, and that the best way to do so was through social media.

It was a very moving experience, and it often made me feel hopeful. But it was also weird and unpleasant some of the time; I was called a publicity whore and worse. After a while I took it hard and stopped giving interviews. Name-calling aside, I felt strange becoming "famous," even briefly, for an impulsive photo of me kissing my boyfriend, regardless of the intent behind it.

I doubt many people even remember the campaign now; such is the nature of viral phenomena. But for just a moment, I had a voice in this discussion. I still sometimes look at the other photos people posted for the campaign: an Israeli-Palestinian gay couple, two parents and a child, other interracial couples kissing. I see them and know we helped build something brief but beautiful.

Funnily enough, my father played a huge role in bringing Jeremy and me closer together in our understanding of the Arab-Israeli conflict. Shortly after the campaign, Dad was visiting me and we had an introductory dinner. My mother had immediately loved Jeremy upon meeting him, which was pretty momentous, considering she almost universally hated every boyfriend I brought home. But Dad was different, for obvious reasons, and I remember being quite nervous. I was worried my father would make an insensitive comment or that Jeremy would inadvertently offend him. Instead, I watched in disbelief as they sat and talked for hours about every topic imaginable.

Of course, the conversation inevitably turned to Israel and Palestine. Jeremy said something irritating and I jumped in to argue with him, but Dad immediately cut me off.

"Sulome," he said sharply. "Butt out. I'll handle this."

The next thing I knew, Jeremy was being thoroughly schooled. Because he was so impressed by my father's experience and knowledge of the Middle East, he barely put up a fight as Dad patiently explained why much of what Jeremy had been taught to believe about this conflict was simply factually inaccurate. I sat back and watched my father change my boyfriend's mind—something I had tried to do for months with little success—and realized Dad was . . . well, kind of a badass. Afterward, Jeremy looked somewhat stunned, as if he didn't know what had hit him.

"Babe," he said to me after Dad left. "Your father is the most fascinating person I've ever met."

"Yeah," I replied. "You know what? Me too."

10. THE RELEASE

The truth will set you free. But not until it is finished with you.
—DAVID FOSTER WALLACE

NOW

Nobody does pompous like a retired Lebanese army officer.

I'm eating lunch at the Le Gray Hotel in downtown Beirut, listening to him tell me things about my father's kidnapping that I already know. I can't identify him, but he used to be about as high up as you can go in the Lebanese army during the eighties—in other words, he's a solid source.

He's barely letting me get a word in edgewise. It's hot as fuck outside and I had an unpleasant interaction with a taxi driver on my way here as we sat in bumper-to-bumper traffic. He wouldn't turn on the AC until I threatened not to pay him, after which he drove slowly in sullen silence, making me late for my appointment. The officer is obviously unaccustomed to waiting for people, so the interview is off to a rocky start. I try to stifle my irritation as he lectures me about how Iran is responsible for all of Lebanon's woes—it's exactly the kind of oversimplification and lack of nuance that characterizes most political discussion about the Middle East.

The army officer does provide some insight into the difficulties faced by the Lebanese government in wartime. The little

aught up in proxy wars that involved much more
rnments such as America, Iran, and Israel. Because
..actured nature, every sect was affiliated with a foreign sponsor, a state of affairs that continues to this day, at the
expense of nationalism. Lebanese politicians are still usually too
busy nursing their bitter little vendettas against each other and
pursuing the interests of other nations to consider what's best for
their country.

He also tells me how he witnessed the stormy relationship
between U.S. officials and the Mossad during the Islamic Jihad's
terror spree, adding further credence to the theory that Israel had
intelligence on the kidnappings and chose not to share it with the
United States.

"I met with a U.S. delegation to find out what had happened
to Buckley about three days after he was kidnapped," the officer explains. "I said Buckley was in the Anjar camp but we didn't have details and weren't a hundred percent sure. So I told them the Israelis
could help because they had a secret service in Barouk and they
knew everything that was happening in the area. [The Americans]
went to Israel. They came back and one of them told me the Israelis
were very impolite, very unhelpful, and he was shocked. So was I. I
told him, 'You give them billions of dollars a year.'"

He pauses to sip his drink.

"When I met William Casey, he was very angry with the Israelis," the officer remarks. "He called them sons of bitches and said
they were watching Americans die."

Strong words, but by all accounts, Casey was deeply disturbed
by Buckley's kidnapping. Then again, Casey expressing frustration
over the lack of interagency cooperation doesn't prove Asgari was
an Israeli mole. I wonder if anybody in D.C. thinks the Israeli government might keep important intelligence from us, even when

Americans are at risk, so I pose that question in a couple of interviews.

Bodine offers her thoughts when we speak. "The Israelis are going to want to know what these people are planning vis-à-vis Israel," she tells me. "There may be a callousness, like if they know about a plan to pick up an American they don't say anything, because to them the bigger mission of the job is to protect Israel. It's America's job to protect Americans. I don't think they would have used their influence to protect or get Americans released in and of itself; to be blunt, it wouldn't have been smart tradecraft on their part."

Not everybody takes the possibility seriously. Vincent Cannistraro, who used to be CIA chief of operations for the Middle East until just before my father was taken, is quite adamant that Ostrovsky's allegations couldn't possibly be true.

"Where it really mattered, [the United States and Israel] were very close," Cannistraro tells me at his house in a D.C. suburb. "When the marines were killed—if Israel knew that that was coming, I don't believe they would've hidden that and I don't think Ostrovsky would know if they had."

But over the phone, Fred Burton, the ex-diplomatic spook, tells me that he doesn't remember the Israelis being particularly helpful to U.S. intelligence at the time.

"One thing you learn early on, Sulome—in this business, each nation is looking out for its own," he says. "Each nation spies on each other. Everybody looks out for their own interest and welfare. Yeah, there are liaison channels and everybody makes nice, but the reality is, there are no friendly intelligence services, so the Israelis would only have told us something they wanted to for a very specific purpose, and that would have been either to trade information or collect information to fill their intelligence gaps. I don't know if they had human assets—their facilitators, the folks that they could use at the time who helped the State of Israel—but it wouldn't surprise me. Iran has always been a critical intel collection point for them. But if they garnered anything, it certainly wasn't shared with us."

Burton has something to add just before we hang up.

"Your father is a good man," he says to me with regret in his voice. "I view that period of time as one of failure in many ways. There was just nothing good to come out of it."

I'm touched by this expression of feeling from someone in his position. "Well, he's alive," I offer. "That's the good thing."

"I know, but he certainly suffered mightily and there were good people trying to get him out," Burton says. "We were just not successful. I view that as a failure on our part, but we certainly cared and still do."

A week later, I receive a package from Fred Burton. It contains a copy of his book *Ghost: Confessions of a Counterterrorism Agent* and a plastic silver bracelet with my father's name on it. I remember that hundreds of people used to wear these bracelets, the same way people now wear pink bracelets for breast cancer—to remind themselves and others that Dad was suffering. It's very moving to think about Burton wearing this, and it gives me a little more faith in our country's spooks.

———

I'm Skyping with the man widely credited with freeing my father: Giandomenico Picco, former conflict negotiator for the United Nations. In his book *Man Without a Gun,* Picco describes how his negotiations with the Islamic Jihad single-handedly resulted in the release of the Western hostages. He doesn't differentiate between the IJO and Hezbollah, but he claims to have met with Mughniyeh in person—quite a dangerous thing to do—and persuaded him to let my father and the others go through sheer force of personality and his connections in Iran.

The first thing I notice is that Picco, who remains a friend of my father's, thinks the hostage crisis ended quite differently than I've hypothesized.

"Someone told me that the crisis wrapped up because Hezbollah coalesced more and wanted to become more politically legitimate, while Iran and Syria were trying to mend ties with the West," I ask. "Do you think that's accurate?"

"No," Picco says firmly. "I agreed on the timing with the Iranians. The price I had to pay was that I would have a committee of professors make a report on who started the war between Iran and Iraq. Nothing to do with Lebanon; nothing to do with hostages. The report worked because by the late eighties, any head of state in the world . . . never said formally or officially that the war had been started by Saddam Hussein, which was for the Iranians very, very important. It occurred to me in '88 after the end of the war, that was a tool I could use . . . that's why I called the report *Truth for Freedom*."

It sounds strange that Iran would trade the hostages they supposedly held on to for years in exchange for a UN report, even if it was condemning Saddam.

"But why do you think the Islamic Jihad stopped taking hostages?" I asked. "It can't have just been because of a report."

"Because that was organized with the Iranians and the Revolutionary Guard," Picco responds. "They freed the hostages because that report from the UN was more important to them. That's what people don't understand."

I don't understand it either, frankly.

"I was taken [to meet Mughniyeh and the IJO] three or four

times over a period of two months," Picco continues. "The first time, they said 'We want something in return.' I said, 'I have negotiated with Iran.' The guy told me—and I assume he was Mughniyeh, I know he was—he said, 'Who cares? I'm Lebanese. I'm not Iranian.'"

"That's really interesting," I murmur. It seems to me that by this point, something important had shifted in the relationship between Iran and the kidnappers. I already know that Rafsanjani and others in the Iranian government had previously been frustrated in their attempts to pressure the IJO into releasing Dad and the other hostages. This bolsters my theory regarding a Hezbollah takeover of the IJO. Once that had taken place, Iran would have much more control over how—and for what price—the hostages were released.

It sounds to me like the Iranians saw another opportunity to benefit from the negotiations; a little something to sweeten a deal many in the government had been trying to make for years. It was clear the hostages had become a serious impediment to their ambitions, a reason for Iran's continuing exile from the international community. So Hezbollah could have absorbed the IJO and with the encouragement of its Iranian sponsors, indicated that it was open to negotiating the hostages' release. This doesn't mean that Iran and Hezbollah were consumed by concern for my father and the other hostages—it just makes sense given the political dynamics of the time.

It also stands to reason that Hezbollah would have tried to figure out how it too could benefit from the final transaction, which is where Israel came in. Picco describes how he convinced the Israeli government to release some Shia prisoners held in Israel in exchange for Hezbollah releasing the hostages. Again contradicting his earlier statement that the hostages were freed solely in exchange for a UN report, Picco describes how he negotiated between Hezbollah and Israel. He says the Israelis were very concerned with looking good, like they were trying to show that they were reasonable and helpful in the negotiations.

"The second time I came to them, the Israelis said, 'No, we don't want to free any more [prisoners]; if we don't let them go, you don't free anybody,'" he tells me. "I said to them, 'Wrong, my friends. I'm not stupid . . . if you're not going to release them, the only thing that happens is that you will not be part of the deal, you cannot say to the world that you were helpful.' I convinced Hezbollah by saying, 'Look, why don't you become smarter than the Israelis? You release the hostages and the Israelis will not be able to claim that they helped.' So I convinced Hezbollah to give up the hostages . . . When the press announced that they were going to be released, Israeli intelligence called me and said, 'How did you do it? Because we did not release anybody.' I said, 'My dear friend, decide what you want to do. Do you want to appear that you helped me or do you want to appear that you obstructed me?' Within two hours, they released the prisoners. They said to me, 'You're the only one who was able to convince us of that.'"

"Right, that makes sense," I tell Picco. "That's a great tactic."

"Yes, but nobody has ever done this with the Israelis," Picco says proudly. "They don't have the guts."

I don't want to offend Gianni because I've always thought him a lovely man and it's clear he put his life on the line to help free my father, but I doubt it was as simple as Iran just wanting a report or Hezbollah trying to get some prisoners released. I ask some other sources why they think the hostage crisis ended.

Crocker, former U.S. ambassador to Lebanon, says there were larger forces at work in the background of Picco's negotiations.

"This was the beginning of something that looked like it might be a new start for the peace process," Crocker explains. "The war was over in 1990 . . . Hezbollah was changing. They had, for the first time in 1992, contested parliamentary elections and gained seats. They were doing some outreach to Western leaders. While certainly showing no signs of getting out of the military game, they were quite obviously interested in establishing themselves as an influential and respected political force within Lebanon."

"What about Iran?" I ask.

"The Islamic Republic was now over a decade old, well established, threatened neither from within or without," Crocker replies. "It was a very different place than it was in the early eighties. I think you had a confluence in a changing region. Hezbollah was looking at Syria, which was looking at Iran, which was looking at both. It must have been some sort of conversation saying what used to be an asset has become a liability."

Under Bashar's father Hafez al-Assad, Syria invaded Lebanon in 1976 at the behest of the Christians, supposedly to restore order to the war-torn country. In reality, their occupation just helped fuel the violence. A treaty of "Brotherhood, Cooperation and Coordination" was signed between Lebanon and Syria in 1991. It allowed the Syrians to continue the occupation, supposedly to prevent Lebanon's chaos from spreading to Syria, and made Syria responsible for protecting Lebanon against external threats. Today, the Syrian civil war is pulling Lebanon into its vortex. Let no one say the Middle East is without irony.

The occupation is part of the reason why so many Lebanese nowadays have no sympathy for the millions of Syrian refugees pouring into their country, fleeing the war. "Look how they treated us," sneered one man in a café near my house when he overheard me talking to my mother about how poorly the refugees are treated in Lebanon. "Did they let us into their country when we had a war? No. They're like cats; when they want something, they come purring, but when you are nice to them, they scratch you. They're cats, and they should be kicked like cats."

Xenophobia aside, after the invasion, the Syrians continued to occupy the country and overtly meddle in Lebanese affairs until 2005, when they were blamed for masterminding the assassination of Lebanese prime minister Rafic Hariri, allegedly with Hezbollah's connivance. A special tribunal formed under Lebanese law to investigate the circumstances of Hariri's assassination has indicted a few of the group's members. Hariri's murder is another crime Hezbollah denies authorizing, claiming Israel engineered the event to destabilize the country and tar the group's image. It's quite a complex story, though, and I think I have enough complexity on my hands here, so I'll leave that investigation to someone else.

It's not clear exactly why my father was freed, but when all was said and done, Dad was put in a car and dropped off on a road somewhere in Beirut. I've heard him speak about it. One of his captors quite sincerely presented him with a bouquet of pink carnations to give my mother. As soon as they drove off, he threw it away, along with his blindfold. Some Syrian soldiers picked him up almost immediately and he was soon taken to the U.S. embassy in Damascus, where a tired little girl was sleeping on a couch, waiting for him to wake her.

———

At the end of January 2015, while I'm in Beirut, Israel carries out an airstrike in the Golan Heights, killing the late Imad Mughniyeh's son as he traveled in Syria with a Hezbollah convoy. A couple of days later, Hezbollah retaliates by taking out an Israeli convoy on the Lebanese border. All fired up to report on an impending war, I send a pitch to one of my editors, and as soon as he accepts it, I pack up and head to Jnoub (southern Lebanon) to find a story.

True to form, Lebanon precariously balances itself on the edge of another massive conflict without actually falling in. There is no

war. But one of the people I interview for that piece is a local Hezbollah official, or *masuul,* in one of the southern towns near the Israeli border. That's all I'll say about him, because I've sworn up and
down throughout this process I will not include any information
that could identify him. I'll just refer to him as the Masuul.

The Masuul and I establish a good rapport during the interview. He's not creepy in the slightest, but I can tell he enjoys talking
to me, though not all my questions please him. "You're straight-
forward," he tells me once. "I like that." He seems kind, although
iron-hard in his political rhetoric. I ask him questions about the
recent flare-up with our neighbor to the south and he's quite open
with me, in that swaggering, bravado-filled way that Hezbollah
members have when asked about their militarily superior enemy.
As we're getting ready to leave when the interview is over, the fixer
I'm using that day happens to mention to the Masuul who my father is, almost offhand.

The Masuul visibly recoils, his face turning ash gray. "Why
didn't you warn me?" he asks my fixer, after a few moments of
open-jawed, blinking silence. "I wasn't expecting that."

My fixer laughs. "Why would I have warned you?"

The Masuul ignores him, instead looking me full in the face.
He doesn't touch my hand, because that would be *haram,* but I can
tell he wants to.

"I feel ashamed," he tells me in Arabic.

"Why would you be ashamed?" I ask, puzzled.

"I think you must hate us."

"Not really, no," I reply honestly. "It was a war, and I'm starting
to find out there were probably more outside forces involved than
anyone really knows about."

The Masuul pauses for a moment. I feel him step across some
line in his mind. "One day I want to introduce you to someone," he

says. "This person will be able to tell you all about what happened. He can give you facts, details, because he was there the whole time. He was one of the people who held your father."

I'm floored. What are the odds? "Please, I need to meet this man," I tell him.

But the Masuul is evasive. "Next time you come here, I will bring him."

———

I visit the Masuul three more times over the course of four months. On one of those trips, I interview him for another story, and manage to sneak in a question about Hezbollah's legacy of terrorism. He looks at the floor while he talks.

"Parts of our past are not clean," he says. "Some of us thought we were doing what was best for our country. But we were manipulated." When pressed for details, the Masuul will only say that the man I am to meet will tell me all about it. But every time my fixer contacts him to follow up, he keeps delaying my meeting with this man. He always swears he will make it happen in the next couple of days, but two trips come and go without the interview. Each time I go home, see Jeremy for a month, and fly right back to Beirut, determined to nail the Masuul down and get him to introduce me to the person who had held my father captive for seven years.

In March, I visit the Masuul at his home again. We chitchat for a while, then I ask him when I can meet this mysterious man. "I know three of these men," the Masuul finally says. "The man I want you to talk to must convince the other two to let him see you. There is a price on his head for what he did. He's very high up, you know, so no cameras or recorders. You'll probably have to be searched to ensure you aren't carrying anything on you."

I nod impatiently. I know the FBI still offers hefty rewards for information leading to the apprehension of the men involved with the kidnappings, hijackings, and bombings—but the possibility of turning in anyone I speak to as a journalist, even my father's captors, never crosses my mind. I'm a reporter and the commitment I make to my sources is sacred. I'd sooner go to jail than turn any of them in; but he doesn't know that. "Yes, that's not a problem, but when will I meet him?"

The Masuul smiles enigmatically. "Soon. And you will get a very big surprise when you do. It'll make your hair turn gray. You'll know his face when you see it. You know who he is."

I walk back to the car, lost in puzzlement. My fixer stays behind to try to get more information out of him while I wait outside. I can hear them talking quietly in Arabic. Finally, my fixer comes outside, with an expression on his face like someone just punched him in the stomach.

"Hey, what's wrong?" I ask him. "You look like you've seen a ghost."

"I'll tell you in the car," he hisses through a smile, waving good-bye to the Masuul. As soon as we get in, I turn to him, tense with curiosity.

"Well?"

"It's him," my fixer says. "He is the man. He's one of the people who kidnapped your father."

I feel the bottom drop out of my world. I've spent hours with the Masuul by this point. I drank his coffee and played with his little daughter. I almost *like* him, for fuck's sake. I can't reconcile that hospitable, honest-seeming man with one of the monsters who destroyed my childhood. I spend the ride home in silence, watching the spring-green mountains of Jnoub rise and fall as we pass them by.

11. THE INTEGRATION

No human being, when you understand his desires, is worthless.
No one's life is nothing. Even the most evil of men and
women, if you understand their hearts, had some generous
act that redeems them, at least a little, from their sins.
—ORSON SCOTT CARD

NOW

The afternoon of May 28, 2015, is dragging its feet. It's the very
last day of my third trip to Lebanon in five months; I have a flight
to catch at eight the next morning. All my efforts to persuade the
Masuul to finally set a date for this interview have proven fruitless.
Desperate, I call my fixer and ask him what we should do.

"Fuck it," he says colorfully. By now, the poor man has spent
an extraordinary amount of time trying to get the Masuul to sit
down with me. In many ways, it's become his quest as well as mine,
although he too has asked me not to include any identifying information about him because he wants to avoid the headache Hezbollah would give him for bringing me around these people. "Let's just
go. He can't ignore us if we're outside his house."

So we jump in the car, drive to Jnoub, and call the Masuul when
we're five minutes away. Arab hospitality being the revered institution it still is in those parts, he can't really say no. When we arrive,

he welcomes us in and we sit down in his living room as he serves us coffee and presses a cigarette on me.

I light it and feel the smoke curl around my face. The Masuul and I look at each other. The moment is like a foundation stone finally shifting into place. It feels as inevitable as a mountain avalanche in winter.

Before we got there, my fixer told me to act as though I didn't know the man the Masuul had spoken about was actually him, but the pretense is immediately dropped by us both. The Masuul must understand that I know who he is by the set of my shoulders when I walk into his house, the confusion in my eyes. He spreads his hands, almost helplessly.

"You should be interviewing the American soldiers on the *New Jersey* who killed our people after they lied and said they were neutral, then took the Israelis' side," he tells me as I jot down his words in my notebook. He's referring to an incident in which the U.S. battleship fired upon Druze and Shia militias in the hills overlooking Beirut. For some reason supposedly having to do with bad gunpowder, the ship's fire was disastrously inaccurate, some shells missing their targets by ten thousand yards. When the dust settled, hundreds of civilians in the Shia suburbs of Beirut lay dead. Many cite the USS *New Jersey* incident as a pivotal moment in the Lebanese civil war, after which the neutrality of the U.S. force in Lebanon came under serious question and Lebanese Muslims began to believe the United States had chosen the side of the Christians and their Israeli sponsors.

"Do you know why we kidnapped your father?" the Masuul asks me. "It was nothing personal. Our fight was not with Terry Anderson or the other hostages. Our fight was with the people who had slaughtered our families."

"But you ruined my family," I tell him.

The Masuul holds my pain up to the light and examines it. I

can tell it hurts him to look at it. He sighs. "When we took your father, we weren't thinking about you," he replies. "You're sitting here in front of me now. You're a decent, good, respectable girl. I like you very much. And I liked your father. He is a good man, the best out of all those we took. But it could have been anyone. If someone else had caught our eye, we would have taken him. I look at you now and I feel for you. I think about your father and I feel for him too. But at the time, we didn't see your father as Terry Anderson, the person. To us, he was America."

"But he didn't do anything to you," I point out. "What made you think kidnapping an innocent man was the right thing to do?"

"We were desperate," the Masuul says simply. "We were a tiger in a cage, without food or water, beaten every day. We just couldn't take any more. We had to do something."

When I ask him about the rumors of American incompetence and Israeli involvement in the kidnappings, his posture becomes stiff and guarded.

"We didn't know anything about the Israelis," he says quickly. "We weren't working with them or anything. But let's just say they ate it up because it made us look bad to the world. We're still paying that price today. But we didn't know."

So he doesn't want to talk about that. I don't blame him. If the allegations about Asgari being an Israeli asset are true, the men involved are now members of Hezbollah, and might be embarrassed at having been penetrated at that level. Also, the last thing any Hezbollah member wants is the intimation that they were working with the enemy. I change the subject.

"You broke my father's mind," I tell him shakily. "He was never the same again. I thought he would be perfect, and I was crushed." My face feels wet. I know I've started to cry. Fuck. I'm surprised I have any tears left at this point in my journey.

"I'm sure," the Masuul says sympathetically. "I didn't expect him to be normal after what he went through.

"At the time, we all felt terrible to know you were born without a father," he continues. I can feel him talking himself out of his shame. "We felt terrible for Terry Anderson because he had a daughter he didn't know. But we did what we had to do to save our people. Eight of the boys in my unit were killed by Americans. I can take you to their graves the next time you come. At least your father is alive. You can see him, talk to him. I can't ever talk to my friends again."

"Do you regret what you did to him?" I ask. I already see the answer in his eyes, but I need to hear the answer he will give me.

"If Terry Anderson comes to me today, to my house, I will embrace him and say I'm sorry for what happened to him," the Masuul replies. Then I hear his voice harden like frost. "But I don't regret what I did. I did it to help my people."

My fixer gestures for me to end the conversation, and I don't trust myself not to say something stupid, so I thank him distantly and get up to leave. As we're walking out the door, the Masuul stops me and takes my hand in his, ignoring his religion, which tells him he's forbidden to touch a woman who isn't his wife.

"Please give Terry Anderson my regards," the man who kidnapped my father tells me with a smile. "He was always my favorite."

———

I try to control my trembling on the drive home. My heart is thrumming. *Fuck them all,* I think. Fuck the Masuul, his friends, Iran, Israel, Hezbollah, America—they all had some part in this, whether direct or indirect. I realize it doesn't really matter to me which of them was "responsible," who is guilty and who's innocent. I finally find myself knee-deep in the gray area of history, where there are no heroes, just people in all their filth and glory. The Masuul did what he did not because of some conspiracy, but because he sacrificed his morals at the altar of nationalism and revenge. Whether Hezbollah and the Islamic Jihad acted separately or together; whichever faction in Iran gave the orders; whether or not there was some manipulation of the circumstances by Israel; however much America floundered and obfuscated—they all tried to use my father's kidnapping to their own advantage. Most of them likely did the same with Pete.

As we speed down the highway to Beirut, I realize I've relinquished an important element in my quest to understand the humanity of the people involved with this event: politics. What drives people to erase their sense of right and wrong, allowing themselves to be manipulated like bits of plastic on a board game. Why places like Lebanon lose their beauty to violence like a flower flung into a storm. I remember something a prisoner in Roumieh once told me during an interview.

"It's all about politics," he said. "That's the virus of this country."

———

I go home for a couple of months, then return to Lebanon, with the intention of meeting the Masuul again. I barely know why, but I need to continue speaking with him. There's so much I know he can tell me, and I can see that he wants to. I have no idea what is driving this man to ignore every single reason and impulse not to trust me. I don't know why he's revealed as much as he has. But I think about the stories he still has to tell, the questions he can answer for me, and I know the two of us are not finished with each other yet.

When I arrive and coordinate with my fixer, we run into an issue. Another journalist we know makes an appearance on Lebanese television and mentions his friendship with none other than retired CIA agent Robert Baer, who was active in Lebanon at the time of my father's captivity and tasked with tracking down the terrorists—including, of course, the Masuul. This journalist also met the Masuul through my fixer and interviewed him for his own stories. The Masuul happens to see the TV show, becomes quite concerned that the journalist is a spy, and suspects me by association. As a result, that trip ends fruitlessly. But I don't give up, and book another flight as soon as I get home.

I give it a month and a half, until I believe the Masuul has calmed down enough to agree to another meeting with me. My fixer sets up a visit to Jnoub as soon as I land. I bring a female journalist friend with me, knowing she'll help break the ice. This time the Masuul seems to be in a good mood, and he obviously finds my friend charming. He has a wide, joyful smile that smacks me across the face every time I see it, because terrorists and kidnappers aren't supposed to smile like that. Knowing how paranoid he is, we chat about other topics for some time. I'm trying to be cautious so as not to arouse his suspicions, but I still manage to steer the conversation around to my father's kidnapping.

"Tell me about how you treated the hostages," I eventually ask, knowing the answer. "Did you hurt them?"

The Masuul's smile vanishes. He shrugs helplessly; his mouth appears empty of words. I feel his impulse to downplay their brutality, and I can see him fight it.

"What can I say, Susu?" he replies finally. My name is difficult for him to pronounce, so he's adopted my fixer's nickname for me. It jars me every time he says it. "I'd like to tell myself we weren't that cruel to them, but I know we treated them very badly. Some of them worse than others, though. Your father, we all respected him. He is a tough man; he was not afraid of us. He always used to try and reason with us, explain to us why what we were doing was wrong."

The Masuul laughs gently. "Terry Anderson is not weak. He is a hard man. He used to be a soldier, right? A marine?"

I nod, silent.

"We were soldiers of a sort. We treated him better than the others."

"I know how you treated him," I say quietly. "He wrote a book. I read it when I was ten." I can feel angry tears simmering beneath the surface of my voice. I'm too worked up to speak Arabic, so my fixer translates, but I feel him shift uneasily next to me. He's trying to soften the blow of the words, but because I understand what he's saying, he has to communicate the message more accurately than I can tell he wants to. I can taste the tension in the room and know my fixer is mentally urging me to turn down the emotion, but it's becoming increasingly difficult to maintain my composure.

The Masuul shakes his head, again at a loss for words. "Susu," he finally says. "What do you want me to say? I don't know what I can tell you except that if I could, I would go back in time and put you in your father's arms myself."

This means little to me, but also more than I want it to.

I switch gears. "Tell me about Ali-Reza Asgari," I say. "Was he the man in charge of the kidnappings?"

The Masuul hesitates, then gives a nervous laugh. "Where did she hear that name?" he asks my fixer.

My fixer grins. "She knows more about this subject than you think."

"You're good," the Masuul says to me, wagging a finger. "You also speak more Arabic than you appear to, right? I bet you speak it as well as him and I."

I give a brief, enigmatic smile. "Who is Ali-Reza Asgari?" I ask again.

He sighs. "What do you want to know about him?"

"I heard he was working with Israel. Is that true?"

"Why do you have to ask me that?" The Masuul groans. "I'm not supposed to talk about that."

"Look, what you did to my father almost destroyed my family," I tell him through my fixer. "I need to understand what happened."

The Masuul sighs. "We didn't know he was," he says reluctantly. "But yes, Asgari was working with Israel. He was one of their dogs. Imad Mughniyeh had no idea; none of us did. It was a shock when we found out."

"Was he part of the Iranian Revolutionary Guard contingent that started Hezbollah?" I ask.

"Not exactly," the Masuul replies. "They say now in the press that he was, but he was actually part of his own group . . . People in Hezbollah knew what was happening and let it go on. You can say Hezbollah was a part of it. But Asgari was working for a cleric's office."

This fits with what I've learned about Asgari and Hashemi breaking off from the IRGC to form their own terror-exporting group in Iran. Hashemi was a cleric and seems to have established the IJO from within Ayatollah Montazeri's office. But what if the Masuul is lying? He does have plenty of motive to place blame for the kidnappings on someone else, and what better scapegoat than his archnemesis, the Israeli government? I find myself wanting to believe his information because it fits in so neatly with what I've learned elsewhere. But I have to again fight my impulse to give in to certainty. I need more information, hard proof that this theory is worthy of my attentions.

Unfortunately, the Masuul looks like he's done talking for the day. "Come back and I'll tell you more," he says. "Bring your friend again."

———

But when my fixer calls him a few days later, the Masuul doesn't pick up the phone; nor does he return the following dozen calls. I return home unsatisfied. The pattern repeats itself; I give him a month and a half to tell himself that I'm not a spy, then when my fixer says the Masuul is ready to meet, I return to Lebanon. Each trip hasn't been a total loss, as I've filed many stories from Beirut, but I'm beginning to grow quite tired of this chase.

Then again, even if he realizes I'm not CIA, this man has every reason to think I'll turn him in for the reward, which is still in the millions, even after all this time. Has he told the others involved about me? Maybe they're instructing him not to meet with me, or perhaps his superiors in Hezbollah don't approve. I'm well aware there's no chance my jaunts down south have gone unnoticed.

When I arrive and my fixer calls to tell me the meeting is set up, I leave my friend behind. I want the truth from the Masuul, without distractions. I don't want him downplaying his actions so as not to appear unfavorably in front of a pretty female journalist.

On this trip, I do something I freely admit to being uncomfortable with, not just because of the danger if I'm discovered, but because it seems ethically questionable to me. I record our interview without the Masuul's knowledge. I want to protect myself from the inevitable accusations that I'm inventing this man and our meetings.

We have to pause the conversation periodically while people

come in and out, asking for favors or submitting paperwork. The Masuul is a high-level Hezbollah official, so he is appointed to oversee local affairs. Each time they leave, I press him for more information.

"Why would the Israelis want to involve themselves in kidnapping foreigners here in Lebanon?" I ask.

"They were the ones who benefited from what we did," says the Masuul. "Now the Shia and Hezbollah are known as terrorists, which is what they wanted."

I sense his discomfort with the topic and realize I need to establish a bond, which is when I do something I generally try to avoid with sources. I give him my personal political opinion.

"I felt that from the start," I tell the Masuul through my fixer. I can feel myself losing whatever objectivity I've managed to hang on to. I know I need to pull back, but I also feel compelled to show him I'm not an enemy, that I understand the struggle of his people despite what he did to my father. In this moment, I'm not a reporter. I'm a person, with the human fallacy of conviction.

This is all so he'll tell me the truth, I say to myself. *I just need to make him trust me.*

"Look, I just want you to know something," I tell him. "I hate what those people [in the Israeli government] did to Lebanon; I think the way they've acted is evil. If the Israelis knew about what was happening or were involved in some way, I want to know about it."

"Don't press me," the Masuul complains. "When I'm not feeling well, I don't like to talk about these things. I promise I'll tell you everything before you leave. You'll take the information with you on the plane."

I've heard that one before.

"Sometimes I don't sleep," he says suddenly. "I think about the past too much. I take four medications just to calm my nerves. The past is hunting me now. What happened cost me my health. If my son knew what happened, if I tell him, maybe when he grows up, he'll think I'm a bad person."

I wouldn't blame him, I think to myself. Listening to this man talk about how hard it was for him to inflict those horrors on other human beings infuriates me, but I try to keep my tone even and pleasant.

"Ask him if it makes it worse for him to talk to me about the past," I tell my fixer. "Or does it help?"

"I haven't told anyone in my life about this," he replies when my fixer translates. "I put it behind me. I never forget it, but I'm older now, I want to move on."

A woman interrupts by coming in, asking for help with a problem. Our conversation pauses.

"Don't think I'm sitting here, smiling and laughing," the Masuul continues when she leaves. "We are human beings, after all. My hair turned white when I was nineteen years old. There was no stability. We'd spend the night in different places. It was chaos; you couldn't trust anyone. Our sect was being destroyed by the war."

"So you must feel guilty," I say. I know he does; I can see it in his face. "That's only human."

"No," the Masuul insists. "I don't feel guilty for doing what I did. I did it for my country and my people. But it was difficult."

So he's denying any shame for what he did. But he's lying to himself about it; that much is clear. Otherwise, why would he be talking to me? What could he possibly be getting out of this?

"If you asked me today if I would do it again, I would tell you no—" he begins.

"Because it didn't work," I interrupt. "It made everything worse for your people."

"But we were beset on all sides," he explains. "The Israelis were attacking us, the *New Jersey* attacked us; the Lebanese army and the Christians were attacking us because they sided with the Israelis. We thought we had no other choice. If no other methods worked, perhaps this would."

The Masuul pauses for a moment, thinking. "What a coincidence," he says with an amazed smile. "I can hardly believe it. We had put all of this behind us, and now I'm sitting here with Terry Anderson's daughter."

"But it's healing in a way, isn't it?" I ask. "At least, it is for me." And this is true; there's a strange catharsis in hearing how the Masuul could have told himself that this was the way to save his country. I'm not sure why, but it's helping me to understand how his mind works. I never justify what he did; I never forget what this man put my father through. I'm speaking to my own personal boogeyman, one of the villains who haunted my childhood—and he looks so much less scary with the light on. His evil is all too human, now that I can see it; but then again, that in itself is frightening.

"If I tell you everything about the hostages, I want you to know one thing," he says intently. "It wasn't personal."

"I know," I reply. *Does he think that makes it any better?* I turn to my fixer. "Tell him, honestly, I can't sit here as a human and tell him I approve—obviously, this is my father—and I never approve of making civilians pay for what their governments have done. But explain to him that I'm also different from most people. I want to understand more than I'm angry. Obviously, there's anger there, because I know what my father went through and how hard it was for him. But I'm not trying to get revenge—nothing like that."

My fixer translates. I continue. "And for me, it's hard to talk to him because I can see that in many ways, he can be a good man. So it's difficult for me to put those things together. But I'm trying to do that—"

The Masuul gets my fixer's attention. They talk rapidly in Arabic—I can only understand some of it; something about the Masuul telling another man who was involved that he was speaking with me and the man's reaction, which doesn't seem to have been positive.

"Tell me what he said," I demand.

"He's saying he talked to a guy who was involved," my fixer replies. "He asked him to meet you."

"The guy said no?"

"[The Masuul] told this guy, 'Since you were there with me, I want you to come sit down and talk to this man's daughter.' The guy told him, 'You are crazy, you're a lunatic talking to her.'"

"Of course he did," I say. "He thinks I'm going to turn them in."

"This guy was telling [the Masuul], 'You must not be in your right state of mind, talking to this girl when you know who her father is,'" my fixer continues.

"You know why your friend said that?" I tell the Masuul, looking him straight in the eye. "Because he doesn't know who I am. You know me."

"But it's hard because this man was my partner," the Masuul complains. "We have history, me and him, I can't just sit there and lie to his face, not telling him that this is happening, that I'm talking to you. For myself, I know that yes, Susu is a good girl. She's honest."

"Of course you had to tell him," I reply in Arabic, though the prospect of another terrorist afraid that I'm going to turn him in to the FBI somewhat worries me. "And of course he went nuts. But what I'm saying is that he's scared because he doesn't know me. This is me. It's clear who I am. I'm an open book."

I think that's what I have going for me here—the fact that I have nothing to hide. I have no intention of turning either of these men in, and I do honestly want to understand them.

"[His friend] still has bad views about Americans—" my fixer begins.

"Sometimes I have bad views about Americans," I counter.

The Masuul's phone goes off, playing a mournful Arabic song.

"He says he can't even discuss it with his friend because his friend hates Americans so much," my fixer whispers to me while the Masuul takes the call. "He's being so honest with us, really. It's incredible."

"Explain to him that no matter what he did to my father, I'm not going to turn him in," I whisper back. "That's not my job . . . to do the government's work for them. I'm a journalist."

My fixer translates. He and the Masuul chatter for a minute. My fixer turns back to me.

"He says his body is paying the price for what he did. His shoulder still hurts from those days. He was in the room with the hostages once. He was wearing plastic shoes and slipped on some diesel fuel, broke his shoulder. He says maybe God was punishing him that day."

"So it was a battle injury?" I say, trying to disguise the bitterness in my voice. It's very sad that the Masuul broke his shoulder, but he and his friends brutalized my father for seven years. However, I need this man to trust me because I want something from him. I don't understand what it is yet, but I know it's immense and powerful, and I think he wants something equally momentous from me.

But my fixer and the Masuul are deep in conversation again, and I can barely get a word in edgewise. I finally manage to get their attention.

"Tell him—and I'm going to be honest here—that this is my problem with what he did," I say. "To this day, my father has nothing against the Shia. He defends them. Explain to him that my problem with what he did is that it wasn't personal. My father had nothing to do with anything."

"But your dad used to talk very big," the Masuul says, laughing. "He used to curse us all sometimes."

"That sounds about right," I reply, not without some pride.

Another woman comes in with something that needs to be done, and my fixer gestures for us to leave. But before we say goodbye, the Masuul stops us and says something to my fixer.

"He doesn't want to tell you too much because he doesn't want to upset you," my fixer tells me. "But he says the next time we come, he'll tell you everything."

12. THE JOYFUL ENTITLEMENT

Make no mistake: peaceful madmen are ahead of the future.
—**GABRIEL GARCÍA MÁRQUEZ**

NOW

When we call him a couple of days later, the Masuul doesn't pick up. We keep trying, to no avail. In the meantime, I file stories as the days inch into weeks, and suddenly it's time for me to return to New York the next morning. Desperate for some closure, I tell my fixer to pick me up and we head to Jnoub. The asshole can try dodging me when I'm outside his door. That tactic worked once; why not give it another shot?

We travel the long, familiar road through green-smelling hills and towns strewn with Hezbollah martyrs' posters. It's well past dark by the time we roll up to the Masuul's home. My fixer calls him as soon as we arrive.

They chatter on the phone. My fixer hangs up, looking somewhat concerned.

"He's not home," he tells me. "He said to meet him a couple of towns over."

So we drive down winding backstreets, get lost, and call the Masuul for directions a couple of times before pulling up to what is unmistakably a Hezbollah headquarters, fortified and set bunker-style into the side of a hill. There must be more than ten trucks and cars parked around it, all military-type vehicles. They're clearly having some sort of meeting. There's probably an Israeli surveillance drone honing in on us as we speak; I imagine waving it a winking smile and suppress a slightly hysterical giggle.

My fixer calls the Masuul; he says he's coming outside. We wait nervously for a few minutes until we see him stride out of the bunker. He's holding a pistol. He saunters to my window and motions for me to open it, which I do.

The Masuul leans on the car door, pistol in hand. I've never seen him like this. His eyes are hard, his smile lost.

He laughs, a short, bitter sound, devoid of humor, then looks at me long and appraisingly. My fixer is whip tense beside me. Jnoub holds its breath.

Finally, the Masuul points the gun in my face with a smile. "Pow," he says playfully, but this is no game. This is a message, a test—one of those moments in which my reaction is absolutely pivotal. The word hangs in the air.

Without allowing myself to calculate for even a second, I take the gun from his hand. Perhaps surprisingly, he allows me to take it. I've held guns before and they always seemed so heavy, but I don't feel the weight of this one.

I point it back at him. "Pow," I reply calmly, smiling into his eyes.

The moment shatters like glass and the tension is sucked from the air. The Masuul relaxes and laughs, shaking his head. He takes back the gun, then turns to my fixer. They chuckle to each other in Arabic. The Masuul gestures at my fixer to translate.

"Holy shit, that was crazy," my fixer says through a clenched smile. "I never saw this man looking that way before. Okay, Susu, he says he's going to give you what you want. He says to tell you he hasn't spoken about this to another person in his life; he swore an oath on the Koran never to speak of it again. They're all being hunted for what they did. He says he needs to know that his name won't be in any of this and no one will be able to identify him. He says he's trusting you."

I don't hesitate. "Tell him he can trust me. I am not here to take him down. That's not my job."

My fixer communicates this; they confer.

"He says he's going to call me in a month or so and tell you to come," my fixer tells me. "He says he's going to tell you things that will turn your hair gray."

———

I make the familiar trip home to see Jeremy. We build a little more of a life together, then I have to break a piece of it off by flying back to Lebanon again. My fixer says the Masuul is ready to meet again, and he has the perfect excuse for a trip.

Apparently, the Masuul, a hunting enthusiast, ordered a dog from a "breeder" in the Beqaa, and my fixer has agreed to deliver it to him in Jnoub, thinking that would be an opportune time to deliver me as well. I use quotation marks for *breeder* because the place we are supposed to pick up the dog is more like a canine torture chamber. The Middle East is not known for its respect of animal rights. The dogs are cringing, skeletal, and smell like the ninth gate of hell. While showing off their wares, the animal abusers masquerading as breeders chase the puppies down, grab them by the scruff of the neck, and shake them or hit them as they cower in trembling heaps.

I am horrified past words. Animals are my red line. I have zero tolerance for the trendy Brooklyn vegans more concerned with humane slaughtering of cows than inhumane slaughtering of people in other countries. That kind of preoccupation with animals seems to me a luxury of the ignorantly privileged. But as far as I'm concerned, the animal kingdom has far more to offer this planet than humankind. Destroy and brutalize each other if we must, but why not leave the animals out? This isn't their fight. They have nothing to do with any of it. I rescue an animal practically every time I'm in Beirut; I've palmed off several scrawny kittens to friends and family over the years. Seeing puppies kicked around like soccer balls makes my blood boil.

My fixer gestures to the Masuul's dog, with clearly no intention of coming any closer. Arab culture is not dog-friendly, and I have a feeling delivering the animal was a task that sounded better to him in theory than it looks in practice. The puppy is a boisterous, friendly fellow, well built and scrappy. The men show off his pointing skills as I try not to look visibly disgusted with them. They confer with my fixer and indicate that we're to take the dog. He picks the poor thing up like a sack of potatoes and heads to the back of the car. I see him fumbling for his keys.

"Wait a second," I call to him. "You're not actually going to put him in the trunk, are you?"

"Sure, why not?" my fixer asks. "He smells like shit. We can leave it open a crack so he can breathe."

"What are you, nuts?" I yell. "That poor little guy isn't getting bounced around like that. Look at him; he's terrified. I'll keep him off the seats but he's not going in the trunk, I can tell you that much."

My fixer grumbles but acquiesces. The dog shivers uncontrollably at my feet. He does smell foul, but he looks so small and afraid.

I put my hand on his little head and whisper soothingly to him as we turn around and begin the drive to Jnoub.

We've been driving for about an hour when the engine starts to smoke. The brakes have been squealing uncontrollably for some time now; every time I express concern, my fixer waves it off until we hit a hidden speed bump and the entire car gives an exhausted, rattling jump.

"Susu," my fixer says, worried now. "I'm not sure if this thing is going to make it there. This fucking car is destroyed." Concerned for the cleanliness of the seats, he's left our usual SUV behind in favor of his beat-up little sedan.

"Doesn't help that you drive it like a tank," I offer. "What should we do?"

We hit another bump; this time I'm certain the vehicle has given up.

"Stop the car," I hiss at him. "Let's please not end up stuck in the middle of nowhere with a dog that smells like ass and no way home. Turn around. We can take him to [the Masuul] tomorrow. No way am I dying in a car crash for this shit."

"I think you're right," he concedes. "But what do we do with the dog?"

I look at him. "*Habibi*, you wouldn't know the first thing to do with this creature. I'll take the fucking dog."

A hair-raising ride home later, I'm leaning over the bathtub scrubbing the smelly puppy clean. He stands there quietly, shaking like a leaf, as I soap him up and rinse him off. He doesn't stop quivering until I put some dog food my fixer bought at my behest into a bowl, after which he eats like he hasn't been fed in weeks. Then he proceeds to attach to me like Velcro for the rest of the night, removing himself from my lap only to do his business all over the house.

When I try to put him on the balcony, he howls like he's being murdered and won't stop until he's pressed up against me again.

So I find myself in bed with my father's kidnapper's dog, whom I decide to call Daniel, after having scrubbed his shit off the floor three times.

How in the blue fuck did I get into this situation? I ask myself.

But it's not the puppy's fault his new master kidnapped my dad. He's so pathetically happy to be shown a paltry bit of kindness that I want to cry a little, but probably not just about the dog. I feel like I've been watching the events of the past six months on TV. Everything feels scripted, as though someone else wrote my life a long time ago and I'm just rereading the pages. For whatever reason, I feel deeply that I'm supposed to be here, in this bed, with this man's dog.

———

The next day, we deliver the dog to the Masuul. I walk Daniel up to his new house on the leash I bought him before we left. Just before I hand him off, I look at the Masuul dead in the eye.

"I have demands," I tell him in Arabic. "We can negotiate."

He gives a startled guffaw, then thanks me and leads the dog away, motioning for me to go into the house, where his son greets me. The boy can't be more than eight years old. There are two younger girls, one just a toddler. The Masuul's wife is a stocky woman with a friendly, if wary, smile. It's clear the Masuul has shared his past with them; when he comes back, he speaks freely in their presence.

He invites us to sit down with them for supper, a simple meal of *labneh* (yogurt) and meat pastries. We eat as I ask him questions.

"Why my father?" I begin. "Are you sure there was no reason you chose him?"

"He could have been anyone," the Masuul replies. "It wasn't personal."

"Don't you see how wrong it is to hurt someone just because of where they were born?" I ask. "It wasn't Dad's fault that the Americans and Israelis attacked your people."

The Masuul sighs. "Today, I can see it wasn't your father's fault, and it's certainly not your fault. But it wasn't our fault we were attacked either. We felt we had no choice."

"Everybody has choices," I say quietly. "You could have made different ones."

"But sometimes people aren't free," he replies. "They think they are, but they're not. We were little people, but there were much bigger players in this game.

"If your father comes here, to my house, I'd have all the village come and greet him," the Masuul continues suddenly. "All the men who kidnapped him would come and say they're sorry. If you ask me now whether I would do this again, I'll say no. It was a very different time; things have changed now."

That reminds me of something I've been meaning to ask. "How much was Hezbollah involved in the whole thing? Tufayli says he had nothing to do with it, that the orders were coming from elsewhere."

"He's lying," says the Masuul immediately. "It's true that Hezbollah wasn't cohesive at the time and our orders were coming from somewhere else. But they all knew and were benefiting from this."

Perhaps Hezbollah believed they were gaining something from the terrorism in the short term, but as I've come to find out, it did much to damage the group's reputation over time. And the Masuul is confirming what I already suspected: that Hezbollah—at least part of its leadership at the time—bears a hefty measure of responsibility for what happened to my father.

Hezbollah says it played no role in the hostage-takings, while conventional narrative dictates that the group engineered the whole thing. As usual, I find that the truth is probably somewhere in between.

We go over some of what we discussed on earlier visits, then the Masuul pauses midsentence and looks at me.

"This is my family," he says simply, pointing at his children and wife. "I've tried to put the past behind me and build something. Please don't take it away from me."

"I'm a journalist," I repeat. "Not a spy, not a government official. I'm not going to take anything away from you."

"But journalists often act as mouthpieces for their governments," the Masuul complains to my fixer, who translates. "Like you—would you ever go on Al-Manar [the Hezbollah television station] and publicly say that Hezbollah did something right?"

"Probably not," I reply honestly. "But that's because I know doing that would prevent me from being taken seriously; it would be seen as me taking sides."

"That's exactly what I mean!" he exclaims.

"What about you?" I counter. "Would you go on CNN and say the U.S. did something right?"

He smiles thinly. "Certainly not."

"See? We all face certain constraints and realities in our jobs. That's just the way the world is. But like my father, I'm a reporter. I have to try and stay in the middle."

"But your father wasn't always neutral," the Masuul tells me. "Some of his writing was very pro-government; he would often repeat their lies."

I consider this for a moment. Dad used to be a marine, after all. Perhaps there's an element of truth to the claim that he may not have always been completely objective.

"We're all human," I say. "I know my father, and I'm certain he did his best to be unbiased. None of us do this perfectly; sometimes we want to believe what we've been told so badly that we make mistakes. If he ever advanced false government rhetoric, it wasn't on purpose."

The Masuul considers this for a moment; then nods. "I just need to know that you will be a journalist, the way you're supposed to be," he tells me. "I need to know that you will not hurt me because I've hurt you."

"I'm not going to hurt you," I tell him. "I don't want to hurt anyone. I will tell the truth as I see it."

Then I feel the words pour out of my mouth, almost unbidden.

"I think we want something from each other," I say. "I want to understand what happened to my father, and you want me to forgive you, don't you?"

"I know you won't ever forget what I've done," the Masuul begins.

"No," I interject. "I won't. But I do forgive you."

And it's true. He had choices and he made the wrong ones. But a seventeen-year-old handed a gun in the middle of a civil war and told to hurt other people because he thinks they hurt him will rarely make the right decisions. That doesn't mean that I excuse or justify what he did. But I understand it better now.

I can also see that he didn't escape from his experience unscathed, that my father and the other hostages haunt him like frail, bearded wraiths. I think he sees them at night, the same way journalists see their ghosts, only the Masuul's specters are vengeful and angry, biting off a piece of him every time they cross his mind.

The Masuul looks at me in wonder. "Thank you," he says eventually. "There are no words for this. I never expected to hear that."

I can see his wife smiling; his kids look confused but happy. I feel a great peace wash over me, cleansing the anger still clinging to the grooves and crevices of my mind. To my surprise, I find that I've completely lost interest in the machinations of countries like Iran and Israel, or the mistakes made by America. I'll probably never know the answers to those questions with certainty after all these years. At this point, I've lost touch with how much of my reporting I can allow myself to believe and frankly I've stopped caring. Governments will always plot and scheme, trying to reap as much political benefit as possible from the tragedies of families such as mine. Asgari may have been an Israeli mole, or he may not have been. Perhaps Hezbollah didn't mastermind the kidnappings, or maybe it did. The United States government probably bungled many opportunities to help Dad—that much I'm fairly certain of. But I've come to understand that this journey hasn't really been about any of that at all. Every question, every lead, has led me to this moment, this place in the vastness of time, when I look my father's kidnapper in the face and give him my forgiveness.

———

On my way back to Beirut, I call Dad on Skype. "Hi, sweetie," he says when he picks up. "Are you home yet?"

"No, Daddy," I whisper, my voice cracking. "I'm still in Lebanon."

"Sulome? I can't hear you. You're still in Lebanon? Are you all right?"

"I'm fine. But, Dad, I got that interview, the one I was telling you about."

His voice changes, becomes flat and empty. "With the man that held me?" Some time ago, I had shared with him the possibility that I might be speaking with one of his captors. Dad wasn't able to place the Masuul by my description of him, but he said that made sense, since he was mostly blindfolded the whole time and there were probably a dozen men who had guarded him at some point throughout those seven years.

"Yes. I talked to him about you," I say. "It was really hard." Then I break. "I love you so much, Daddy. I'm so sorry. For everything. I love you."

"Sweetheart," my father tells me. "The fact that you got one of these men to trust you enough to tell you anything about this at all is astonishing. What you just did is the very height of journalism. I can't tell you how proud of you I am."

I feel some long-ignored part of me unclench. The cold southern air pours through the open car window, settling on my body like dust. I hear my blood in my ears. In that moment, my father is everything I need him to be, and I am a daughter he is proud of.

EPILOGUE

It is no measure of health to be well adjusted
to a profoundly sick society.
—JIDDU KRISHNAMURTI

January 25, 2016

The U.S. government may have saved my life today.

I'm in Beirut, just after my final visit with the Masuul. I've been trying to go to Syria for two weeks now, to report on Hezbollah's starvation siege of Madaya, a rebel-controlled city in the west of the country. My fixer managed to talk some of his friends into letting a couple of other journalists and myself illegally cross the border with them in a Hezbollah military convoy. The siege of Madaya has been reported extensively, but primarily by phone—it's simply too dangerous to get that close, and Hezbollah isn't generally so obliging to foreign press. But once again, my fixer's connections appear to be solid—everything seems to be lining up.

Why would I enter a country ravaged by a conflict that's claimed so many journalists and aid workers, including my friend Pete? Is any story worth the potential consequences of a decision like that? All I can say is that my existence has revolved around war since before I was born, and I've danced right up to the edge of it, but have still never actually seen what it looks like.

Jeremy asked me to marry him on my birthday last June and I

said yes—something I scarcely believe is happening, given my relationship history. But I plan to have children with him and won't put them through the agony of fearing for my life, so the time frame in which I feel comfortable taking a risk like this is diminishing. I want to see the demon that's been capering just outside my line of sight for so long. I feel compelled to stare it in the face just once before my life changes forever.

So I've been preparing to go into Syria. We were supposed to make the trip yesterday, but the cease-fire between rebel fighters and Hezbollah was broken in a town close to Madaya, making it too dangerous to chance a border crossing. We decide to cool it and wait until we receive word that the situation has calmed down, which is what I'm doing when my U.S. phone rings suddenly.

"Hello, is this Ms. Sulome Anderson?" a very official-sounding male voice asks.

"This is she, may I ask who's calling?"

"I'm a special agent with the U.S. embassy. I need to ask you a question, ma'am."

"Yes . . . ?" I offer, completely befuddled.

"Are you planning a trip to Syria in the next couple of days?"

I'm dumbfounded. How the fuck would the American embassy know about my travel plans? Was it a friend with a big mouth? A concerned citizen?

"Um . . . why?" is all that comes out of my mouth. Smooth. Glad he can't see my expression, because poker face is the opposite of what's going on right now.

"We need you to come in today, ma'am," the embassy official tells me. "It's urgent."

Feeling like I've been called into the principal's office, I jump in a cab and ride to the embassy compound. There's a sharp chill in the air, and my breath smokes when I exhale. The agent I spoke with on the phone earlier is waiting at the gate. He leads me into a spare, cold little room, where an attractive but serious-looking female FBI agent is waiting.

I sit on a couch and lean forward expectantly. They both look at me for a moment.

"Ms. Anderson, we called you in because it's come to our attention that you're planning to go into Syria this week," the man begins.

"I know, I shouldn't, right?" I say, half smiling. This must be the usual cautionary spiel they give anyone dumb enough to cross the border illegally.

The smile is not returned.

"No, ma'am, you don't understand," the female agent says to me. "We heard your name through intel. The Syrian regime knows you're coming, as well as your history, and means to harm you. When we learned of this, we tracked down your number—you didn't register with the embassy; you should do that, you know—and called you in so we could strongly advise you not to go."

I take this in. I did provide my fixer with a photocopy of my passport to give to the Hezbollah guys we were planning to go with. Is it possible the paper ended up in the hands of Bashar al-Assad's notoriously brutal regime? If it did, that would bode poorly for my personal safety. It's widely believed that the Syrian government has been holding a freelance American journalist, Austin Tice, since 2012.

And given who my father is, I'd make a powerful bargaining chip for any ruthless political actor hoping to acquire a U.S. hostage. The American government would face a shit storm of epic proportions if I was taken, and might do all sorts of things to get me back. Assad could repeat what is widely believed was done to Tice and have his thugs pose as jihadi rebels, kidnap me, then throw me in a Syrian jail, and pretend he has no idea where I am—until he wants something, in which case I would make an even more valuable commodity than Dad was to his captors. And by the time I got out, even if I managed to escape being gang-raped, which seems unlikely given the regime's tendency to use such tactics, I'd be lucky to have held on to even a shred of my sanity.

The lady FBI agent is rattling off a list of other, more generic reasons I shouldn't go—there's no U.S. embassy in Syria, if something happened to me I'd be on my own, etc.

"We can't stop you, but we strongly feel that you should reconsider this trip," she finishes, holding my gaze. "It's our job to tell you that we feel you would be in great danger if you decide to continue with it."

I assure them I will think about it, thank them, then they see me out. I feel almost numb as I wait for the taxi. Somewhat incredibly, I'm still finding myself debating whether or not I should proceed with the trip. *Perhaps they're just trying to scare me,* I think. Maybe the regime wouldn't take such a risk. They could be aware that I'm coming but mean me no harm.

My internal monologue continues along these lines for the rest of the afternoon. As I've just about made up my mind to go through with the story, my phone goes off again. Jeremy is calling me on Skype.

"Hi, baby," he says when I pick up. "I miss you. When are you coming home?"

With those words, everything changes. I've left my return ticket open so I'll have some flexibility when the Syria trip goes through. I also haven't told Jeremy I'm planning to go there, mostly because I know his reaction will be less than positive.

But what if the embassy's warnings are true? What if I walked into Madaya and never came out? What would that do to my fiancé, to my mother, my family, and my friends? How would Dad feel if he picked up the phone to find out his daughter is facing the same horrors he experienced for seven years? What's the likelihood that any of them would emerge from that scenario with their psyches intact?

"I'm leaving tomorrow," I find myself saying. "I want to come home."

———

But what's going to happen in a couple of weeks, or months, after I've grown bored with the placid routine of life in the States and a bomb goes off in Dahiyeh or there's another flare-up with Israel on the border? I know the answer to that. A big part of me will want to get on the next plane so I can tell people about how my mother's country is descending into the darkness. But this job has become harder for me lately, and even when I'm in New York, I frequently find myself staring at some horror on my computer screen, fighting back angry tears. When you see, right up close, how ugly people can be, after a while the little kindnesses they are capable of start to feel like smoke in a hurricane—pretty but insubstantial, and powerless against the forces that batter everything around us.

My family life has become easier to navigate. Dad and I laugh a lot together, and I sometimes give lectures to his journalism classes via Skype. My mother still follows me from New York to Beirut and vice versa, determined to talk me out of this job. Jeremy and I just moved into a big old house in Brooklyn with a pretty yard that's bright with flowers in the summer. We have a big dopey puppy and we fight sometimes, but at night he holds me close, and for the first time in my life I don't feel alone. I know I've found someone to sit with in a warm, dry place, away from the storm.

I'll never be able to turn away from Lebanon. It's become a part of my identity, and I'd miss it like I'd miss an amputated limb. But for now, for at least a little while, I want to find something lovely and simple to call my own. I want to be able to enjoy walking into a room and knowing exactly who I am and why I'm there, in a way I never have before.

That being said—as much as I tell myself I want a normal life, the conflict bug itches, and I become bored and restless without the high stakes of the Middle East. I have a feeling this is a war I'll be fighting with myself for some time.

Much of what I've written in this book could be the ravings of a woman driven out of her mind by circumstance; I imagine many people will say that. Perhaps it's all just the product of a fevered imagination racked with delusions and my words are completely removed from the ordered existence we can all believe in.

Or maybe it's all of us who are crazy. From the sneering pundits to the politicians who've sacrificed their morals one by one to the bored reality-TV stars to the religion-drunk militants who believe God lives behind a machine gun—when I feel hopeless it seems like maybe this whole fucking world is off its meds. Maybe most of us are clinging to the dream of a reality we can accept as we're moved around like bits of tinfoil on a grimy basement floor. Maybe we're vividly hallucinating safety in a world that's slowly metamorphosing into a snake, the kind that eats its own tail.

Some of us have seen the snake up close, smelled its breath, and counted the yellow teeth in its ravaged head. We've become familiar with the tedious, everyday brutalities of conflict—the word *animals* hissed through the teeth, the way a refugee's tent smells when it burns at night. We know what happens when the links between human beings begin to fray. All of us, including those of us who see these things firsthand—we should listen harder when we're told it's time to wake up.

My fixer once told me a story about his time as a teenage soldier in Hezbollah during the war. He and his friend were guarding the road to the airport and a Christian family drove up: a husband, wife, and their two children. They were trying to flee the country, like so many Lebanese at the time. My fixer's friend made the family get out and lined them up. A common wartime practice involved stopping people at checkpoints, looking at their IDs, and shooting them on the spot if they were members of a different sect. His friend was getting ready to kill unarmed civilians as they stood there, quivering and begging for their lives.

My fixer says he stopped his friend from shooting the family. The two of them got into a fight. His friend was so amped up that he put his gun to my fixer's head. But my fixer finally managed to talk him down, put the family back in the car, and sent them on their way.

A couple of years ago, that same friend called him. They hadn't spoken in years.

"Thank you for stopping me from killing those people," his friend said. "I wouldn't have been able to live with myself if I had done it."

This is the nature of war. Journalists see the insanity that possesses people when their world suddenly turns hell-like and human life loses its value. Some make the right choices under those circumstances; others, like the Masuul, make the wrong ones. As with the victims and the perpetrators of conflict, some reporters manage to keep their souls intact. Many don't.

For the moment, I want to sit in my garden in Brooklyn and watch the sun through the leaves. I might return to Beirut in a month, or I might not.

SOURCE LIST

1   Ninety-six foreign hostages kidnapped during the Lebanese hostage crisis, *The Mirage of Peace: Understanding the Never-Ending Conflict in the Middle East* by David Aikman, page 65.

1   Ten hostages killed in the Lebanese hostage crisis, *Encyclopedia of Social Movement Media* by John D. H. Downing, page 70.

2   Hezbollah fights Islamic State alongside Bashar al-Assad in Syria, "Hezbollah Recruiting Push Comes Amid Deeper Role in Syria," Associated Press, December 18, 2015.

2   Hezbollah prepares for conflict with Israel, "Analysis: Israel's Next War with Hezbollah Will Be Swifter and Decisive," *Jerusalem Post*, March 7, 2016.

2   Beirut's garbage crisis, "Lebanon: 'River of Trash' Chokes Beirut Suburb as City's Garbage Crisis Continues," CNN, February 25, 2016.

3   Forty-four killed in November 2015 Beirut attacks, "Lebanon Mourns 44 Killed in Beirut Bombing," Agence France-Presse, November 13, 2015.

3   130 killed in Paris terror attack, "Paris Terror Attacks: In Memoriam of the Victims," CNN.

3   ISIS threatens attacks on Times Square, Washington, D.C., "Islamic State Releases Video Threatening Attack on New York City," *USA Today*, November 19, 2015.

3   San Bernardino terror attack kills twenty-two people, "Everything We Know About the San Bernardino Terror Attack Investigation So Far," *Los Angeles Times*, December 14, 2015.

3   Donald Trump threatens to issue ID badges for Muslim Americans, "Donald Trump's Horrifying Words About Muslims," CNN, November 21, 2015.

3   Donald Trump threatens to ban Muslims from immigrating to the U.S., "Donald Trump's Call to Ban Muslim Immigrants," *The Atlantic*, December 7, 2015.

8   Hezbollah on U.S. State Department's list of Foreign Terrorist organizations.

17   Terry Anderson's release, "Anderson, Last U.S. Hostage, Is Freed by Captors in Beirut," *New York Times,* December 5, 1991.

28   Kahan Commission in *Israel's Lebanon War* by Ze'ev Schiff and Ehud Ya'ari, page 284.

28–29   Declassified U.S. government documents on the Sabra and Shatila massacres, "A Preventable Massacre," *New York Times,* September 16, 2012.

29–30   Phalange allied with Israel, *Beware of Small States* by David Hirst, pages 23–27.

29   Pierre Gemayel impressed by the Nazis after attending '32 Berlin Olympics, *Pity the Nation* by Robert Fisk, page 65.

30   Arafat flees Lebanon, *Pity the Nation* by Robert Fisk, page 332.

30   Aylet Shaked's "little snakes" Facebook post, "Israel's New Justice Minister Considers All Palestinians to Be 'The Enemy,'" *Washington Post,* May 7, 2015.

31–32   *Los Angeles Times* review of *Den of Lions* by Terry Anderson, October 24, 1993.

43   Twelve killed and twenty-seven wounded in '82 French embassy bombing, "Beirut Bomb kills 12 at French Embassy," *New York Times,* May 25, 1982.

43   Lebanese Shia look to Iran for support, U.S. Library of Congress country studies, Iran.

43   Shiites clash with the Christian South Lebanon Army, *In the Path of Hizbullah,* Ahmad Nizar Hamzeh, page 93.

44   Death toll from 1983 American embassy blast, "U.S. Embassy in Lebanon Devastated by Bomb Blast; Dozens Killed, Pro-Iran Group Named," *Facts on File World News Digest,* April 22, 1983.

44   The U.S.-led multinational peacekeeping force was seen by many as supportive of Israel, *Lebanon 1982–1984,* Rand Corporation report.

44   Terry Anderson covered embassy attack, "U.S. Embassy in Beirut Bombed, 39 Dead," Associated Press, April 19, 1983.

44   Ryan Crocker survived 1983 Beirut blast, G. W. Bush's speech awarding Crocker Medal of Freedom, January 18, 2009.

45   Fifty-eight French paratroopers killed in 1983 barracks bombing, "France Remembers 58 Soldiers Killed in Drakkar, Beirut," RFI, October 24, 2013.

45   Beirut marine barracks bombing the single deadliest day in U.S. Marine

Corps history since Iwo Jima, "Recalling the Deadly 1983 Attack on the Marine Barracks," *USA Today,* October 23, 2013.

46–47 Hezbollah's 1985 manifesto, Council on Foreign Relations, "An Open Letter, the Hizbullah Program," January 1, 1988.

48–49 David Dodge obituary, details of abduction, "David Dodge, an Early Lebanon Hostage, Dies at 86," *New York Times,* January 20, 2009.

48–49 Arafat searches for David Dodge, "Lebanon and PLO Join in Search for American," *New York Times,* July 21, 1982.

49 Phalangists abducted the four Iranian diplomats, *The Iran-Iraq War* by Pierre Razoux and Nicolas Elliott, page 271.

49 Dodge interrogated about missing Iranian diplomats, *Hezbollah: Born with a Vengeance* by Hala Jaber, page 100.

49–50 Benjamin Weir kidnapped in May '84, "Benjamin Weir's Secret Passage," *Time,* September 30, 1985.

50 Buckley abducted March '84, "Hostages in Lebanon: Israelis Are Guarded; Another Seven Americans Held Hostage in Lebanon," *New York Times,* June 27, 1985.

50 Buckley's treatment and the videos of him sent to U.S. embassies, "The Spy Who Never Came in from the Cold," *Canada Free Press,* October 25, 2006.

53 Mughniyeh's motives regarding the Kuwait 17, *Iran's Revolutionary Guard* by Steven O'Hern, page 61.

53 Mustafa Badr al-Din arrested in Kuwait in 1983, "Top Suspect in Hariri Murder Familiar Name in Kuwait Jail," *Al Rai,* July 2, 2011.

53–54 Terry Anderson's FOIA battle with the government to declassify documents related to his kidnapping, "My Dad's Long, Frustrating Battle with the U.S. Government to Learn About His Own Kidnapping," by Sulome Anderson, *Vice,* June 5, 2015.

56 Hezbollah's emergence, use of suicide bombings, "In Search of Hezbollah," *New York Review of Books,* April 29, 2004.

57 Hezbollah seen as responsible for the Islamic Jihad's terrorism, "The Origins of Hezbollah," *Atlantic,* October 23, 2013.

57 Hezbollah replaces Amal, "Hezbollah's Ascent and Descent," Carnegie Middle East Center, June 5, 2015.

67 Hamza akl Hamieh hijacks Kuwait Airways flight 561 in 1982 and Libyan Arab Airlines Zurich–Tripoli in 1981, *Sacred Rage: The Wrath of Militant Islam* by Robin Wright, page 46.

68 Al-Sadr disappeared in Libya in August 1978, "Lebanon's FM to Interview Qaddafi's Top Spy About Sadr's Fate," *Ya Libnan,* September 3, 2012.

69-70 Early Zionist leaders had designs on Lebanon, *Beware of Small States* by David Hirst, pages 22–23.

71 Palestinian violence against Israelis is well-publicized, "Two Israeli Jews Stabbed, One Fatally, by Two Palestinians in Jerusalem," *New York Times,* December 23, 2015.

71 Israeli soldier shoots Palestinian boy in the back as he flees, "Palestinian Teenager 'Shot in Back by Senior Israeli Soldier While Fleeing,'" *The Guardian,* July 8, 2015.

71 Israeli soldiers shoot Palestinian children, "Israeli Army Shoots Dead Palestinian Child in West Bank," *Al Jazeera,* October 5, 2015.

71 Israeli settler runs over Palestinian child, "Palestinian Girl Hit by Israeli Car Driver Dies," *Al Arabiya,* October 20, 2014.

74 Most casualties in the 2006 war between Israel and Lebanon were civilians, "Why They Die: Civilian Casualties in Lebanon During the 2006 War," Human Rights Watch, September 5, 2007.

75-76 Ashura 1983, two killed and fifteen wounded, civil war in Lebanon 1975–1979, History of the Middle East Database.

76 Israel disregards the increasing hostility of Lebanese Shia, *A High Price: The Triumphs and Failures of Israeli Counterterrorism* by Daniel Byman, page 315.

77 Iran's Revolutionary Guard trained Hezbollah members in the early eighties, *The Shia Revival* by Vali Nasr, page 115.

77 Hezbollah was reorganized into a cohesive entity with Iran's help in the late eighties, *Hezbollah: Organizational Development, Ideological Evolution and a Relative Threat Model,* by Michael T. Jackson.

77 Hezbollah denies responsibility for the IJO's terrorism, "Do Terrorists Usually Claim Responsibility for Their Attacks?" *Slate,* March 10, 2014.

78 Abbas Musawi and Sobhi al-Tufayli were secretaries-general of Hezbollah, *A Privilege to Die,* by Thanassis Cambanis, page 112.

80 TWA flight 847 hijacked by Islamic Jihad, "Terror Aboard Flight 847," *Time,* June 24, 2001.

90 "Regarding Iran Contra," Excerpts from the Tower Commission.

92 Fear of Soviet influence on Iran, "The Soviet Union and Iran," *Foreign Affairs,* Spring 1983.

92 Shah of Iran deposed, replaced by Islamic regime, "Iran 1979: A Revolution That Shook the World," *Al Jazeera,* February 11, 2014.

92 Fifty-two hostages released minutes after Reagan is sworn in, "Reagan Takes Oath as 40th President; Promises 'An Era of National Renewal,'

Minutes Later, 52 Hostages in Iran Fly to Freedom After 444-Day Ordeal," *New York Times,* January 21, 1991.

94 David Kimche obituary, *Guardian,* March 10, 2010.

94 Kimche-McFarlane meeting and initial Israel-U.S. deal regarding selling arms to Iran, Understanding the Iran-Contra Affair, Brown University.

94 Kimche suggested Ghorbanifar to McFarlane as go-between with Iran, Understanding the Iran-Contra Affair, Brown University.

95 McFarlane choses North as point man for the arms deals, *The Final Report of the Independent Counsel for Iran/Contra Matters,* Lawrence Walsh, August 4, 1993.

95 McFarlane agrees to work with Ghorbanifar, "The Front," *American Prospect,* March 20, 2005.

95 Reagan administration's support of the Contras, "Regarding Iran Contra," excerpts from the Tower Commission.

95 Unclear which faction in Iran had influence over the hostage-takers, *Getting the Hostages Out: Who Turns the Key?,* Rand Corporation report, May 1990.

95–96 North and McFarlane bring Bible to Iran, "McFarlane Took Cake and Bible to Teheran, Ex-CIA Man Says," *New York Times,* January 11, 1987.

96 *Ash-Shiraa* breaks arms-for-hostages deals, "Iran-Contra: Who Leaked Ronald Reagan's 1985–1986 Arms-for-Hostages Deals?," National Security Archives, November 4, 2014.

96 *Ash-Shiraa* accused of being a mouthpiece for Syria, *How the Iran-Contra Story Leaked,* declassified CIA report, summer 1989.

96 *Ash-Shiraa* accused of being a Mossad asset, "Ari Ben-Menashe," World Heritage Encyclopedia.

101 Abolhassan Banisadr believes in October Surprise narrative, "Bani-Sadr, in U.S., Renews Charges of 1980 Deal," *New York Times,* May 7, 1991.

101 Yitzhak Shamir says October Surprise took place, "Shamir's October Surprise Admission," Consortium News.

101 Israel-Iran arms deal; Argentinian plane crash in Soviet Union, "$27 Million, Israel, Iran Arms Deals Told," *Chicago Tribune,* July 27, 1981.

101–102 PBS interview, Nick Veliotes, declassified documents describing McFarlane's attempts to channel weapons to Iran via Israel pre-Iran-Contra, How Neocons Messed up the Mideast, Consortium News, February 15, 2013.

103 "Captive CIA Agent's Death Galvanized Hostage Search," *Washington Post,* November 25, 1986.

104 Iran-Contra changed U.S. hostage negotiation policy, "The Illusion of a Hostage Policy," *New Yorker,* February 3, 2015.

104 U.S. hostage policy of "quiet diplomacy" and silence in the press, "The Families of Hostages Are Told to Keep Quiet. They Shouldn't," *Washington Post,* June 12, 2015.

106 Terry Waite's kidnapping and blame placed on Oliver North, "Reviews/ Television; On Terry Waite and the Arms-for-Hostages Deal," *New York Times,* November 26, 1991.

108 *Decoy in a Deadly Game: Terry Waite and Ollie North: The Untold Story of the Kidnapping—and the Release* by Gavin Hewitt.

119 Sabra's conflict with former Lebanese president Elias Hrawi, "Calmest Cabinet Session for 31 Years Avoids All Slapstick," *Daily Star,* July 7, 1998.

120 *Ash-Shiraa* is pro-Syrian, "After the Ayatollah," *Foreign Policy,* Spring 1987.

122 Hezbollah officially announces its role in Syrian war, "Hezbollah's Role in Syrian Conflict Ushers New Reality for Its Supporters," *Guardian,* May 24, 2013.

123 Battling ISIS has increased Hezbollah's popularity, "How ISIS Terror Benefits Hezbollah," *Now Lebanon,* November 12, 2015.

123 "Beirut Editor 'Never Imagined' Scoop Would Be So Big," *Washington Post,* December 10, 1986.

123 Hashemi's fundamentalism, "The Case of Mehdi Hashemi," by Evan Siegel.

123 Hussein-Ali Montazeri, "Profile: Iran's Dissident Ayatollah," BBC, January 30, 2003.

123 Hashemi headed IRGC's Office of Liberation Movements, *Iran's Revolutionary Guard: The Threat That Grows While America Sleeps* by Steven O'Hern, page 71.

124 Hashemi took control of Montazeri's armed followers in 1981, Iran Report, RFE/RL August 9, 1999.

124 OLM was transferred to Ministry of Foreign Affairs in 1984; Hashemi went to Qom and set up Office for Global Revolution, *Iran: A Country Study,* U.S.Library of Congress, 1987.

124 Links between Hashemi and the Islamic Jihad, Hashemi spreads Islamic revolution to other countries, "Newspapers Report U.S.-Iran Contacts," *Harvard Crimson,* November 5, 1986.

124 Hashemi goes rogue, *Iran and the United States: An Insider's View on the Failed Past and the Road to Peace* by Seyed Hossein Mousavian and Shahir Shahidsaless, page 93.

124 Asgari as Hashemi's point man, *Navigating Iran, From Carter to Obama* by Ofira Seliktar, page 49.

124 Asgari sent to Lebanon in 1982, "As U.S. Looks to Nuclear Deal, Book Faults Handling of Iranian Defector," *New York Times,* May 18, 2014.

124 Asgari's meeting with Assad: *Navigating Iran: From Carter to Obama* by Ofira Seliktar, page 49.

124 Asgari's connections to the IJO's terrorism, *The Good Spy: The Life and Death of Robert Ames* by Kai Bird, pages 374–375.

125 Declassified CIA documents regarding Hashemi's conflict with Rafsanjani and his role in leaking Iran-Contra, "Iran-Contra: Who Leaked Ronald Reagan's 1985–1986 Arms-for-Hostages Deals?," National Security Archives, November 4, 2014.

125 "Americans Pawns in Iran Power Struggle: 3 Hostages Apparently Held by Foes of Talks," *Los Angeles Times,* November 14, 1986.

125 Montazeri loses favor with Khomeini after Hashemi's execution, "Filling Montazeri's Shoes in Iran," *Guardian,* December 29, 2009.

127 *Ash-Shiraa*'s links to radical elements in Iran, Sabra's inside information on hostages, "Iranians Seized for Waite Trade, Says Magazine," Associated Press, May 1, 1987.

128 Ghorbanifar claims Iranians seized Weir from his captors by force, "From an Iranian Middleman, His Side of the Story," *New York Times,* June 23, 1987.

128 Hala Jaber's interview with Naim Qassem regarding hostage-takings, *Hezbollah: Born with a Vengeance* by Hala Jaber, page 143.

141 United States once supported Saddam Hussein, "Exclusive: CIA Files Prove America Helped Saddam as He Gassed Iran," *Foreign Policy,* August 26, 2013.

141 United States helped Taliban rise to power, "U.S. Gave Silent Backing to Taliban Rise to Power," *Guardian,* August 10, 2001.

141 American support of Mubarak, "How Did the U.S. Get in Bed with Mubarak?," *Salon,* January 29, 2011.

141 CIA sponsored coup against Mossadegh in Iran, "CIA Admits Role in 1953 Iranian Coup," *Guardian,* August 19, 2013.

143 *Hezbollah: Mobilization and Power* by Aurélie Daher.

157 Mustafa Zein as a CIA source in Lebanon, *The Good Spy: The Life and Death of Robert Ames* by Kai Bird.

157–158 Salameh was a high-ranking member of Fatah and Black September, "Life and Death of a Terrorist," *New York Times,* July 10, 1983.

158 Palestinian versus Israeli death tolls, "This Chart Shows Every Person Killed in the Israel-Palestine Conflict Since 2000," *Vox,* July 14, 2014.

160–161 SAVAK established by the shah and CIA in 1957, *Iran: A Country Study,* U.S. Library of Congress, page 276.

164 *The Sunday Times* reports that Asgari was working for Western intelligence and Mossad, "Defector Spied on Iran for Years," *Sunday Times,* March 11, 2007.

164 *The Washington Post* reports that Asgari is in the United States, claims by Iran that he was kidnapped by the CIA and Mossad, "Former Iranian Defense Official Talks to Western Intelligence," *Washington Post,* March 8, 2007.

164–165 Asgari provides intelligence to Israel, "Iran's Ministry of Intelligence and Security: A Profile," Federal Research Division, U.S. Library of Congress.

172 Al-Musawi replaced Tufayli as secretary-general of Hezbollah in 1991, Tufayli's ouster, *Hizb'allah in Lebanon: The Politics of the Western Hostage Crisis* by Magnus Ranstorp, page 105.

177 Hezbollah and Lebanese forces busted an Israeli spy ring in 2009, "Robert Fisk: The Mysterious Case of the Israeli Spy Ring, Hizbollah and the Lebanese Ballot," *Independent,* May 21, 2009.

177 Hezbollah turned Mossad officer "Prisoner X" into a double agent, "Spy in Cell 15: The Real Story Behind Israel's 'Prisoner X,'" *Der Spiegel,* March 26, 2013.

177 Hezbollah busts CIA ring in 2011, "Hezbollah Station Identifies 10 Supposed CIA Officers," *New York Times,* December 13, 2011.

178 Samir Geagea's imprisonment for war crimes, "Geagea Released from Jail," *Al Jazeera,* July 26, 2005.

179 Jumblatt concerned with freeing Terry Waite, "Jumblatt Efforts to Free Waite Reported," *Los Angeles Times,* August 15, 1987.

179 Walid Jumblatt's stance against Bashar al-Assad in Syria war, "PSP to Rally in Support of Syrian People, Expulsion of Syrian Ambassador," *Naharnet,* August 30, 2012.

179 SSNP assassinated Kamal Jumblatt in 1977, "Assassinations in Lebanon: A History (1970s to the Present)," About News.

182 Roumieh prison riot March 2013, "Islamist Inmates Riot in Roumieh After Prison Visit Is Denied," *Daily Star,* March 2, 2013.

182 ISIS-Nusra clashes along Lebanese border as of Jan 2016, "ISIS-Nusra Clashes Resume on Lebanese Border," *Daily Star,* January 30, 2016.

184 Sharia law enacted by ISIS in Arsal, "ISIS Running Sharia Court in Arsal in Bid to Win Hearts and Minds," *Daily Star,* February 7, 2015.

194 Crew members of USS *Liberty* believe attack was deliberate, "New Revelations in Attack on American Spy Ship," *Chicago Tribune,* October 2, 2007.

195 American marines in Beirut harassed by Israelis, letter from commandant, *Israel Charged with Systematic Harassment of U.S. Marines,* Washington Report on Middle East Affairs.

195 Marine captain draws gun on Israeli lieutenant colonel, "A Marine, Pistol Drawn, Stops 3 Israeli Tanks," *New York Times,* February 3, 1983.

199–200 Publication of Ostrovsky's book *By Way of Deception* initially banned, "N.Y. Judge Bans Book; Injunction Says Spy Exposé 'Would Hurt Israel,'" *Washington Post,* September 13, 1990.

203–204 The Lavon Affair, *Ben-Gurion's Spy: The Story of the Political Scandal That Shaped Modern Israel* by Shabtai Teveth, page 81.

204 Israeli agents in Lavon Affair awarded certificates of appreciation by Katzav, "Israel Honors 9 Egyptian Spies," Reuters, March 30, 2005.

206 ISIS names Peter Kassig as next to die in Alan Henning video, "ISIS Releases Two Videos, Including Beheading of Briton Alan Henning," *Vocativ,* October 3, 2014.

216 For William Casey, finding Buckley was an "absolute priority," "Why the CIA Killed Imad Mughniyeh," *Politico,* February 9, 2015.

218–219 *Man Without a Gun* by Giandomenico Picco.

222 Syrian occupation of Lebanon, "Middle East: Syria and Lebanon," Council on Foreign Relations, February 18, 2005.

223 Hezbollah denies Hariri murder, blames Israel, "The Hariri Murder: Hizbullah Presents Its Case Against Israel," Qifa Nabki, August 8, 2010.

223 Israel kills son of Mughniyeh in Golan Heights airstrike, "Israel Strike in Syria Kills Mughniyeh's Son, Nine Others," *Daily Star,* January 18, 2015.

223 Hezbollah attacks Israeli convoy in Shebaa Farms, "Two Israeli Soldiers Killed in Hezbollah Missile Attack," *Al Jazeera,* January 28, 2015.

226 FBI still offers rewards for information leading to the kidnappers, Rewards for Justice.

228 USS *New Jersey* fires on Druze and Shia militia in hills above Beirut, "U.S. Battleship Pounds Hills Held by Syrians in Lebanon; Britain, Pulling Out Troops," *New York Times,* February 9, 1984.

228 Accuracy of *New Jersey*'s guns called into question, *A Glimpse of Hell: The Explosion on the USS Iowa and Its Cover-Up* by Charles C. Thompson II, page 140.

228 *New Jersey* incident called into question the neutrality of U.S. forces in Lebanon, *Lebanon: A Country Study,* Library of Congress report, 1987.

255–256 Starvation siege of Madaya, "Starving Syrians in Madaya Are Denied Aid amid Political Jockeying," *New York Times,* January 10, 2016.

257 Austin Tice believed to be held by the Syrian regime, "Mystery Surrounds American Missing in Syria," *Al Jazeera,* October 8, 2015.

ABOUT THE AUTHOR

Sulome Anderson is a journalist based between Beirut, Lebanon, and New York City. Her work has appeared in *New York* magazine, *Vice, The Atlantic, Foreign Policy,* and *Vox.* She has covered subjects ranging from Syrian refugee child brides to an ISIS presence in Lebanon and has also worked in Egypt and Turkey, where she reported on anti-government protests. Her goal is to draw attention to individuals marked by conflict and remind her readers that these people, whether victims or villains, are as human as they are.